ECCE ROMANI

A LATIN READING PROGRAM

I•B

ROME AT LAST

THIRD EDITION

PRENTICE HALL
Glenview, Illinois
Needham, Massachusetts
Upper Saddle River, New Jersey

ISBN: 0-673-57589-6

8 9 10 07

This North American edition of *Ecce Romani* is based on *Ecce Romani: A Latin Reading Course,* originally prepared by The Scottish Classics Group © copyright The Scottish Classics Group 1971, 1982, and published in the United Kingdom by Oliver and Boyd, a division of Longman Group.

Photo Credits appear on page 185.

Cover illustration: Yao Zen Liu
Text art: Yao Zen Liu
Maps: Laszlo Kubinyi

PRENTICE HALL

REVISION EDITOR: GILBERT LAWALL
University of Massachusetts, Amherst, Massachusetts

AUTHORS AND CONSULTANTS

Peter C. Brush
Deerfield Academy
Deerfield, Massachusetts

Sally Davis
Arlington Public Schools
Arlington, Virginia

Pauline P. Demetri
Cambridge Ridge & Latin School
Cambridge, Massachusetts

Jane Hall
National Latin Exam
Alexandria, Virginia

Thalia Pantelidis Hocker
Old Dominion University
Norfolk, Virginia

Glenn M. Knudsvig
University of Michigan
Ann Arbor, Michigan

Maureen O'Donnell
W.T. Woodson High School
Fairfax, Virginia

Ronald Palma
Holland Hall School
Tulsa, Oklahoma

David J. Perry
Rye High School
Rye, New York

Deborah Pennell Ross
University of Michigan
Ann Arbor, Michigan

Andrew F. Schacht
Renbrook School
West Hartford, Connecticut

Judith Lynn Sebesta
University of South Dakota
Vermillion, South Dakota

The Scottish Classics Group
Edinburgh, Scotland

David Tafe
Rye County Day School
Rye, New York

Rex Wallace
University of Massachusetts
Amherst, Massachusetts

Allen Ward
University of Connecticut
Storrs, Connecticut

Elizabeth Lyding Will
Amherst College
Amherst, Massachusetts

Philip K. Woodruff
Lake Forest High School
Lake Forest, Illinois

CONTENTS

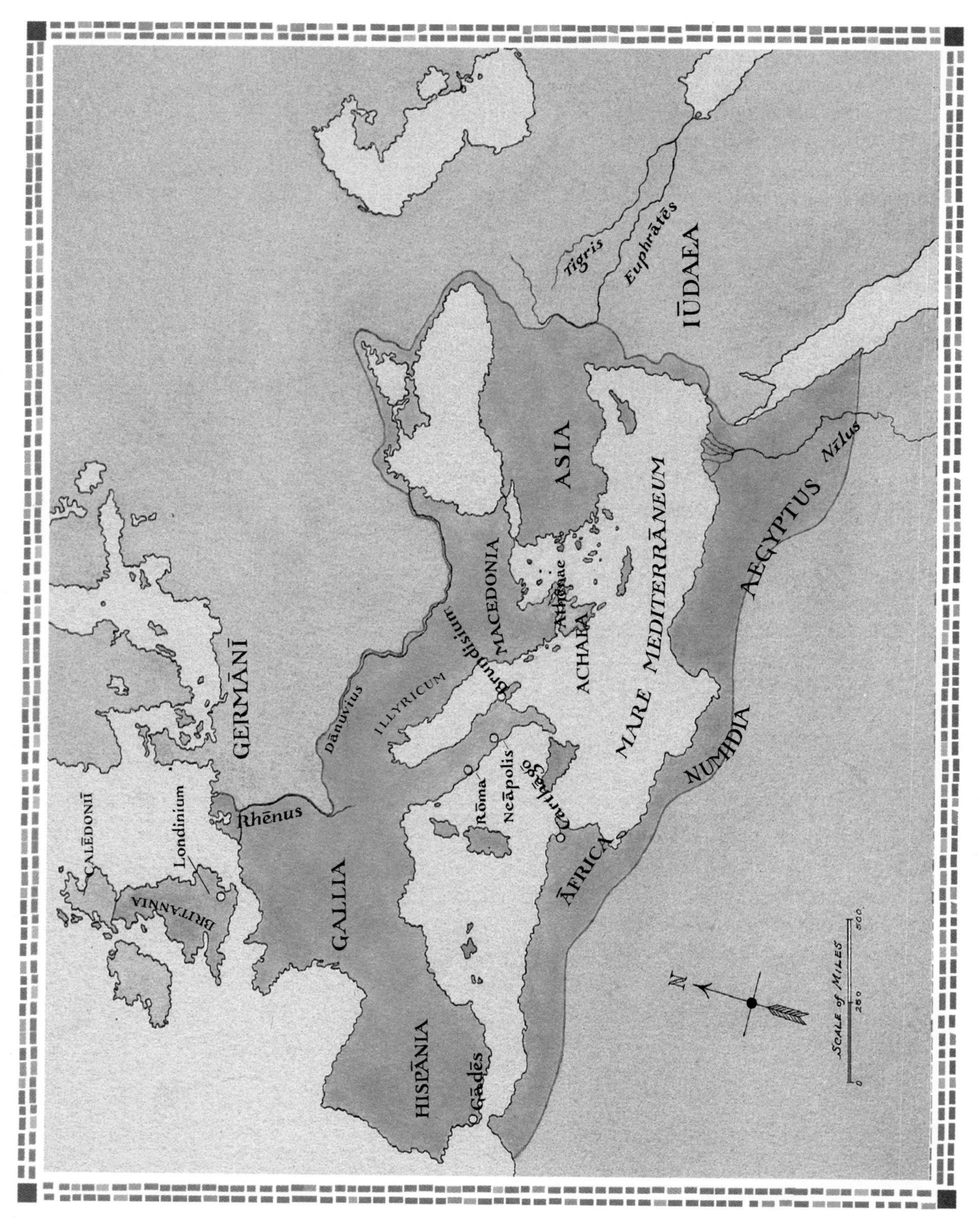

The Roman Empire, A.D. 80

INTRODUCTION

Welcome to the second part of the first level of *ECCE ROMANI.* In this book you will follow the adventures of the family of Cornelius as they complete their journey to Rome and as Eucleides shows the children around the city and takes them to the chariot races in the famed Circus Maximus. The book begins with the family spending a night at an inn, where Cornelius and the boys hear a terrifying tale of murder. You will learn of both the splendors and the dangers of life in Rome as Eucleides takes the children on a tour of the great buildings of the city and as Marcus has a nightmarish dream of being attacked by ruthless thieves.

While following this story, you will learn much about the cultural life of the Romans as you experience life in an ancient inn, travel over ancient roads, and view the excitement of life in the great city. You will learn about the aqueducts that the Romans constructed to make urban life possible by providing an adequate supply of water, and you will witness one of the most popular forms of entertainment in Rome, the fiercely competitive chariot races. By reading the passages from Latin authors in *The Romans Speak for Themselves* that accompany Chapters 19, 21, 23, 25, and 27 of *ECCE ROMANI*, you will gain insight into how the ancient Romans themselves viewed the products and practices of their culture, and you may draw comparisons with the culture of your own world today.

You will also be introduced to life on the frontiers of the Roman empire in northern Europe and in north Africa, and you will begin to explore the process of cultural assimilation through which Roman practices and values came to be accepted in lands far removed from the city of Rome.

You will expand your knowledge as you follow the development of Roman history from the establishment of a republican form of government after the expulsion of the last of the kings in 509 B.C. through a period of legendary heroes and the consolidation of Roman power in Italy to Rome's victory over its archenemy Carthage and the extension of Roman power into the eastern Mediterranean world, with Rome becoming the leader of a far-flung empire.

As you continue to study Latin words and their English derivatives, you will be making many connections and comparisons between these two languages. You will learn the meaning of Latin expressions that have been taken over directly into English, and you will learn the meaning of prefixes that were attached to Latin words and that continue to be used in our English today.

CHAPTER 18

ARRIVAL AT THE INN

Raeda in fossā haerēbat. Cornēliī per viam ībant ad caupōnam quae nōn procul aberat. Cornēlia, quae nōn iam lacrimābat, cum Eucleide ambulābat. Puerōs, quod praecurrēbant, identidem revocābat Cornēlius. Aurēlia, quamquam in caupōnā pernoctāre adhūc nōlēbat, lentē cum Cornēliō ībat.

Mox ad caupōnam appropinquābant. Nēminem vidēbant; vōcēs tamen hominum audiēbant.

Subitō duo canēs ē iānuā caupōnae sē praecipitant et ferōciter lātrantēs Cornēliōs petunt. Statim fugit Sextus. Stat immōbilis Marcus. Aurēlia perterrita exclāmat. Cornēlius ipse nihil facit. Cornēlia tamen nōn fugit sed ad canēs manum extendit.

"Ecce, Marce!" inquit. "Hī canēs lātrant modo. Nūllum est perīculum. Ecce, Sexte! Caudās movent."

Eō ipsō tempore ad iānuam caupōnae appāruit homō obēsus quī canēs revocāvit.

"Salvēte, hospitēs!" inquit. "In caupōnā meā pernoctāre vultis? Hīc multī cīvēs praeclārī pernoctāvērunt. Ōlim hīc pernoctāvit etiam lēgātus prīncipis."

"Salvē, mī Apollodōre!" interpellāvit Eucleidēs. "Quid agis?"

"Mehercule!" respondit caupō. "Nisi errō, meum amīcum Eucleidem agnōscō."

"Nōn errās," inquit Eucleidēs. "Laetus tē videō. Quod raeda dominī meī in fossā haeret immōbilis, necesse est hīc in caupōnā pernoctāre."

"Doleō," inquit caupō, "quod raeda est in fossā, sed gaudeō quod ad meam caupōnam nunc venītis. Intrāte, intrāte, omnēs!"

3 **praecurrō, praecurrere,** *to run ahead*
5 **homō, hominis,** m., *man*
7 **sē praecipitant,** (*they*) *hurl themselves, rush*
8 **fugiō, fugere,** *to flee*
9 **manum,** *hand*
10 **hī canēs,** *these dogs*
modo, adv., *only*
11 **cauda, -ae,** f., *tail*
12 **appāruit,** (*he*) *appeared*
obēsus, -a, -um, *fat*
revocāvit, (*he*) *called back*
14 **pernoctāvērunt,** (*they*) *have spent the night*
ōlim, adv., *once (upon a time)*
lēgātus, -ī, m., *envoy*
15 **Quid agis?** *How are you?*
16 **Mehercule!** *By Hercules! Goodness me!*
nisi errō, *unless I am mistaken*
agnōscō, agnōscere, *to recognize*
19 **doleō, dolēre,** *to be sad*

Exercise 18a
Respondē Latīnē:

1. Quō ībant Cornēliī?
2. Volēbatne Aurēlia in caupōnā pernoctāre?
3. Quid canēs faciunt?
4. Quālis homō ad iānuam caupōnae appāruit?
5. Quālēs cīvēs in caupōnā pernoctāvērunt?
6. Cūr necesse est in caupōnā pernoctāre?

FORMS

Adjectives: 1st/2nd Declension and 3rd Declension

You learned in Chapter 16 that some adjectives have endings like those of 1st and 2nd declension nouns. There are also other adjectives, which have 3rd declension endings, as shown in the right hand column in the following chart:

Number	1st and 2nd Declensions			3rd Declension		
Case	Masc.	Fem.	Neut.	Masc.	Fem.	Neut.
Singular						
Nominative	magn***us***	magn***a***	magn***um***	omn***is***	omn***is***	omn***e***
Genitive	magn***ī***	magn***ae***	magn***ī***	omn***is***	omn***is***	omn***is***
Dative	magn***ō***	magn***ae***	magn***ō***	omn***ī***	omn***ī***	omn***ī***
Accusative	magn***um***	magn***am***	magn***um***	omn***em***	omn***em***	omn***e***
Ablative	magn***ō***	magn***ā***	magn***ō***	omn***ī***	omn***ī***	omn***ī***
Vocative	magn***e***	magn***a***	magn***um***	omn***is***	omn***is***	omn***e***
Plural						
Nominative	magn***ī***	magn***ae***	magn***a***	omn***ēs***	omn***ēs***	omn***ia***
Genitive	magn***ōrum***	magn***ārum***	magn***ōrum***	omn***ium***	omn***ium***	omn***ium***
Dative	magn***īs***	magn***īs***	magn***īs***	omn***ibus***	omn***ibus***	omn***ibus***
Accusative	magn***ōs***	magn***ās***	magn***a***	omn***ēs***	omn***ēs***	omn***ia***
Ablative	magn***īs***	magn***īs***	magn***īs***	omn***ibus***	omn***ibus***	omn***ibus***
Vocative	magn***ī***	magn***ae***	magn***a***	omn***ēs***	omn***ēs***	omn***ia***

Be sure to learn these forms thoroughly.

NOTES

1. Some 1st and 2nd declension adjectives end in ***-er*** in the masculine nominative singular, e.g., **miser**, and keep the **-e-** before the **-r** in all other forms. The feminine and neuter of this adjective are **misera** and **miserum**. Compare the 2nd declension noun **puer**, gen., **puerī**, which also keeps the **-e-** in all of its forms.

   Some 1st and 2nd declension adjectives that end in ***-er*** in the masculine nominative singular drop the **-e-** in all other forms, e.g., **noster, nostra, nostrum**; gen., **nostrī, nostrae, nostrī**. Compare the 2nd declension noun **ager**, gen., **agrī**.

2. Most 3rd declension adjectives have identical forms in the masculine and feminine, as does **omnis** above.

3. The ablative singular of 3rd declension adjectives ends in ***-ī*** (not ***-e***), and the genitive plural ends in ***-ium***. The neuter nominative and accusative plurals end in ***-ia***. Compare these endings with those of 3rd declension nouns that you learned in Chapters 11, 13, and 15.

4. You have met the following 3rd declension adjectives:

brevis, -is, -e, *short*
immōbilis, -is, -e, *motionless*
incolumis, -is, -e, *unhurt, safe and sound*
omnis, -is, -e, *all, the whole, every, each*
Quālis, -is, -e...? *What sort of...?*

In future vocabulary lists, most 3rd declension adjectives will be given in this way, with the masculine nominative singular form spelled out in full and only the endings given for the feminine and neuter nominative singular forms.

BUILDING THE MEANING

Nouns and Adjectives: Agreement II

You learned in Chapter 16 that adjectives agree with the nouns they modify in gender, case, and number. Consider the following sentence:

Multās vīllās, multōs agrōs, multās arborēs vident.

Since **vīllās** is a feminine noun in the accusative plural, **multās** has a feminine accusative plural ending. Similarly, **multōs** is masculine accusative plural agreeing with **agrōs**, and **multās** is feminine accusative plural agreeing with **arborēs**. An adjective will agree with the noun it describes in gender, case, and number.

You already know that 1st and 2nd declension adjectives may be used to modify nouns of any declension (see the example above). Third declension adjectives may also be used to describe nouns of any declension:

Omnēs vīllās, omnēs agrōs, omnēs arborēs vident.

Note that the adjective **omnēs** has the same endings all three times in this sentence while two different forms, **multās** and **multōs**, are used in the sentence above. Why is this?

There are three agreement clues of gender, case, and number that will help you to decide which noun an adjective modifies.

1. Sometimes any one of the three *agreement* clues will show which noun an adjective modifies:

Māter bonōs puerōs laudat. *The mother praises the good boys.*

Māter and **puerōs** are different in gender, case, and number, and therefore all the clues in **bonōs** are decisive.

2. Sometimes only two of these clues are present:

Māter bonās puellās laudat. *The mother praises the good girls.*

In this sentence **māter** and **puellās** have the same gender, but either of the two other clues (case and number) will help.

3. In the following sentences only one of the *agreement* clues is present:

Māter bonam puellam laudat. *The mother praises the good girl.*

Since **māter** and **puellam** have the same gender and number, only the case of **bonam** is decisive.

> Mātrem bonum puerum laudāre iubēmus.
> *We order the mother to praise the good boy.*

Here, it is the gender alone that is decisive.

> Mātrem bonās puellās laudāre iubēmus.
> *We order the mother to praise the good girls.*

Here, only the number is decisive.

4. You will find examples where none of the clues of agreement will help you. When this happens, you must rely on *sense*:

> Puellam ignāvam epistulam scrībere iubēmus.
> *We order the lazy girl to write the letter.*

Note that in English we usually place adjectives immediately before the nouns they modify, e.g., "the good boys," "the good girls." In Latin the more significant word comes first, and usually this is the noun and not the adjective. Thus the most frequently occurring order of words in Latin would be **puerī bonī** and **puellae bonae**. The adjective may, however, be placed before the noun for emphasis, as in the sentences in 1, 2, and 3 above.

Words expressing *number* and *quantity* are often thought of as being very significant or important and so precede the nouns they modify, thus **omnēs puerī** and **magna aedificia**.

Note also that an adjective modifying the object of a preposition will sometimes precede the preposition in Latin, e.g., **magnīs in aedificiīs**, *in big buildings*.

Exercise 18b

Identify all 3rd declension adjectives in the sentences below. Tell what noun each modifies and what gender, case, and number each is. Read aloud and translate:

1. Omnēs viātōrēs ad caupōnās vesperī adveniēbant.
2. Apollodōrus est dominus omnium servōrum quī sunt in caupōnā.
3. In omnī urbe magna aedificia sunt.
4. Aurēlia nōn est fēmina fortis, nam in caupōnīs perīculōsīs pernoctāre nōn vult.
5. Omnēs līberī erant laetī quod Syrus, raedārius bonus, raedam celerrimē agēbat.
6. Cornēlia laudat Marcum, puerum fortem, quī omnēs lupōs magnā in silvā repellit.
7. Puer fortis canēs nōn timet.
8. Canēs manum puellae fortis olfaciunt.
9. Sextus omnēs arborēs ascendere vult.
10. Brevia itinera laetī saepe facimus.

omnis, -is, -e, *all, every*
viātor, viātōris, m., *traveler*
vesperī, *in the evening*
fortis, -is, -e, *brave, strong*
olfaciō, olfacere, *to catch the scent of, smell, sniff*

LEGENDARY HEROES OF EARLY ROME

Once Tarquinius Superbus had been expelled for tyranny in 509 B.C., the monarchy was replaced by a republican form of government, in which two consuls, elected annually, held equal power and ruled with the advice of the senate. For the next 250 years, Rome's history was one of constant struggle and conflict, as she vied with other city-states for supremacy in Italy. The story of Rome's conquests is studded with patriots, whose actions reflect the character of early Rome and emphasize the virtue of **pietās**, firm loyalty and devotion to one's country, gods, and family. The stories of these patriots were told by the Roman historian Livy (1st century B.C.–1st century A.D.), on whom the following accounts are based.

Horatius Cocles defending the bridge
"Horatius Cocles Defending the Bridge," oil on canvas, Charles Le Brun, Dulwich Picture Gallery, London, England

HORATIUS AT THE BRIDGE

The king of Clusium in Etruria, Lars Porsenna, was goaded by Tarquinius Superbus into leading an army to attack Rome and restore the monarchy. As the Etruscans advanced to cross the Pons Sublicius, the access route into the city across the Tiber, they were thwarted by one man, Horatius Cocles. He instructed his fellow citizens to demolish the bridge behind him, promising to hold back the attack of the enemy as well as one man could. The sight of a single armed man standing at the entrance to the bridge astounded the Etruscan army. Two comrades helped Horatius stave off the first attack and then retired into the city over what still remained of the bridge. Horatius taunted the Etruscans and with his shield blocked the many spears they threw at him as they advanced. As the last of the bridge fell, the loud crash behind him and the cheers of the Romans inside the city stopped the advancing enemy in their tracks. "Father Tiber," prayed Horatius, "receive these weapons and this soldier in your kind waters!" and he jumped into the river and swam through a shower of spears to safety with his fellow citizens in the city.

MUCIUS SCAEVOLA

Porsenna then decided to besiege the Romans into submission. Gaius Mucius, a young Roman noble, got permission from the senators to infiltrate the Etruscan camp and kill the king. Mucius happened to arrive at the camp on the soldiers' payday. As he mingled with the crowd, he noticed that two similarly dressed important people were talking with the troops from a raised platform. Since Mucius realized he could not ask someone in the crowd, "Which one is King Porsenna?" he made a guess, pulled his sword, and slew the king's scribe. Seized by the royal bodyguards and dragged before the king, he said, "I am a Roman citizen. They call me Mucius. As an enemy I wanted to kill my enemy, nor do I have less courage for death than for killing." When the furious king threatened to have Mucius burned alive, "Watch this," he said, "so you may know how cheap the body is to men who have their eye on great glory." With that, Mucius plunged his right hand into the fire on an altar and held it there. The king, astounded because Mucius showed no feeling of pain, jumped up and ordered his guards to pull him from the fire. "Go back," said Porsenna, "since you do more harm to yourself than to me." After informing the king that he was but one of a number of young Romans who had sworn to assassinate the king, Mucius returned to Rome, where he received rewards of honor and the cognomen Scaevola, "Lefty."

CLOELIA

Frightened by the news that others like Mucius Scaevola would attempt to kill him, Porsenna offered to withdraw his troops in exchange for Roman hostages. Cloelia was one of the girls included among the hostages. Inspired by Mucius' act of heroism, when she realized that the Etruscan camp was near the Tiber, Cloelia led a group of girls to elude their guards, swim across the river in a shower of spears, and reach safety on the Roman side. Incensed, Porsenna demanded Cloelia's return, only to honor her by sending her home with other hostages of her choosing and calling her deed greater than those of Cocles and Mucius. After friendship had thus been restored and the treaty renewed, the Romans honored Cloelia by setting up in the Forum a statue of a girl seated on a horse.

History and myths of antiquity are full of legendary women, some of whom are pictured here.
"Great Women of Antiquity," Frederick Dudley Walenn, Christopher Wood Gallery, London

CINCINNATUS

Lucius Quinctius Cincinnatus was a model Roman citizen-farmer, a statesman idolized in legend for virtues other than being a fine patriot and military leader. In 458 B.C., the Aequi, a neighboring people with whom the Romans had been fighting for half a century, had surrounded a Roman army and its commander, a consul, near Mt. Algidus in the Alban Hills southeast of Rome. Deeming the other consul not up to the challenge of rescuing the besieged army, the senate decreed that Cincinnatus should be named dictator, a special office that in times of crisis permitted them to put the best qualified citizen in charge of the state for up to six months. The senate's representatives found Cincinnatus at his four-acre farm across the Tiber, intent on his work of digging ditches and plowing. After an exchange of greetings, they asked him to put on his toga and hear the senate's instructions. The startled Cincinnatus ordered his wife to run to their hut and fetch his toga. Once he had wiped off the dust and sweat and put on his toga, the senators hailed him as dictator, asked him to come to the city, and explained the dangerous circumstances of the army. The next day Cincinnatus ordered every citizen of military age to muster on the Campus Martius, armed, provided with five days' supply of food, and each carrying twelve poles to be used for building a palisade. With this army Cincinnatus marched from Rome and arrived at Mt. Algidus at midnight. In the darkness he deployed his troops in a circle, surrounding the enemy. On command, his army started shouting as they dug a trench and built a palisade that fenced the Aequi in between the two Roman armies. The enemy quickly surrendered. Within days Cincinnatus resigned his dictatorship and returned to his farm. Here, indeed, was a Roman driven by **pietās** rather than a hunger for wealth or power.

The Romans passed along legendary anecdotes such as these about their heroes from generation to generation as an inspiration to their children.

WORD STUDY V

Latin Suffixes *-(i)tūdō* and *-(i)tās*

Some Latin adjectives may form nouns by adding the suffix ***-(i)tūdō*** or the suffix ***-(i)tās*** to their bases. The base of a Latin adjective may be found by dropping the ending from the genitive singular, e.g., the base of **magnus** (genitive, **magnī**) is **magn-**. Nouns formed in this way are in the 3rd declension, they are feminine, and they convey the meaning of the adjective in noun form:

Adjective			Base	Noun
Nom.	*Gen.*			
magnus	**magnī**	*big, great*	**magn-**	**magnitūdō, magnitūdinis**, f., *size, greatness*
obēsus	**obēsī**	*fat*	**obēs-**	**obēsitās, obēsitātis**, f., *fatness*

In English words derived from these nouns, ***-(i)tūdō*** becomes *-(i)tude* and ***-(i)tās*** becomes *-(i)ty*. The meaning of the English derivative is usually the same as that of the Latin noun, e.g., *magnitude* (size), *obesity* (fatness).

Exercise 1

Give the Latin nouns that may be formed from the bases of the adjectives below. In numbers 1–4, use the suffix ***-(i)tūdō***, and in numbers 5–10, use the suffix ***-(i)tās***. Give the English word derived from each noun formed, and give the meaning of the English word:

1. **sōlus, -a, -um**
2. **multus, -a, -um**
3. **longus, -a, -um**
4. **sollicitus, -a, -um**
5. **ūnus, -a, -um**
6. **brevis, -is, -e**
7. **īnfirmus, -a, -um**
8. **timidus, -a, -um**
9. **vīcīnus, -a, -um**
10. **hūmānus, -a, -um**

Errāre est hūmānum. ***To err is human.*** **(Seneca)**
Manus manum lavat. ***One hand washes the other.*** **(Petronius, *Satyricon* 45)**

Nōn omnia possumus omnēs. ***We cannot all do everything.*** **(Vergil, *Eclogues* VIII.63)**

Latin Suffixes *-īlis, -ālis, -ārius*

The suffixes ***-īlis, -ālis,*** and ***-ārius*** may be added to the bases of many Latin nouns to form adjectives. The base of a Latin noun may be found by dropping the ending from the genitive singular, e.g., the base of **vōx** (genitive, **vōc*is***) is **vōc-**. Adjectives formed in this way mean *pertaining to* the meaning of the noun from which they are formed:

Noun			Base	Adjective
Nom.	*Gen.*			
vir	**vir*ī***	*man*	**vir-**	**virīlis, -is, -e,** *manly*
vōx	**vōc*is***	*voice*	**vōc-**	**vōcālis, -is, -e,** *pertaining to the voice*
statua	**statu*ae***	*statue*	**statu-**	**statuārius, -a, -um,** *pertaining to statues*

Some adjectives ending in ***-ārius*** are used as nouns, e.g., **statuārius, -ī,** m., *sculptor*. Can you think of similar words made from the nouns **raeda, -ae,** f., *coach*, and **tabella, -ae,** f., *tablet, document*?

English words derived from these adjectives make the following changes in the suffixes:

-īlis becomes *-il* or *-ile*, e.g., **virīlis**, *virile*
-ālis becomes *-al*, e.g., **vōcālis**, *vocal*
-ārius becomes *-ary*, e.g., **statuārius**, *statuary*

The meaning of the English derivative is similar to or the same as that of the Latin adjective, e.g., **virīlis** in Latin and *virile* in English both mean "manly." Sometimes the English word ending in *-ary* may be used as a noun, e.g., *statuary*, "a group or collection of statues," "sculptor," or "the art of sculpting."

Exercise 2

For each English word below, give the following:

a. the Latin adjective from which it is derived
b. the Latin noun from which the adjective is formed
c. the meaning of the English word.

You may need to consult a Latin and an English dictionary for this exercise.

auxiliary	principal
civil	puerile
literary	servile
nominal	temporal

Combining Suffixes

Some English words end with a combination of suffixes derived from Latin. For example, the English word *principality* (domain of a prince) is derived from the Latin **prīnceps, prīncipis**, m., by the combination of the suffixes ***-ālis*** (*-al* in English) and ***-itās*** (*-ity* in English).

Exercise 3

For each word below, give the related English noun ending in the suffix *-ity*. Give the meaning of the English word thus formed and give the Latin word from which it is derived:

civil	immobile
dual	partial
facile	servile
hospital	virile

English Replaced by Latin Derivatives

In the following exercise, the italicized English words are not derived from Latin. Note that these words are usually simpler and more familiar than the Latin derivatives that replace them. Latin can help with the meanings of many of these more difficult English words.

Exercise 4

Replace the italicized words with words of equivalent meaning chosen from the pool on the next page. Use the Latin words in parentheses to determine the meanings of the English words in the pool:

1. Staying at an inn was much too *risky* for Aurelia.
2. While he was away, Cornelius left the children in the *guardianship* of Eucleides.
3. Although the driver *handled* the reins skillfully, he was unable to avoid disaster.
4. It was *easy to see* that Eucleides was a friend of the innkeeper.
5. The *runaway* slave was captured and returned to the farm.
6. The innkeeper offered his *friendly welcome* to the Cornelii.
7. The heat made the slaves' work more *burdensome*.
8. The Via Appia is full of *traveling* merchants, who sell their wares from town to town.
9. Cornelia cast a *sorrowful* glance as she waved goodbye to Flavia.
10. This *country* inn was host to all the local farmers.

custody (**custōs**)	hospitality (**hospes**)
itinerant (**iter**)	fugitive (**fugere**)
apparent (**appārēre**)	perilous (**perīculum**)
doleful (**dolēre**)	onerous (**onus**)
manipulated (**manus**)	rustic (**rūsticus**)

Latin Words in English

Some Latin words are used in English in their Latin form. Many of these words have become so familiar in English that they are pluralized using English rules:

senator plural: *senators*
area plural: *areas*

Others retain their Latin plurals, e.g.:

alumnus plural: *alumni*
alumna plural: *alumnae*
medium plural: *media*

Sometimes both an English and a Latin plural are used:

index plurals: *indexes, indices*
memorandum plurals: *memorandums, memoranda*

Occasionally the use of two plurals reflects more than one meaning of the word. For example, the word *indexes* usually refers to reference listings in a book, whereas *indices* are signs or indicators, e.g., "the indices of economic recovery."

Exercise 5

Look up these nouns in both an English and a Latin dictionary. For each noun, report to the class on similarities or differences between the current meaning in English and the original meaning in Latin. Be sure to note carefully the English plurals and their pronunciation:

antenna
appendix
campus
consensus
crux
focus
formula
stadium
stimulus

CHAPTER 19

SETTLING IN

Cūnctī in caupōnam intrāvērunt.

"Nōnne cēnāre vultis?" inquit caupō. "Servī meī bonam cēnam vōbīs statim parāre possunt."

"Ego et Cornēlia hīc cēnāre nōn possumus," inquit Aurēlia. "Dūc nōs statim ad cubiculum nostrum." 5

Servōs caupō statim iussit cēnam Cornēliō et Marcō et Sextō parāre. Ipse Aurēliam et Cornēliam ad cubiculum dūxit. Aurēlia, ubi alterum duōrum lectōrum vīdit, gemuit.

"Hic lectus est sordidus," inquit. "Neque ego neque Cornēlia mea in sordidō lectō dormīre potest. Necesse est alium lectum in cubiculum movēre."

Caupō respondit, "Cūr mē reprehendis? Multī viātōrēs ad meam caupōnam venīre 10 solent. Nēmō meam caupōnam reprehendit."

Iam advēnit Eucleidēs. Ubi Aurēlia rem explicāvit, Eucleidēs quoque caupōnem reprehendit.

Caupō mussāvit, "Prope Viam Appiam caupōnam meliōrem invenīre nōn potestis. In caupōnā meā nūllī lectī sunt sordidī." 15

Sed servōs iussit alium lectum petere. Brevī tempore servī alium lectum in cubiculum portāvērunt. Caupō iam cum rīsū clāmāvit, "Ecce, domina! Servī meī alium lectum tibi parāvērunt. Nōnne nunc cēnāre vultis?"

"Ego nōn iam ēsuriō," inquit Cornēlia. "Volō tantum cubitum īre."

"Ego quoque," inquit Aurēlia, "sum valdē dēfessa." 20

Nōn cēnāvērunt Aurēlia et Cornēlia, sed cubitum statim iērunt. Aurelia mox dormiēbat sed Cornēlia vigilābat.

1 **intrāvērunt,** *(they) entered*
2 **cēnō, cēnāre,** *to dine, eat dinner*
cēna, -ae, f., *dinner*
vōbīs, *for you*
6 **iussit,** *(he) ordered*
Cornēliō, *for Cornelius*
7 **dūxit,** *(he) led*
lectus, -ī, m., *bed*
8 **hic lectus,** *this bed*
sordidus, -a, -um, *dirty*
12 **rem explicāre,** *to explain the situation*
14 **melior,** *better*
17 **tibi,** *for you*
19 **ēsuriō, ēsurīre,** *to be hungry*
cubitum īre, *to go to bed*
20 **valdē,** adv., *very, exceedingly, very much*
21 **iērunt,** *they went*
22 **vigilō, vigilāre,** *stay awake*

Exercise 19a

Respondē Latīnē:

1. Quid servī caupōnis parāre possunt?
2. Vultne Aurēlia statim cēnāre?
3. Quid fēcit Aurēlia ubi lectum vīdit?
   Quid fēcit...? *What did...do?*
4. Quid servī in cubiculum portāvērunt?
5. Cūr Cornēlia cēnāre nōn vult?
6. Quid fēcērunt Aurēlia et Cornēlia?

FORMS
Verbs: Perfect Tense I

Compare the following pairs of sentences:

Caupō **mussat.**	*The innkeeper* ***mutters.***
Caupō **mussāvit.**	*The innkeeper* ***muttered.***
Dāvus servōs **iubet** canēs dūcere.	*Davus* ***orders*** *the slaves to lead the dogs.*
Caupō servōs **iussit** cēnam parāre.	*The innkeeper* ***ordered*** *the slaves to prepare dinner.*
Marcus **gemit.**	*Marcus* ***groans.***
Aurēlia **gemuit.**	*Aurelia* ***groaned.***
Marcus nūntium in vīllam **dūcit.**	*Marcus* ***leads*** *the messenger into the house.*
Cornēliam ad cubiculum **dūxit.**	*He* ***led*** *Cornelia to the bedroom.*

In each of the pairs of examples listed above, the verb in the first example is in the present tense and the verb in the second example is in the *perfect tense*.

Meanings and translations of the perfect tense:

1. The perfect tense ("perfect" comes from Latin **perfectus**, *completed*) refers not to an action that *is happening* (present tense) or that *was happening* (imperfect tense; "imperfect" = "not completed"), but to an action that *happened* or to something that someone *did* in past time:

Present:

Caupō **mussat.**	*The innkeeper* ***mutters.***

Imperfect:

Caupō **mussābat.**	*The innkeeper* ***was muttering/used to mutter.*** (imperfect = continuous or repeated action in past time)

Perfect:

Caupō **mussāvit.**	*The innkeeper* ***muttered.*** (perfect = a single action, completed in the past)

Note that in questions, emphatic statements, or denials we may use the helping verb "did" in translating a verb in the perfect tense:

Cēnāvitne Aurēlia?	***Did*** *Aurelia* ***eat*** *dinner?*
Cēnāvit Aurēlia.	*Aurelia* ***did eat*** *dinner.*
Aurēlia nōn **cēnāvit.**	*Aurelia* ***did*** *not* ***eat*** *dinner.*

2. The perfect tense may also refer to an action that someone *has completed* as of present time:

Servus meus alium lectum tibi **parāvit**.	*My slave **has prepared** another bed for you.*
Hīc multī cīvēs praeclārī **pernoctāvērunt**.	*Many famous citizens **have spent the night** here.*

In the perfect tense, the ending of the 3rd person singular is ***-it***; the ending of the 3rd person plural is ***-ērunt***.

In many verbs, the stem for the perfect tense ends in **-v-** or **-s-** or **-u-** or **-x-**:

mussā**v-** iu**ss-** gem**u-** dū**x-**

The perfect endings are then added to the perfect stem:

mussāv***it***	iuss***it***	gemu***it***	dūx***it***
mussāv***ērunt***	iuss***ērunt***	gemu***ērunt***	dūx***ērunt***

The perfect stems of some verbs are recognized not by letters such as those given above but by a lengthened vowel:

Iam Eucleidēs **advenit**. (present)	*Now Eucleides **arrives**.*
Iam Eucleidēs **advēnit**. (perfect)	*Now Eucleides **arrived**.*

Note how **currō** forms its perfect stem; its perfect tense is **cucurrit**, and its perfect stem is **cucurr-**. This is called a *reduplicated stem.*

Sometimes there are no letters such as **-v-**, **-s-**, **-u-**, or **-x-** or any other marker for the perfect stem, and the perfect stem is the same as the present. Third conjugation verbs of this sort are spelled the same in the 3rd person singular in the present and the perfect tenses, and only the context can tell you the tense of the verb (find an example in lines 12–13 of the story).

Exercise 19b

Give the missing forms and meanings to complete the following table:

Perfect Tense		**Infinitive**	**Meaning**
Singular	*Plural*		
intrāvit	intrāvērunt	intrāre	to enter
______	custōdīvērunt	______	______
timuit	______	______	______
______	cēnāvērunt	______	______
______	trāxērunt	______	______
mīsit	______	______	______

(continued)

Perfect Tense		Infinitive	Meaning
Singular	*Plural*		
spectāvit	______	______	______
doluit	______	______	______
______	mānsērunt	______	______
______	voluērunt	______	______
haesit	______	______	______

Exercise 19c

Read aloud and translate:

Cornēliī per viam ad caupōnam lentē ambulābant.

Sextus, "Nōnne ille tabellārius equōs vehementer incitāvit, Marce?"

Cui respondit Marcus, "Ita vērō! Eōs ferōciter verberāvit. Equī cisium celeriter trāxērunt. Raedārius noster, 'Cavē, sceleste!' magnā vōce exclāmāvit. Tum raedam dēvertēbat, sed frūstrā. Tabellārius tamen neque cisium dēvertit 5 neque raedam vītāvit. Itaque equī raedam in fossam trāxērunt. Gemuit raedārius; gemuērunt pater et māter; lacrimāvit Cornēlia."

"Pater tuus certē īrātus erat," interpellāvit Sextus. "Statim virgam arripuit et miserum raedārium verberābat. Cornēlia, ubi hoc vīdit, iterum lacrimāvit. 'Pater! Pater!' inquit. 'Nōlī miserum hominem verberāre!'" 10

"Tum pater," inquit Marcus, "Cornēliam tacēre iussit. Omnēs sollicitī caelum spectāvērunt quod iam advesperāscēbat. Pater igitur Eucleidem nōs ad caupōnam dūcere iussit."

2 **vehementer,** adv., *very much, violently, hard*
3 **cui,** *to whom, to him, to her*
8 **certē,** adv., *certainly*
arripuit, *he seized*
9 **hoc,** *this*

Exercise 19d

Locate all of the verbs in the perfect tense in the story in Exercise 19b. Copy them onto a sheet of paper in six columns, each headed with one of the markers of the perfect stem ("**-v-**," "**-s-**," "**-u-**," "**-x-**," "lengthened vowel," and "no stem marker").

ADDITIONAL READING:

The Romans Speak for Themselves: Book I: "Stopping at an Inn," pages 53–58.

ROMAN LIFE VIII

GRAFFITI FROM ANCIENT INNS

Numerous graffiti were scratched or painted on the walls of inns and taverns in Pompeii, and many of them have been recovered by archaeologists while excavating this city that was destroyed by the eruption of Mount Vesuvius in A.D. 79. Some of the graffiti were written by the proprietors, others by the guests. They concern food, drink, conditions at the inn, and experiences of the guests. Sometimes they are prose, sometimes verse, and sometimes they are in dialogue form. Here is a sample:

I

Viātor, audī. Sī libet, intus venī:
tabula est aēna quae tē cūncta perdocet.
Traveler, listen. Come inside if you like:
there's a bronze tablet which gives you all the information.

II

Assibus hīc bibitur; dīpundium sī dederis, meliōra bibēs;
quattus sī dederis, vīna Falerna bibēs.
A drink is had here for one as; *if you pay two, you'll drink better (wines);*
if you pay four, you'll drink Falernian.

III

Tālia tē fallant utinam mendācia, caupō:
tū vēndis aquam et bibis ipse merum.
I hope these deceptions get you into trouble, innkeeper:
you sell water and drink the pure wine yourself.

IV

Mīximus in lectō. Fateor, peccāvimus, hospes.
Sī dīcēs, "Quārē?" Nūlla matella fuit.
I wet the bed. I have sinned, I confess it, O host.
If you ask why: there was no chamber-pot.

Scene from an inn at Pompeii. Sausages and meat hang from the rack.

ROMAN LIFE IX

ROMAN TRAVEL

Gaius Cornelius and his family traveled by land from Baiae to Rome along a section of the Via Appia, which ran south from Rome to Brundisium—a distance of 358 miles or 576 kilometers. It was part of a network of major highways that radiated from the Golden Milestone (**mīliārium aureum**), in the Forum at Rome, to all parts of the Empire. These roads, originally built by the legions to make easy movement of troops possible, were laid on carefully made foundations with drainage channels at both sides and were usually paved with slabs of basalt. Although land travel was safer and easier than at any time before the "Railway Age," it was nevertheless extremely slow by modern standards. The **raeda** seldom averaged more than five miles or eight kilometers per hour; a man walking might manage twenty-five miles or forty kilometers a day; an imperial courier on urgent business might, with frequent changes of horse, manage to cover over 150 miles or 240 kilometers in twenty-four hours. Since carriage wheels had iron rims and vehicles lacked springs, a journey by road was bound to be uncomfortable.

The Roads of Roman Italy

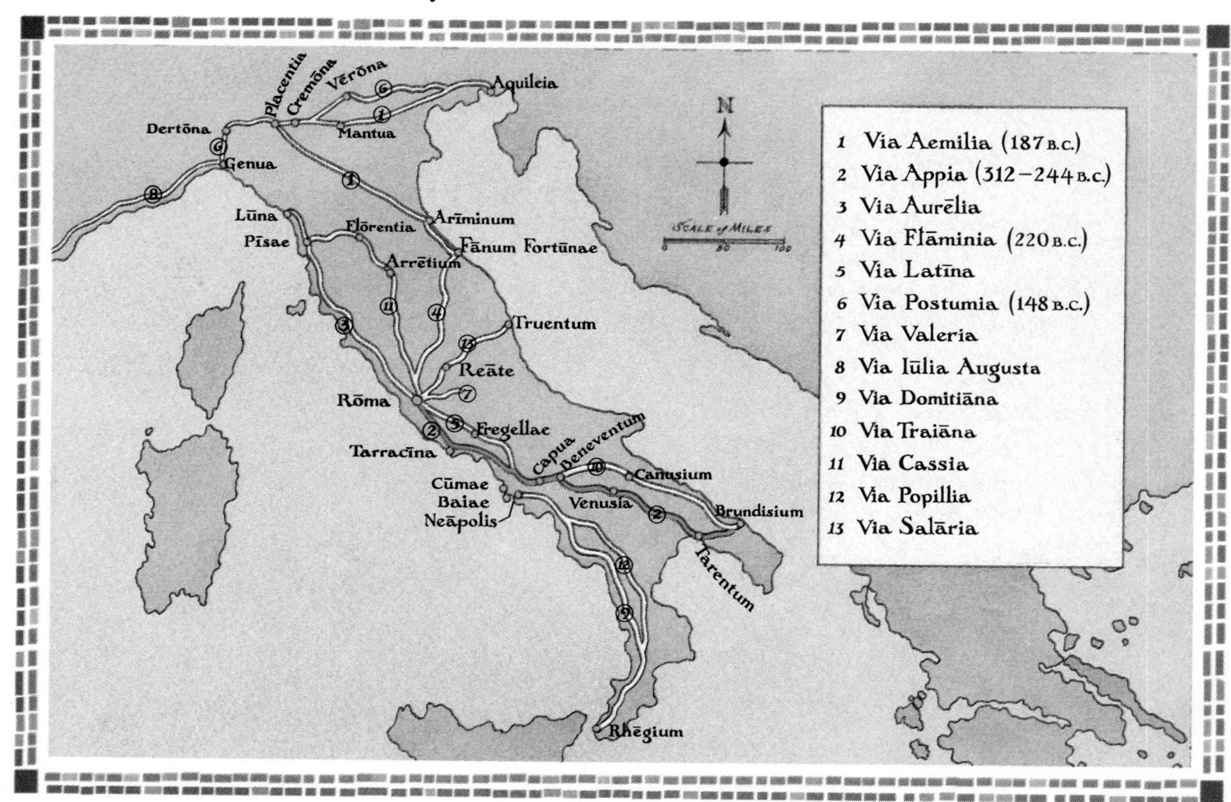

Some **raedae** were open or covered only with a canopy and would subject travelers to clouds of dust and attacks of insects. Others were enclosed with leather, cloth, or wood but could be uncomfortable in hot weather.

Whether a journey was over land or water, the trip was filled with hazards and discomforts. The following passage illustrates some of these discomforts:

> When I had to make my way back from Baiae to Naples, to avoid the experience of sailing a second time, I easily convinced myself that a storm was raging. The whole road was so deep in mud that I might as well have gone by sea. That day I had to endure what athletes put up with as a matter of course: after being anointed with mud, we were dusted with sand in the Naples tunnel. Nothing could be longer than that prison-like corridor, nothing dimmer than those torches that do not dispel the darkness but merely make us more aware of it. But even if there were light there, it would be blacked out by the dust which, however troublesome and disagreeable it may be in the open, is, as you can imagine, a thousand times worse in an enclosed space where there is no ventilation and the dust rises in one's face. These were the two entirely different discomforts that we suffered. On the same day and on the same road we struggled through both mud and dust.
>
> Seneca, *Moral Epistles* LVII

Roman mosaic seascape showing travel by boat

Landscape Crossed by the Nile, Palestrina, mosaic, Museo Archeologico Prenestino, Palestrina

HORACE'S JOURNEY

The Roman poet Horace describes a journey that he took on the Appian Way from Rome to Brundisium in 38 or 37 B.C. He describes some of the hazards with which travelers might be faced:

> After I had left great Rome, I put up in Aricia in a humble inn. My companion was Heliodorus, a teacher of rhetoric. From there we went to Forum Appii, a town packed with boatmen and grasping innkeepers. We were idle enough to take this part of the journey in two stages; for the more energetic it is only one; the Appian Way is less tiring for leisurely travelers. Here, because of the water, which is very bad, I suffered an upset stomach; and it was in a bad temper that I waited for my companions to finish their evening meal. As we were about to go on board, the boatmen began to argue. A whole hour went past while the fares were being collected and the mule harnessed. The vicious mosquitoes and marsh-frogs made sleep impossible while the boatman, who had drunk too much cheap wine, sang of his absent girlfriend, and a passenger joined in the singing.
>
> At last the weary passengers fell asleep; and the idle boatman turned the mule out to graze, fastened its halter to a stone, and lay on his back snoring.

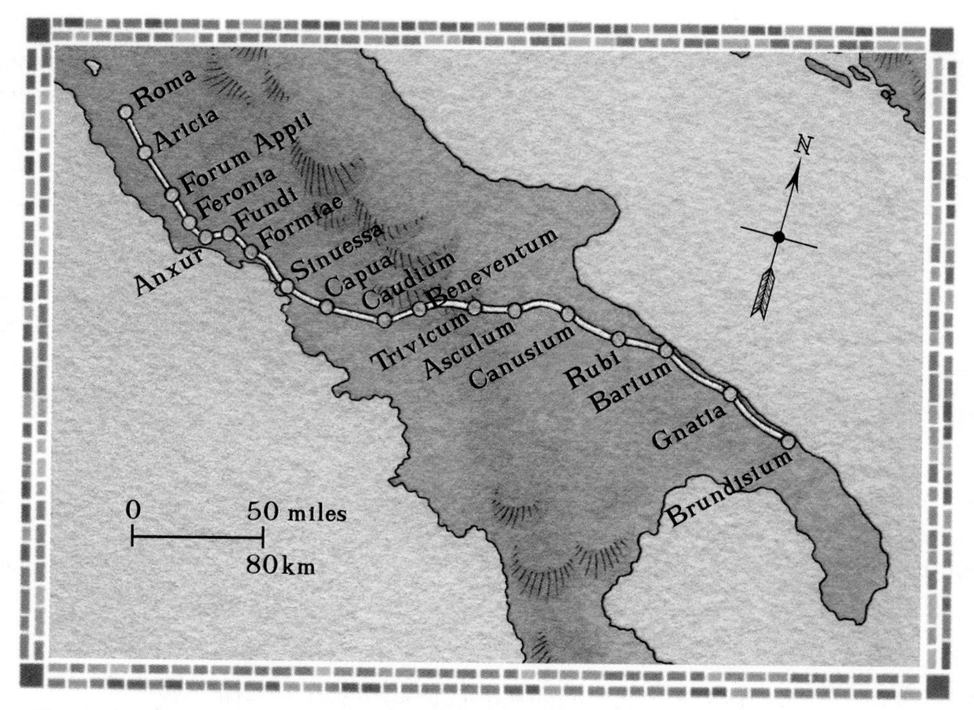

The Road from Rome to Brundisium

At dawn we realized we weren't moving. A hot-tempered passenger leapt up and beat the boatman and the mule with a stick. When at last we disembarked, it was almost ten o'clock. With due reverence and ceremony we washed our hands and faces in the fountain of Feronia. After lunch we "crawled" the three miles to Anxur, which is perched on rocks that shine white in the distance. There our very good friend Maecenas was due to meet us. As my eyes were giving me trouble, I smeared black ointment on them. Meanwhile, Maecenas arrived with that perfect gentleman, Fonteius Capito. We were glad to leave Fundi behind, with its self-appointed "praetor" Aufidius Luscus. How we laughed at the official get-up of the ambition-crazy clerk, his toga praetexta and the tunic with the broad stripe. At last, tired out, we stayed in the city of Formiae, where Murena provided accommodation and Capito a meal.

The next day we reached Sinuessa and were met by Varius, Plotius, and Vergil—friends to whom I was most attached. Then a small villa next to the Campanian bridge gave us shelter; and the official purveyors, as they were obliged to do, provided us with wood and salt. After we left here, our pack-mules were unsaddled early at Capua. Maecenas went to play ball, Vergil and I to sleep; for ball games are bad for a man with sore eyes and an upset stomach. After Capua, Cocceius received us in a house with ample provisions built above the inns of Caudium.

From here we made our way right on to Beneventum, where the overworked innkeeper nearly burned the place down while roasting lean thrushes on a spit. Soon after leaving Beneventum, I saw again the familiar mountains of my native Apulia. We would never have struggled over those mountains if we had not found lodgings at Trivicum. There the smoke made our eyes water, for they put green branches on the fire, leaves and all. There also I waited until midnight for a deceitful girl who never showed up. What a fool I was!

From here we sped on twenty-four miles in carriages, intending to lodge in the small town of Ausculum. Here they charge for the cheapest of all commodities—water. The bread, however, is very good indeed, so that the experienced traveler usually takes some away in his bag; for the bread at Canusium is as hard as a stone, and the water supply is no better.

From here we arrived at Rubi, tired out—as was to be expected—for the stage was long and the road conditions difficult because of heavy rain. After this the weather was better, but the road worse as far as Barium, a fishing town. Then Gnatia provided us with laughter and amusement: the people tried to convince us that in the temple there frankincense melts without a flame. I don't believe it!

Brundisium is the end of my long account and of my long journey.

Horace, *Satires* I.5 (abridged)

Chance Encounter

Ubi Cornēlia et māter cubitum iērunt, Marcus et Sextus cum Cornēliō mānsērunt. Cum Cornēliō cēnāre et post cēnam ad mediam noctem vigilāre in animō habuērunt, nam omnia vidēre et omnia audīre voluērunt.

Marcus, "Ēsuriō, pater," inquit. "Ēsurīsne tū quoque, Sexte?"

"Ita vērō!" respondit Sextus. 5

"Semper ēsurītis, tū et Marcus!" exclāmāvit Cornēlius.

"Licetne nōbīs," inquit Marcus, "hīc cēnāre?"

Paulisper tacēbat pater, sed tandem, "Estō!" inquit. "Tibi et Sextō licet hīc cēnāre. Post cēnam tamen necesse est statim cubitum īre."

Rīsērunt puerī quod laetī erant. "Gaudēmus, pater," inquit Marcus, "quod nōs in 10 cubiculum nōn statim mīsistī. Voluimus enim hīc manēre et aliōs viātōrēs spectāre."

Tum Cornēlius caupōnem iussit cibum parāre. Brevī tempore servus cibum ad eōs portāvit. Dum puerī cibum dēvorant, subitō intrāvit mīles quīdam. Cornēlium attentē spectāvit. "Salvē, vir optime!" inquit. "Salvēte, puerī! Cūr vōs in hanc caupōnam intrāvistis? Cūr nōn ad vīllam hospitis īstis? Nōnne tū es senātor Rōmānus?" (continued) 15

1 **mānsērunt,** (they) *stayed*
2 **post,** prep. + acc., *after*
medius, -a, -um, *mid-, middle of*
  media nox, *midnight*
7 **Licetne nōbīs...?** *Is it allowed for us...? May we...?*
8 **paulisper,** adv., *for a short time*
Estō! *All right!*
11 **mīsistī,** *you have sent*
voluimus, *we wanted*
enim, conj., *for*
13 **Dum...dēvorant,** *While...were devouring*
mīles, mīlitis m., *soldier*
14 **vir optime,** *sir*
  optimus, -a, -um, *best, very good*

Exercise 20a
Respondē Latīnē:

1. Quid Marcus et Sextus facere voluērunt?
2. Ēsuriuntne puerī?
3. Licetne Marcō et Sextō in caupōnā cēnāre?
4. Cūr puerī laetī sunt?
5. Quis intrāvit dum puerī cibum dēvorant?

"Senātor Rōmānus sum," respondit Cornēlius. "Nōs in hanc caupōnam intrāvimus quod raeda nostra in fossā haeret immōbilis. In agrīs nocte manēre nōlēbāmus, sed numquam anteā in caupōnā pernoctāvimus. Certē in agrīs pernoctāre est perīculōsum."

Tum mīles, "Etiam in caupōnā pernoctāre saepe est perīculōsum."

"Cūr hoc nōbīs dīcis?" rogāvit Cornēlius. "Estne hic caupō homō scelestus? Dē Apollodōrō quid audīvistī?" 20

"Dē Apollodōrō nihil audīvī, sed semper est perīculōsum in caupōnā pernoctāre. Vōsne audīvistis illam fābulam dē caupōne nārrātam? Ille caupō hospitem necāvit."

"Minimē!" inquit Cornēlius. "Illam fābulam nōn audīvī. Cūr igitur nōbīs illam nōn nārrās dum cēnāmus?" 25

16 **in hanc caupōnam,** *into this inn*
18 **numquam,** adv., *never*
anteā, adv., *before*
20 **dīcō, dīcere,** *to say, tell*
23 **illam,** *that famous*
fābula, -ae, f., *story*
nārrātus, -a, -um, *told*
necō, necāre, *to kill*
25 **nārrō, nārrāre,** *to tell (a story)*

Respondē Latīnē:

1. Cūr Cornēlius in agrīs pernoctāre nōlēbat?
2. Quid mīles dē Apollodōrō audīvit?
3. Quid fēcit caupō in fābulā?

FORMS

Verbs: Perfect Tense II

You have now met all the endings of the perfect tense:

Singular	1	*-ī*	Plural	1	*-imus*
	2	*-istī*		2	*-istis*
	3	*-it*		3	*-ērunt*

These are the endings of the perfect tense of *all* Latin verbs, e.g.:

Singular	1	mīs*ī*	Plural	1	mīs*imus*
	2	mīs*istī*		2	mīs*istis*
	3	mīs*it*		3	mīs*ērunt*

Exercise 20b

Using the chart above, supply the appropriate perfect tense endings, read aloud, and translate:

1. Ego līberōs in hortō petīv______; tū eōs in silvā invēn______.
2. Ubi tunica Sextī in rāmīs haerēbat, nōs omnēs rīs______.

3. Quō iit Cornēlia? Ego et Marcus patrem hoc rogāv______, sed ille nihil respond______.
4. Quamquam Sextus fu______ molestus, servī eum nōn verberāv______.
5. Ubi heri fu______, Marce et Cornēlia? Pater et māter nōs iuss______ hīc manēre.
6. Postquam vōs cēnāv______, cubitum īre volu______.
7. Heri nōs in urbe erāmus, sed mātrem ibi nōn vīd______.
8. "Unde vēn______, amīcī?" rogāv______ caupō. "Quō nunc ītis?"
9. Tūne Cornēlium vīd______, ubi tū Rōmam advēn______? Ego certē eum nōn vīd______.
10. Ille, postquam haec audīv______, ē caupōnā sē praecipitāv______.

ille, *he*
heri, *yesterday*
postquam, *after*
haec, *these things, this*

BUILDING THE MEANING

Subordinate Clauses with the Conjunction *dum*

Look at the following sentences:

Dum Cornēliī **cēnant**, mīles fābulam nārrat.
***While** the Cornelii **eat dinner**, the soldier tells a story.*

Dum Cornēliī **cēnābant**, mīles fābulam nārrābat.
***While/As long as** the Cornelii **were eating dinner**, the soldier was telling a story.*

In the first sentence, both verbs are in the present tense, and the sentence describes two actions that are taking place at the same time.

In the second sentence, both verbs are in the imperfect tense, and the sentence describes two actions that were taking place over the same period of time in the past. In sentences of this kind, *as long as* is often a good translation for **dum**.

Now look at the following sentence:

Dum puerī cibum **dēvorant**, subitō intrāvit mīles quīdam. (20:13)
***While** the boys **were devouring** dinner, suddenly a certain soldier entered.*

Here the conjunction **dum** introduces a subordinate clause with its verb in the present tense (**dēvorant**), and the verb of the main clause is in the perfect tense. The subordinate clause describes an action that was continuing over a period of time in the past when suddenly a single, simple action occurred, namely, the soldier entered. Contrary to expectation, Latin uses the present tense and not the imperfect in subordinate clauses introduced by **dum** when the verb of the main clause is in the perfect tense. Translate as above: *While the boys **were devouring** dinner….*

Uses of the Infinitive (Consolidation)

You have met the following uses of the infinitive in your reading:

a. Complementary infinitive:

Marcus arbōrēs **ascendere** nōn vult.
*Marcus does not want **to climb** trees.*

Multī viātōrēs ad meam caupōnam **venīre** solent.
*Many travelers are accustomed **to come** to my inn.*
Many travelers are in the habit of coming to my inn.

b. Infinitive with impersonals:

Nōbīs necesse est statim **discēdere**. (9:13–14)
*It is necessary for us **to leave** immediately.*
We must leave immediately.

Vōbīs licet hīc **cēnare**.
*It is allowed for you **to dine** here.*
You may dine here.

The verbal phrase **necesse est** and the verb **licet** are said to be *impersonal*, because we may supply a subject, *it*, and translate them with the impersonal phrases *it is necessary* and *it is allowed.* The infinitives, however, are actually the grammatical subjects, and we may translate very literally and rather awkwardly as follows:

***To leave** immediately is necessary for us.*
***To dine** here is allowed for you.*

c. Infinitive as subject of the verb **est**:

Certē in agrīs **pernoctāre** est perīculōsum. (20:18)
***To spend the night** in the fields is certainly dangerous.*
*It is certainly dangerous **to spend the night** in the fields.*

The infinitive is here being used as a *verbal noun*, and as such it is neuter in gender, hence the neuter complement **perīculōsum**.

d. Accusative and infinitive with verbs such as **docēre** and **iubēre**:

Aurēlia **Cornēliam** docet vīllam **cūrāre**. (6:11)
*Aurelia teaches **Cornelia** (how) **to take care of** the country house.*

Ancillam iubet aliās tunicās et stolās et pallās in cistam **pōnere.** (10:2)
*She orders **a slave-woman to put** other tunics and stolas and pallas into a chest.*

Exercise 20c

In the story at the beginning of this chapter, locate all infinitives and explain their uses.

Exercise 20d

Read aloud and translate. Explain uses of **dum** and of infinitives:

1. Cūr, Marce et Sexte, ad mediam noctem vigilāre in animō habētis?
2. Omnia vidēre et audīre volumus quod numquam anteā in caupōnā pernoctāvimus.
3. Dum puerī in caupōnā erant, dormīre nōlēbant.
4. Cūr voluistī hīc pernoctāre, Marce?
5. Cūr in caupōnā pernoctāvistis, puerī? Licetne fīliō senātōris in caupōnam intrāre?
6. Cornēlius servum in cubiculum īre iussit.
7. In viā pernoctāre perīculōsum est.
8. Dum Cornēlius et puerī cēnant, intrāvit mīles quīdam.
9. Vōbīs in caupōnā cēnāre licet.
10. Ego et tū cubitum īre nōluimus.

Exercise 20e

Using story 20 and the charts of forms showing perfect tense endings as guides, give the Latin for:

1. Cornelia: "I wanted to go to bed."
2. Boys: "We stayed with Cornelius."
3. Boys: "We intended to stay awake until midnight."
4. Cornelius: "Why do you laugh, boys?"
5. Soldier: "Why, sir, did you enter this inn?"
6. Cornelius: "I entered this inn because my carriage is stuck in a ditch."

Sign over a wine shop in Pompeii

ROMAN HOSPITALITY

Because inns were dirty and often dangerous, well-to-do Romans tried to avoid staying in them. Instead, they tried to plan their journey so that they could stay at the **vīlla** of a **hospes**. This word means "host" or "guest," but it is also translated as "friend," although in this special sense it has no exact equivalent in English. It describes a relationship established between two families in the past and kept up by every succeeding generation. As a result of such a relationship, a traveler could go to the house of his "family friend"—whom in some cases he personally might never have met—and claim **hospitium** for the night, producing, if need be, some token such as a coin that had been halved as proof of the link between the two families. Members of the host's family, if they happened to be traveling in a district in which their guest's family owned a **vīlla**, could claim similar rights of hospitality. It could extend to other situations. For instance, if a Roman had business interests in one of the provinces, someone residing there might look after them for him. In return, he might have some service done for him in Rome. Cornelius, you may remember, is taking care of Sextus while his father is in Asia.

Open-air dining room of a villa

Open-air triclinium of House of Neptune and Amphitrite at Herculaneum, Museo e Gallerie Nazionali di Capodimonte, Naples

FORMS

Verbs: Principal Parts

When we refer to a Latin verb, we normally give the four principal parts, from which all forms of that verb may be derived. Since Chapter 10 you have been seeing the first two principal parts of verbs in vocabulary lists. All four principal parts of the verb **parō** are:

parō: 1st person singular, present tense =
I prepare, I am preparing, I do prepare

parāre: present infinitive =
to prepare, to be preparing

parāvī: 1st person singular, perfect tense =
I prepared, I did prepare, I have prepared

parātus, -a, -um: perfect passive participle (verbal adjective) =
having been prepared, prepared, ready

	Present	Infinitive	Perfect	Perfect Passive Participle	Meaning of the Verb
1st Conj.	párō	paráre	parávī	parátus	*to prepare*
2nd Conj.	hábeō	habḗre	hábuī	hábitus	*to have*
3rd Conj.	míttō	míttere	mī́sī	míssus	*to send*
-iō	iáciō	iácere	iḗcī	iáctus	*to throw*
4th Conj.	aúdiō	audī́re	audī́vī	audī́tus	*to hear*

NOTES

1. The perfect stem is found by dropping the ***-ī*** from the end of the third principal part of the verb. The perfect endings are then added directly to this stem.

2. The fourth principal part of a Latin verb will usually be the *perfect passive participle*, which has the forms of a 1st and 2nd declension adjective. You have seen examples of this form in sentences such as the following from Chapter 10:

   Gaius ipse ascendere est **parātus**. (10:14)
   Gaius himself is **ready** *to climb [into the carriage].*

You have seen these other examples: **perterritus, -a, -um,** *frightened, terrified* (5:8); **commōtus, -a, -um,** *moved* (14:17); and **nārrātus, -a, -um,** *told* (20:23). You will study the perfect passive participle more fully later in the course.

3. Intransitive verbs do not have perfect passive participles, and the *future active participle* will be given as the fourth principal part instead:

   veniō, venīre, vēnī, ventūrus, *to come*

The future active participle **ventūrus** may be translated *being about to come*. You will study this form later.

4. The principal parts of most verbs of the 1st, 2nd, and 4th conjugations follow the patterns on the previous page.

5. In future vocabulary lists, the principal parts of verbs of the 1st, 2nd, and 4th conjugations that follow the set patterns will appear as follows:

   parō, -āre, -āvī, -ātus, *to prepare*
   habeō, -ēre, -uī, -itus, *to have, hold*
   audiō, -īre, -īvī, -ītus, *to hear*

   As you learned in Chapter 10, the infinitive shows to which conjugation a verb belongs.
   When verbs of the 1st, 2nd, and 4th conjugations do not follow the set patterns, their principal parts will be given in vocabulary lists in full:

   lavō, lavāre, lāvī, lautus, *to wash*

6. There is no set pattern for 3rd conjugation verbs. Their principal parts will be given in vocabulary lists in full:

   dūcō, dūcere, dūxī, ductus, *to lead*

7. The principal parts of irregular verbs will be given in full with the notation *irreg.*:

   sum, esse, fuī, futūrus, irreg., *to be*
   eō, īre, iī or **īvī, itūrus,** irreg., *to go*

The perfect tense of irregular verbs is formed by adding the perfect endings to the perfect stem in the same way as for all other verbs, e.g., **fu*ī*, fu*istī*, fu*it***, etc.

Note, however, that in the perfect tense forms of the verb **īre**, formed from the stem **i-**, the double **i**'s become **ī** before **s**:

	Sing.	Pl.
1	íī	íimus
2	ī́stī	ī́stis
3	íit	iḗrunt

This verb also has forms from the stem **īv-**: īvī, īvistī, īvit, etc.

8. It is very important that you learn the principal parts of Latin verbs.
   To help you do this, the principal parts of new verbs that do not follow the set patterns or are irregular will be given in separate verb lists following the stories in which they first appear from this point on.

The principal parts of verbs that you have already met that do not follow the set patterns or are irregular will also be given in these separate verb lists following the stories in which they first reappear from this point on.

New verbs that follow the set patterns in the 1st, 2nd, and 4th conjugations will be given with their principal parts abbreviated in the regular vocabulary lists.

Exercise 20f

Read aloud and translate each verb form given at the left below. Then deduce and give the first three principal parts for each verb:

	1st Sing. Present	Present Infinitive	1st Sing. Perfect
necāmus, necāvimus	necō	necāre	necāvī
intrant, intrāvērunt			
errās, errāvistī			
tenēs, tenuistī			
mittunt, mīsērunt			
manēmus, mānsimus			
iubet, iussit			
discēdimus, discessimus			
haeret, haesit			
dormiunt, dormīvērunt			
petunt, petīvērunt			
custōdīmus, custōdīvimus			
gemitis, gemuistis			

Can you give the first three principal parts for the following?

estis, fuistis			

509–265 B.C.

THE EARLY REPUBLIC

The Roman Republic grew steadily from 509 B.C., when the election of Lucius Junius Brutus and Lucius Tarquinius Collatinus as its first consuls signaled its birth, until 264 B.C., the start of the First Punic War. Rome expanded physically, until through military conquests she gained control of all of Italy south of the Rubicon River. Political growth came about through the adaptation of the constitution to meet the changing needs of society and circumstances. This constitution was not a formal, written document but a set of practices and policies. A major cause of change was the long, yet successful, struggle of the common people, the plebs, to acquire legal and political equality with the upper-class patricians.

THE CONSULS AND THE MAGISTRATES

The two consuls, essentially co-presidents, were both heads of the civil government and generals of the Roman army. The election of two leaders to a one-year term of office was a consciously dramatic change from the election of a single king for life, one that assured that no one person could have unlimited power.

As time went on, to assist the consuls in managing the affairs of state, other officers were named: praetors, who directed the judicial system; aediles, who supervised commerce and public works; tribunes, who championed the lower classes; and quaestors, who handled financial matters. These magistrates, like the consuls, were elected annually. To maintain the balance of power, two or more individuals generally bore the same title and either shared the same duties or performed matching roles in the government. As Rome grew and the Roman government had greater responsibilities to fulfill, the number of quaestors, aediles, and praetors was increased. Censors, moreover, were chosen every five years to revise the list of members of the Senate and carry out the census that assigned citizens to specific classes. In times of crisis, a dictator could be appointed to take over the government for a period of no more than six months, as did Cincinnatus. An ambitious Roman's political career might carry him up the steps of a series of offices, the **cursus honōrum:** election as quaestor, followed by appointment to the Senate, then terms as praetor, consul, and censor. After being quaestor one might also become a tribune of the plebs or an aedile before becoming a praetor.

The Centuriate assembly (**comitia centuriāta**) had its origin in the army, which was originally divided into centuries or groups of a hundred men. It passed laws, ratified treaties, issued declarations of war, and elected consuls, praetors, aediles, the censors, and the priests of the state religion. A citizen was assigned to his century or voting block in the Centuriate assembly according to his wealth, originally equalling the amount of military equipment he could afford. The cavalry or horsemen, **equitēs**, made up the eighteen richest of the 193 centuries. The next richest class made up eighty centuries of infantry or foot soldiers. At the bottom of the ranking were the citizens who owned no property, the proletariat, all heaped into one century. Each century cast a single vote, determined by the majority of the entire group, like the American electoral college. Since the ninety-eight votes of the two wealthiest classes could constitute the majority when the entire assembly voted, and since clients in the lower ranks usually voted according to the wishes of their richer patrons, it is easy to guess how the voting went.

The Tribal assembly **(comitia tribūta)**, an outgrowth of the Council of Plebeians, issued plebiscites, which eventually were as binding as laws passed by the Centuriate assembly. It also elected aediles and the tribunes, who, with their power of veto, could intercede in the passage of laws and in practices that were unjust to the plebeians.

The Senate, an advisory council whose members were former magistrates, controlled finances and foreign policy. In practice, they were the major influence in the government, for the magistrates followed the senators' advice and matters were brought before the assemblies only after the Senate had voiced its approval.

Rome and Its Warring Environs, 509–265 B.C.

A Roman Victory depicted by Peter Paul Rubens

"A Roman Triumph," oil on canvas, Peter Paul Rubens, National Gallery, London, England

THE CITIZEN ARMY

For Rome to survive its continual battles with her neighboring states, especially those in the hills, a larger citizen army was needed. The plebeian class provided that human resource, and once they had assumed the burden of military duty, they began to demand full equality as citizens. Military successes brought spoils of war and property grants and made the lower class more prosperous and ambitious. The wealthier plebeians especially were eager to attain equality with the patricians. By organizing a mass strike and refusing to perform their military service, the plebeians could force changes. Their leadership came from the tribunes, originally military officers, who gained acceptance as plebeian representatives before the Senate. As a first step, existing legal practices were codified and written down on bronze tablets. This first collection of Roman law, the Laws of the Twelve Tables, guaranteed every Roman citizen the right to justice. The Tribal assembly became an official body, with formal powers to pass plebescites and elect aediles and tribunes. Then the right to hold office, including the consulship, allowed the plebeians to become senators. And once the plebiscites of the Tribal assembly came to be equal to laws passed by the Centuriate assembly, Rome achieved a fairly representative form of government, in which a senatorial aristocracy of patricians and wealthy plebeians formed the new ruling class of citizens.

THE CONQUEST OF ITALY

The progress of the Roman military conquest of Italy is not a simple story, since the conquered did not always stay conquered. A new generation was likely to bring a new war with an old foe. The first victories came in the struggle to survive against the threats of neighbors: the Sabines, Aequi, and Volsci from the mountains inland; the Etruscans, pushing across the Tiber from the north; the Latins to the south. When the Gauls invaded Italy from the north in 390 B.C., going so far as to occupy all of Rome except the Capitoline Hill, the Romans, under the command of the legendary Camillus, led a unified Italian force that chased out the invaders, who were interested more in plunder than conquest. The Romans then revamped their military operations. A standing army was formed. The legions, now armed with spears and short swords, arranged in units or maniples that could maneuver quickly and attack in three waves, proved more effective than the old phalanx formation. The practice of establishing a camp with a fixed plan, even when the army was on the move over the growing network of Roman roads, provided a safety-measure of defense.

Following the military conquest of their neighbors and the Gallic invaders, the Romans faced new opponents. They confronted the Samnites and the Greek cities in southern Italy. When Pyrrhus, king of the Greek nation of Epirus, was invited to assist his fellow Greeks in repelling the Romans, he brought such novelties as elephants to Italy, but could win battles only at the expense of great losses to his manpower. After his famous Pyrrhic victory at Asculum (279 B.C.), the king reckoned the human cost and made his legendary remark, "One more victory like this, and we shall be truly ruined." After Pyrrhus went home to Greece, Rome was left master of Italy. From the time of the Gallic invasion, moreover, Rome ceased to be simply a vengeful conqueror and adopted the policy of forming an alliance with each city she won. These allies gave Rome military allegiance and control of foreign policy, but they retained home rule in the governing of their own states. To many neighbors, too, Rome offered Roman citizenship. Elsewhere throughout Italy, she planted colonies that provided a Roman presence. Thus Rome became not simply a strong city-state, but the head of a confederacy of cities in Italy.

MURDER

Mīles hanc fābulam nārrāvit.

Duo amīcī, Aulus et Septimus, dum iter in Graeciā faciunt, ad urbem Megaram vēnērunt. Aulus in caupōnā pernoctāvit, in vīllā hospitis Septimus. Mediā nocte, dum Septimus dormit, Aulus in somnō eī appāruit et clāmāvit. "Age, Septime! Fer mihi auxilium! Caupō mē necāre parat." 5

Septimus, somniō perterritus, statim surrēxit et, postquam animum recuperāvit, "Nihil malī," inquit. "Somnium modo fuit."

Deinde iterum obdormīvit. Iterum tamen in somnō Aulus suō amīcō appāruit; iterum Septimō clāmāvit, "Ubi ego auxilium petīvī, tū nōn vēnistī. Nēmō mē adiuvāre nunc potest. Caupō enim mē necāvit. Postquam hoc fēcit, corpus meum in plaustrō posuit et 10 stercus suprā coniēcit. In animō habet plaustrum ex urbe crās movēre. Necesse est igitur crās māne plaustrum petere et caupōnem pūnīre."

(continued)

4 **somnus, -ī**, m., *sleep*
eī, *to him*
6 **somnium, -ī**, n., *dream*
animum recuperāre, *to regain one's senses, be fully awake*
7 **nihil malī,** *nothing of a bad thing, there is nothing wrong*
malus, -a, -um, *bad*
8 **obdormiō, -īre, -īvī, -ītūrus,** *to go to sleep*
10 **corpus, corporis**, n., *body*
11 **stercus, stercoris**, n., *dung, manure*
suprā, adv., *above, on top*
12 **māne**, adv., *early in the day, in the morning*
pūniō, -īre, -īvī, -ītus, *to punish*

6 **surgō, surgere, surrēxī, surrēctūrus,** *to get up, rise*
7 **sum, esse, fuī, futūrus,** irreg. *to be*
9 **adiuvō, adiuvāre, adiūvī, adiūtus,** *to help*
10 **pōnō, pōnere, posuī, positus,** *to place, put*
11 **coniciō, conicere, coniēcī, coniectus,** *to throw*

Exercise 21a

Respondē Latīnē:

1. Ubi est Megara?
2. Ubi pernoctāvit Aulus? Ubi erat amīcus Aulī?
3. Quandō Aulus Septimō appāruit? **Quandō...?** *When...?*
4. Quid fēcit Septimus postquam animum recuperāvit?
5. Ubi caupō corpus Aulī posuit? Quid in animō habuit?

Iterum surrēxit Septimus. Prīmā lūce ad caupōnam iit et plaustrum petīvit. Ubi plaustrum invēnit, stercus remōvit et corpus extrāxit. Septimus, ubi amīcum mortuum vīdit, lacrimāvit. Caupō scelestus quoque lacrimāvit, nam innocentiam simulābat. 15
Septimus tamen caupōnem statim accūsāvit. Mox cīvēs eum pūnīvērunt.

Postquam mīles fābulam fīnīvit, silentium fuit. Subitō Cornēlius exclāmāvit, "Agite, puerī! Nōnne vōs iussī post cēnam cubitum īre? Cūr ad cubiculum nōn īstis?"

Sed Sextus, "Nōs quoque fābulam mīlitis audīre voluimus. Nōn dēfessī sumus. Nōn sērō est." 20

Hoc tamen dīxit Sextus quod cubitum īre timēbat. Dum enim fābulam mīlitis audiēbat, caupōnem spectābat. Cōgitābat, "Quam scelestus ille caupō vidētur! Certē in animō habet mediā nocte mē necāre. Necesse est vigilāre."

Etiam Marcus timēbat. Cōgitābat tamen, "Sī hic caupō est scelestus, gaudeō quod mīles in caupōnā pernoctat. Eucleidēs certē nōs adiuvāre nōn potest." 25

Invītī tandem puerī cubitum iērunt, vigilāre parātī. Mox tamen sēmisomnī fuērunt. Brevī tempore obdormīvit Marcus.

13 **prīmus, -a, -um,** *first*
lūx, lūcis, f., *light*
prīmā lūce, *at dawn*
14 **mortuus, -a, -um,** *dead*
15 **simulō, -āre, -āvī, -ātus,** *to pretend*
17 **fīniō, -īre, –īvī, -ītus,** *to finish*
20 **sērō** adv., *late*
22 **cōgitō, -āre, -āvī, -ātus,** *to think*
vidētur, (*he*) *seems*
26 **invītus, -a, -um,** *unwilling*

13 **eō, īre, iī** or **īvī, itūrus,** *to go*
petō, petere, petīvī, petītus, *to look for, seek, head for, aim at, attack*
14 **inveniō, invenīre, invēnī, inventus,** *to come upon, find*
removeō, removēre, remōvī, remōtus, *to remove, move aside*
extrahō, extrahere, extrāxī, extractus, *to drag out, take out*
15 **videō, vidēre, vīdī, vīsus,** *to see*
18 **iubeō, iubēre, iussī, iussus,** *to order, bid*
19 **volō, velle, voluī,** irreg., *to wish, want, be willing*
21 **dīcō, dīcere, dīxī, dictus,** *to say, tell*
25 **possum, posse, potuī,** irreg., *to be able; I can*

Respondē Latīnē:

1. Quid Septimus prīmā lūce fēcit?
2. Quandō lacrimāvit Septimus?
3. Cūr lacrimāvit caupō?
4. Quid cīvēs fēcērunt?
5. Quid Sextus timēbat?
6. Cūr Marcus gaudet?
7. Quōmodo puerī cubitum iērunt?
8. Quid Marcus et Sextus in animō habuērunt?

Exercise 21b

The following sentences contain errors of fact in the light of the last story you read. Explain these errors and give new Latin sentences that correct them:

1. Duo puerī, Aulus et Septimus, urbem Rōmam intrāvērunt.
2. Aulus et Septimus frātrēs Marcī erant.
3. Septimus mediā nocte surrēxit quod ēsuriēbat.
4. Aulus auxilium petīvit quod lectus sordidus erat.
5. Cīvēs, postquam Septimum necāvērunt, corpus sub stercore cēlāvērunt.
6. Caupō Septimum accūsāvit postquam cīvem mortuum invēnit.
7. Septimus cīvēs pūnīre in animō habuit quod scelestī erant.
8. Cīvēs corpus in caupōnā sub lectō invēnērunt.
9. Marcus cubitum īre timuit quod silentium erat.
10. Cornēlius caupōnem pūnīvit quod Marcus eum accūsāvit.

Vēnī, vīdī, vīcī. *I came, I saw, I conquered.* (**Julius Caesar, after the battle of Zela, 47 B.C.; reported in Suetonius,** ***Julius Caesar*** **XXXVII**)

Nihil sub sōle novum. *There's nothing new under the sun.* (**Vulgate,** ***Ecclesiastes*** **I.10**)

Mēns sāna in corpore sānō. *A sound mind in a sound body.* (**Juvenal X.356**)

Greece

Exercise 21c

Using the lists of principal parts given in the vocabularies on pages 39 and 40, give the Latin for:

1. What did you want, boys?
2. They got up suddenly.
3. The boys went to bed at last.
4. Septimus looked for the wagon.
5. What have you seen, girls?
6. We went to the inn.
7. What did you say, Marcus?
8. We ordered Cornelia to go to sleep.
9. What have they found?
10. He placed the body in the wagon.

Exercise 21d

Read aloud and translate. Identify the tense of each verb:

1. Marcus sub arbore sedēbat sed subitō surrēxit.
2. Iam advesperāscēbat et viātōrēs aedificia urbis cōnspexērunt.
3. Dāvus in hortō saepe labōrābat.
4. Servī cēnam parāvērunt et nunc cēnāre possumus.
5. Aurēlia in caupōnā pernoctāre nōluit.
6. "Ego," Cornēlius inquit, "in caupōnā numquam pernoctāvī."
7. Cornēlia manum ad canem identidem extendēbat.
8. Sextus ā cane fūgit.
9. Quamquam Marcus dormiēbat, Sextus obdormīre nōn potuit.

nōlō, nōlle, nōluī, irreg., *to be unwilling, not to wish, refuse*

Exercise 21e

Read aloud and translate:

SEXTUS CAN'T SLEEP

Sextus tamen nōn obdormīvit, nam dē mīlitis fābulā cōgitābat. Itaque diū vigilābat et dē Aulō mortuō cōgitābat. Tandem, "Marce!" inquit. "Tūne timuistī ubi illam fābulam audīvistī?"

Sed Marcus nihil respondit. Iterum, "Marce!" inquit. "Tūne caupōnem spectābās?" Iterum silentium! Deinde Sextus, iam timidus, "Marce! Marce!" (5) inquit. "Cūr tū obdormīvistī? Cūr tū nōn vigilāvistī?"

Subitō sonitum in cubiculō audīvit Sextus. "Ō mē miserum! Audīvitne sonitum Aulus ille miser ubi caupō eum necāre parābat? Quālis sonitus fuit?"

Sonitum Sextus iterum audīvit. "Ō Eucleidēs!" inquit. "Cūr ad cubiculum nōndum vēnistī? Ō pater! Cūr mē in Italiā relīquistī? Voluistīne ita mē ad mortem (10) mittere? In Asiam ad tē īre volō. Ibi enim nūllum est perīculum, sed perīculōsum est hīc in Italiā habitāre."

Multa sē rogābat Sextus, nam, quamquam puer temerārius esse solēbat, nunc mediā nocte in cubiculō tremēbat.

Itaque Sextus, per tōtam noctem vigilāre parātus, diū ibi sedēbat. "Quōmodo iam ē manibus caupōnis scelestī effugere possum? Suntne omnēs caupōnēs scelestī? Fortasse caupō mē, fīlium cīvis praeclārī, necāre in animō habet. Quamquam Aulus aurum habuit, ego tamen nihil habeō, neque aurum neque pecūniam." 15

Ita cōgitābat Sextus. Iterum sonitum audīvit. Timēbat sed tandem surrēxit invītus, nam omnēs cubiculī partēs īnspicere volēbat. Mox tamen rīsit. Ecce! Sub lectō erat fēlēs, obēsa et sēmisomna. Prope fēlem Sextus mūrem mortuum vīdit. Mussāvit Sextus, "Nōn necesse est hoc corpus sub stercore cēlāre!" 20

7 **sonitum,** *sound*
10 **ita,** adv., *thus, so, in this way*
ad mortem, *to my death*
 mors, mortis, gen. pl., **mortium,** f., *death*
13 **sē rogābat,** *(he) asked himself, wondered*
15 **tōtus, -a, -um,** *all, the whole*
18 **aurum, -ī,** n., *gold*
19 **pecūnia, -ae,** f., *money*
22 **fēlēs, fēlis,** gen. pl., **fēlium,** f., *cat*
mūs, mūris, m., *mouse*

4 **respondeō, respondēre, respondī, respōnsūrus,** *to reply*
10 **relinquō, relinquere, relīquī, relictus,** *to leave*
14 **tremō, tremere, tremuī,** *to tremble*
15 **sedeō, sedēre, sēdī, sessūrus,** *to sit*
16 **effugiō, effugere, effūgī,** *to run away, escape*
21 **īnspiciō, īnspicere, īnspexī, īnspectus,** *to examine*
rīdeō, rīdēre, rīsī, rīsus, *to laugh (at), smile*

Exercise 21f

In the first 12 lines of the passage above, locate the following in sequence:

1. All verbs in the present tense.
2. All verbs in the imperfect tense.
3. All verbs in the perfect tense.
4. All infinitives.

ADDITIONAL READING:
The Romans Speak for Themselves: Book I: "Ghosts," pages 59–64.

EAVESDROPPING

It was quite dark. Cornelia was still wide awake. All kinds of exciting sounds were floating up from the inn downstairs, inviting her to go down and have a look. She slipped out of bed, put a shawl around her shoulders, and tiptoed into the corridor where Eucleides was on guard.

"Take me downstairs, Eucleides," she wheedled. "I've never seen the inside of an inn before." This was quite true, because an upper-class Roman away from home preferred to stay in a friend's villa and avoided inns if possible.

Eucleides took a lot of persuading, but Cornelia could always get around him; he soon found himself downstairs, looking into the main room, with Cornelia peering from behind his arm.

It was pretty dark inside, despite the lamps. The atmosphere was thick with smoke and reeked of garlic. On the far side Cornelia could see her father; and nearer were other customers seated on stools at rough tables, and an evil-looking group they were.

"Stay away from them, Cornelia," whispered Eucleides. "Those rogues would murder their own mothers for a silver **dēnārius**."

But Eucleides needn't have worried because they were all absorbed in what was going on at the far end of the low room, where a girl was dancing. Above the hum of conversation her singing could be heard to the accompaniment of a rhythmic clacking noise she seemed to be making with her fingers. "Makes that noise with castanets," whispered Eucleides. "Dancing girl from Spain, probably Gades."

But one person was not paying much attention to the entertainment—the **tabellārius**, whose reckless driving had forced their **raeda** into the ditch. He had not come out of the incident unscathed. One of his horses had gone lame, and he was making the most of the enforced delay, drinking the innkeeper's best Falernian wine.

As Cornelia and Eucleides entered, the innkeeper was bringing forward a young man to introduce him to the courier. "This is Decimus Junius Juvenalis, Sir, a soldier like yourself." The **tabellārius**, unbending slightly as a rather haggard young man came forward wearing the insignia of a junior officer, dismissed the innkeeper with a look and said pleasantly enough, "Greetings, young man! Where are you from?"

"I'm on my way back from service in Britain, sir. What a place! They don't have any climate there, just bad weather! Mist, rain, hail, snow—the lot! Hardly a blink of sunshine!"

"Let me see!" said the **tabellārius**. "Who's governor of Britain these days? A chap called Agricola, I hear."

"That's right!" replied Juvenalis. "A madman, if you ask me. He's not content with conquering the bit of Britain that's near Gaul, where you can get something profitable, like silver or wool or hides or those huge hunting dogs. Before I left he had gone to the very edge of the world where the Caledonii live. They say that there, in the middle of

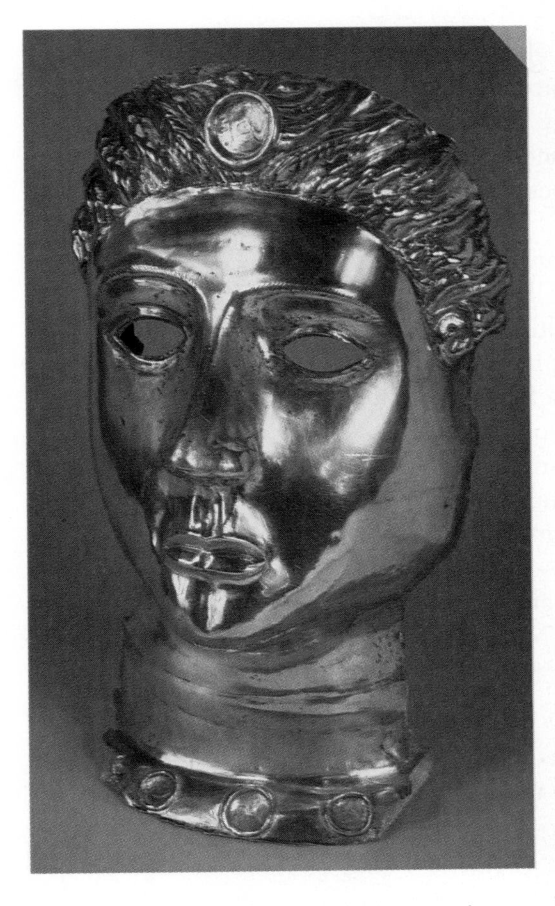

From silver mined in places like Britain the Romans fashioned beautiful pieces such as this mask.
Silver mask, Louvre, Paris, France

winter, the sun doesn't shine at all! But I can't vouch for that myself!"

"I've been to Britain too," said the **tabellārius**, much interested. "I'm not an ordinary **tabellārius**, you know. I personally carry dispatches only if they are confidential messages from—"

And here he whispered something in Juvenalis' ear which Cornelia could not catch.

The innkeeper sidled up again with some more wine.

"We get lots of interesting people stopping here on the Via Appia," he confided. "Not only military gentlemen like yourselves, or that scum of humanity there"—jerking his thumb toward the dancer's audience—"but special envoys to the Emperor himself. When Nero was Emperor, we had one of this new Jewish religious sect who lodged here on a journey all the way from Judaea, to be tried by the Emperor himself no less! He was called Paul or something—"

Suddenly Cornelia felt her ear seized between finger and thumb and looked around into the eyes of a very angry Aurelia. She found herself upstairs and back in bed before she knew what had happened.

Exercise 21g Read aloud and translate:

EARLY THE NEXT MORNING

Nōndum lūcēbat, sed Cornēlia, ut solēbat, iam surgēbat. Tunicam induit et tacitē ē cubiculō exiit, quod mātrem excitāre nōlēbat. Ē cubiculīs caupōnae nihil nisi silentium. Omnēs adhūc dormiēbant, sed Cornēlia audīre poterat vōcem ancillae quae iam in culīnā labōrābat. Cornēlia igitur ad culīnam appropinquāvit et fēminam cōnspexit. Dum Cornēlia spectat, fēmina cibum coquit et cantat. 5
Cornēlia intrat.

CORNĒLIA: Nōnne tū es fēmina quae saltat? Quid tibi nōmen est?

ANCILLA: Ita verō! Saltātrīx sum. Mē appellant Ēlissam. Quis es tū?

CORNĒLIA: Ego sum Cornēlia. Quis tē saltāre docuit?

ANCILLA: (*cum rīsū*) Ubi in urbe Gādibus habitābam cum parentibus, māter mē cum crotalīs saltāre, cantāre, multa alia facere docuit. 10

CORNĒLIA: Sī tū saltātrīx es, cūr cibum coquis?

ANCILLA: Fortasse sum saltātrīx; ancilla tamen sum.

CORNĒLIA: Tū ancilla es? Quōmodo ad Italiam vēnistī?

ANCILLA: Pīrātae mē in Hispāniā cēpērunt et ad Italiam tulērunt. Apollōdorus mē in urbe Rōmā ēmit. 15

CORNĒLIA: Cūr nōn effugis et ad Hispāniam redīs?

ANCILLA: Quōmodo effugere possum? Nūllōs amīcōs in Italiā habeō et ad Hispāniam sōla redīre nōn possum. Praetereā Apollodōrus dominus bonus est quod ipse servus fuit. Mē numquam verberat et omnia dat quae volō. 20

CORNĒLIA: Praeter lībertātem.

ANCILLA: Ita vērō! Praeter lībertātem.

4 **culīna, -ae,** f., *kitchen*
5 **cantō, -āre, -āvī, -ātus,** *to sing*
7 **saltō, -āre, -āvī, -ātūrus,** *to dance*
8 **saltātrīx, saltātrīcis,** f., *dancer*
appellō, -āre, -āvī, -ātus, *to call, name*
10 **Gādēs, Gādium,** f. pl., *Gades, Cadiz, a town in Spain*
11 **crotalum, -ī,** n., *castanet*
15 **pīrāta, -ae,** m., *pirate*
21 **praeter,** prep. + acc., *except*
lībertās, lībertātis, f., *freedom*

5 **cōnspiciō, cōnspicere, cōnspexī, cōnspectus,** *to catch sight of*
11 **doceō, docēre, docuī, doctus,** *to teach*
15 **capiō, capere, cēpī, captus,** *to take, capture*
ferō, ferre, tulī, lātus, irreg., *to bring, carry*
16 **emō, emere, ēmī, ēmptus,** *to buy*
20 **dō, dare, dedī, datus,** *to give*

"Noblewoman Playing a Cithara," wall painting, Metropolitan Museum of Art, New York

Garum → wishtrashire

REVIEW IV: CHAPTERS 18–21

Exercise IVa: Agreement of Adjectives and Nouns

Complete the following sentences with 3rd declension adjectives to match the English cues. Make the adjective agree with the underlined noun. Read aloud and translate:

1. <u>Cornēliī</u> ē raedā dēscendērunt ______. (unhurt)
2. Pater <u>fīliam</u> ______ laudāvit. (brave)
3. <u>Puer</u> ______ lupum repellit. (brave)
4. In ______ <u>caupōnā</u> lectī sunt sordidī. (every)
5. ______ <u>caupōnēs</u> nōn sunt scelestī. (All)
6. <u>Puella</u> ______ stat et manum ad canem extendit. (motionless)
7. Prīnceps ______ <u>senātōrēs</u> Rōmam redīre iussit. (all)
8. ______ <u>Cornēliī</u> Rōmam rediēbant. (all)
9. Servī per agrōs cum <u>canibus</u> ______ currunt. (brave)
10. Cornēlia et Flāvia sunt <u>puellae</u> strēnuae et ______. (brave)

Review the present, imperfect, and perfect tenses of regular verbs and of the irregular verbs **esse, velle, nōlle,** and **īre** in the charts on pages 137–138 before doing exercises IVb–IVd.

Exercise IVb: Identification of Verb Forms; Principal Parts

Identify the tense, person, and number of each of the following verb forms. Then give the principal parts of each verb:

		Tense	Person	Number
1. veniēbātis		______	______	______
	______	______	______	______
2. cōgitāvistis		______	______	______
	______	______	______	______
3. coniciēbam		______	______	______
	______	______	______	______
4. iussērunt		______	______	______
	______	______	______	______
5. surrēxī		______	______	______
	______	______	______	______
6. removēbās		______	______	______
	______	______	______	______
7. clāmāvistī		______	______	______
	______	______	______	______
8. obdormiēbāmus		______	______	______
	______	______	______	______

Exercise IVc: Imperfect, Present, and Perfect Tenses

Change the following irregular verbs to the present tense and then to the perfect tense. Keep the same person and number:

	Present	Perfect
1. volēbam	______	______
2. erāmus	______	______
3. volēbās	______	______
4. ībant	______	______
5. erās	______	______
6. ībās	______	______
7. nōlēbat	______	______
8. ībātis	______	______
9. erant	______	______
10. nōlēbātis	______	______

Exercise IVd: Uses of *Dum* and of Infinitives

Read aloud and translate. Explain uses of **dum** and of infinitives:

1. Dum Cornēliī ad caupōnam appropinquant, subitō canis appāruit.
2. Cornēliī in caupōnā pernoctāre in animō habuērunt.
3. Perīculōsum nōn est in hāc caupōnā pernoctāre.
4. Cornēliōs caupō intrāre iussit.
5. Aurēlia et Cornēlia in caupōnā cēnāre nōluērunt.
6. Puerīs licet vigilāre et mīlitis fābulam audīre.
7. Dum mīles fābulam nārrābat, puerī vigilābant et audiēbant.
8. "Hic lectus est sordidus," inquit Aurēlia. "Necesse est alium lectum petere."
9. Aurēlia et Cornēlia in cubiculō manent, dum servī alium lectum petunt.
10. Aurēlia in lectō sordidō dormīre nōluit.
11. Dum Aurēlia et Cornēlia in cubiculō manent, servī alium lectum in cubiculum portāvērunt.

Exercise IVe: Translation

Read aloud and translate:

MUCIUS GIVES A LESSON IN ROMAN VIRTUE

Porsenna, rēx Clūsīnōrum, urbem Rōmam iam diū obsidēbat. Rōmānī igitur, quod cibum in urbem ferre nōn poterant, famē perībant. Tum mīles quīdam Rōmānus, Gaius Mūcius nōmine, quī cīvēs et patriam servāre volēbat, Porsennam necāre cōnstituit.

Itaque Mūcius ad senātōrēs Rōmānōs iit et, "Tiberim trānsīre," inquit, "et castra hostium intrāre in animō habeō. Ibi rēgem Porsennam necāre volō." 5

Respondērunt senātōrēs, "Sī hoc temptāre vīs, tibi licet." Laetus domum rediit Mūcius. Gladium arripuit et sub tunicā cēlāvit. Trāns Tiberim festīnāvit et castra hostium fūrtim intrāvit. Ibi magnam multitūdinem mīlitum vīdit. Ad mēnsam ante mīlitēs sedēbant duo hominēs. Alter pecūniam mīlitibus dabat, alter spectābat. Cōgitābat Mūcius, "Uter est rēx? Nōnne ille est, quī omnia facit? Necesse est illum necāre!" 10

Mūcius ad mēnsam appropinquāvit et virum gladiō necāvit. Stupuērunt omnēs mīlitēs. Ē castrīs effugiēbat Mūcius sed mīlitēs eum cēpērunt.

"Ō sceleste!" inquiunt. "Cūr scrībam rēgis necāvistī?" 15

"Rēgem, nōn scrībam, necāre volēbam," respondit Mūcius.

Rēx, ubi haec audīvit, īrātus erat et mīlitēs iussit Mūcium pūnīre. Superbē respondit Mūcius: "Cīvis Rōmānus sum. Mē Gaium Mūcium vocant. Castra intrāvī quod urbem Rōmam servāre in animō habēbam. Mē cēpistī sed poenās nōn timeō." 20

Eō ipsō tempore stābat Mūcius prope āram et ignem. Subitō dextram manum in ignem iniēcit. Rēx statim surrēxit et mīlitēs iussit virum ab igne trahere. "Quamquam," inquit, "hostis es, tē ad cīvēs tuōs iam remittō quod vir fortissimus es."

Postquam Mūcius Rōmam rediit, rem tōtam nārrāvit. Cīvēs Mūcium nōn modo laudābant sed, quod iam sinistram modo manum habēbat, eum appellāvērunt Scaevolam. 25

1 **rēx, rēgis,** m., *king*
Clūsīnī, -ōrum, m. pl., *the people of Clusium*
2 **famē perīre,** *to die of hunger*
3 **patria, -ae,** f., *native land*
servō, -āre, -āvī, -ātus, *to save*
5 **Tiberis, Tiberis,** m., *the Tiber River*
6 **castra, -ōrum,** n. pl., *camp*
hostēs, hostium, m. pl., *the enemy*
8 **gladius, -ī,** m., *sword*
trāns, prep. + acc., *across*
9 **multitūdō, multitūdinis,** f., *crowd*
10 **mēnsa, -ae,** f., *table*
ante, prep. + acc., *in front of*
mīlitibus, *to the soldiers*
11 **Uter…?** *Which (of the two)…?*
ille, *that one*
13 **stupeō, -ēre, -uī,** *to be amazed*
15 **scrība, -ae,** m., *scribe*
17 **superbē,** adv., *proudly*
18 **vocō, -āre, -āvī, -ātus,** *to call*
19 **poenae, -ārum,** f. pl., *punishment*
21 **āra, -ae,** f., *altar*
ignis, ignis, gen. pl., **ignium,** m., *fire*
dexter, dextra, dextrum, *right*
23 **fortissimus, -a, -um,** *very brave*
26 **sinister, sinistra, sinistrum,** *left*
27 **Scaevola, -ae,** m., *Scaevola (nickname derived from the adjective* **scaevus, -a, -um,** *left)*

1 **obsideō, obsidēre, obsēdī, obsessus,** *to besiege*
4 **cōnstituō, cōnstituere, cōnstituī, cōnsitūtus,** *to decide*
5 **trānseō, trānsīre, trānsiī** or **trānsīvī, trānsitus,** irreg., *to cross*
22 **iniciō, inicere, iniēcī, iniectus,** *to throw (into)*
23 **remittō, remittere, remīsī, remissus,** *to send back*

FROM THE INN TO ROME

Iam diēs erat. Prīmā lūce raedārius auxiliō servōrum caupōnis raedam ē fossā extrāxit et ad caupōnam admōvit. Tum servī cistās Cornēliōrum raedāriō trādidērunt. Intereā in caupōnā, dum omnēs sē parābant, Sextus, iam immemor terrōris nocturnī, mīlitis fābulam Cornēliae nārrābat; Eucleidēs mandāta servīs dabat. Cornēlius ipse Aurēliae et līberīs clāmābat, "Agite, omnēs! Nōlīte cessāre! Tempus est discēdere." 5

Tandem cūnctī ē caupōnā vēnērunt et in raedam ascendērunt.

"Valē!" clāmāvērunt puerī.

"Valēte!" respondit caupō, quī in viā stābat. "Nōlīte in fossam iterum cadere! Nōn in omnibus caupōnīs bene dormīre potestis."

Tum raedārius habēnās sūmpsit et equōs verberāvit. Tandem Rōmam iterum petēbant. 10

In itinere Sextus omnia dē mūre mortuō Marcō explicāvit; Cornēlius mīlitis fābulam uxōrī nārrāvit. Iam urbī appropinquābant, cum subitō puerī ingēns aedificium cōnspexērunt.

(continued)

1 **auxiliō,** *with the help*
2 **raedāriō,** *to the coachman*
3 **sē parāre,** *to prepare oneself, get ready*
immemor, immemoris + gen., *forgetful*
nocturnus, -a, -um, *happening during the night*
4 **Cornēliae,** *to Cornelia*
mandātum, -ī, n., *order, instruction*
9 **bene,** adv., *well*
10 **habēnae, -ārum,** f. pl., *reins*
12 **uxōrī,** *to his wife*
cum, conj., *when*
ingēns, ingentis, *huge*

2 **admoveō, admovēre, admōvī, admōtus,** *to move toward*
trādō, trādere, trādidī, trāditus, *to hand over*
5 **discēdō, discēdere, discessī, discessūrus,** *to go away, depart*
6 **ascendō, ascendere, ascendī, ascēnsus,** *to climb, climb into (a carriage)*
8 **stō, stāre, stetī, statūrus,** *to stand*
cadō, cadere, cecidī, cāsūrus, *to fall*
10 **sūmō, sūmere, sūmpsī, sūmptus,** *to take, take up*

Exercise 22a

Respondē Latīnē:

1. Cui Sextus mīlitis fābulam nārrābat?
2. Quid Eucleidēs faciēbat?
3. Quid dīxit caupō ubi Cornēliī discēdēbant?
4. Quid fēcit raedārius?
5. Quid Sextus Marcō explicāvit?
6. Quid puerī cōnspexērunt?

Marcus patrem, "Quid est illud?" rogāvit.
Atque Sextus, "Quis in illō aedificiō habitat?" 15
Cui Cornēlius, "Nēmō ibi habitat," cum rīsū respondit. "Est sepulcrum Messallae Corvīnī quī erat ōrātor praeclārus. Hīc sunt sepulcra multōrum et praeclārōrum cīvium quod Rōmānīs nōn licet intrā urbem sepulcra habēre."
Mox alterum aedificium magnum vīdērunt.
"Estne id quoque sepulcrum, pater?" rogāvit Marcus. 20
"Ita vērō!" Cornēlius respondit. "Est sepulcrum Caeciliae Metellae. Nōnne dē Caeciliā Metellā audīvistī?"
Sed Marcus patrī nihil respondit. Iam enim urbem ipsam vidēre poterat. "Ecce Rōma!" clāmāvit.
"Ecce Rōma! Ecce Rōma!" clāmāvērunt Sextus et Cornēlia. 25
Tum Cornēlius, "Brevī tempore ad Portam Capēnam adveniēmus et Titum, patruum vestrum, ibi vidēbimus. Epistulam enim per servum mīsī et omnia eī explicāvī. Titus mox nōs prope Portam excipiet."

14 **illud,** *that*
15 **atque,** conj., *and, also*
16 **sepulcrum, -ī,** n., *tomb*
18 **intrā,** prep. + acc., *inside*
26 **adveniēmus,** *we will come*
patruus, -ī, m., *uncle*
27 **vester, vestra, vestrum,** *your* (pl.)
vidēbimus, *we will see*
28 **excipiet,** *he will welcome*

28 **excipiō, excipere, excēpī, exceptus,** *to welcome, receive*

Respondē Latīnē:

1. Cūr sepulcra nōn sunt intrā urbem?
2. Cuius est alterum sepulcrum? **Cuius**...? Whose...?
3. Audīvitne Marcus dē Caeciliā Metellā?
4. Quis Cornēliōs ad Portam Capēnam excipiet?

Amīcus omnibus amīcus nēminī. ***A friend to everyone is a friend to no one.***

FORMS

Nouns: Cases and Declensions: Dative Case

Look at the following sentences:

1. Mandāta **servīs** dabat. (22:4)
He was giving orders ***to the slaves.***
2. Omnia **Marcō** explicāvit. (22:11)
He explained everything ***to Marcus.***

3. Cornēlius fābulam **uxōrī** nārrāvit. (22:11–12)
*Cornelius told the story **to his wife**.*

4. Servī meī bonam cēnam **vōbīs** parāre possunt. (19:2–3)
*My slaves are able to prepare a good dinner **for you**.*

The Latin words in bold type are all in the *dative case* and may be translated using *to*... or *for*....

Here is a table showing the groups of nouns and cases, including the dative:

Number Case	1st Declension	2nd Declension				3rd Declension		
	Fem.	Masc.	Masc.		Neut.	Masc.	Fem.	Neut.
Singular								
Nom.	puell*a*	serv*us*	puer	ager	bacul*um*	pater	vōx	nōmen
Gen.	puell*ae*	serv*ī*	puer*ī*	agr*ī*	bacul*ī*	patr*is*	vōc*is*	nōmin*is*
Dat.	puell*ae*	serv*ō*	puer*ō*	agr*ō*	bacul*ō*	patr*ī*	vōc*ī*	nōmin*ī*
Acc.	puell*am*	serv*um*	puer*um*	agr*um*	bacul*um*	patr*em*	vōc*em*	nōmen
Abl.	puell*ā*	serv*ō*	puer*ō*	agr*ō*	bacul*ō*	patr*e*	vōc*e*	nōmin*e*
Voc.	puell*a*	serv*e*	puer	ager	bacul*um*	pater	vōx	nōmen
Plural								
Nom.	puell*ae*	serv*ī*	puer*ī*	agr*ī*	bacul*a*	patr*ēs*	vōc*ēs*	nōmin*a*
Gen.	puell*ārum*	serv*ōrum*	puer*ōrum*	agr*ōrum*	bacul*ōrum*	patr*um*	vōc*um*	nōmin*um*
Dat.	puell*īs*	serv*īs*	puer*īs*	agr*īs*	bacul*īs*	patr*ibus*	vōc*ibus*	nōmin*ibus*
Acc.	puell*ās*	serv*ōs*	puer*ōs*	agr*ōs*	bacul*a*	patr*ēs*	vōc*ēs*	nōmin*a*
Abl.	puell*īs*	serv*īs*	puer*īs*	agr*īs*	bacul*īs*	patr*ibus*	vōc*ibus*	nōmin*ibus*
Voc.	puell*ae*	serv*ī*	puer*ī*	agr*ī*	bacul*a*	patr*ēs*	vōc*ēs*	nōmin*a*

Be sure to learn the new dative forms thoroughly.

NOTES

1. In each declension dative and ablative plurals have the same endings.
2. The datives of the pronouns are as follows:

Singular		Plural	
Nominative	*Dative*	*Nominative*	*Dative*
ego	**mihi**	**nōs**	**nōbīs**
tū	**tibi**	**vōs**	**vōbīs**
is, ea, id	**eī**	**eī, eae, ea**	**eīs**
Quis...?	**Cui...?**	**Quī...?**	**Quibus...?**

Here is a table showing the adjectives, including the dative case:

Number / Case	1st and 2nd Declensions			3rd Declension		
	Masc.	**Fem.**	**Neut.**	**Masc.**	**Fem.**	**Neut.**
Singular						
Nom.	magn***us***	magn***a***	magn***um***	omn***is***	omn***is***	omn***e***
Gen.	magn***ī***	magn***ae***	magn***ī***	omn***is***	omn***is***	omn***is***
Dat.	magn***ō***	magn***ae***	magn***ō***	omn***ī***	omn***ī***	omn***ī***
Acc.	magn***um***	magn***am***	magn***um***	omn***em***	omn***em***	omn***e***
Abl.	magn***ō***	magn***ā***	magn***ō***	omn***ī***	omn***ī***	omn***ī***
Voc.	magn***e***	magn***a***	magn***um***	omn***is***	omn***is***	omn***e***
Plural						
Nom.	magn***ī***	magn***ae***	magn***a***	omn***ēs***	omn***ēs***	omn***ia***
Gen.	magn***ōrum***	magn***ārum***	magn***ōrum***	omn***ium***	omn***ium***	omn***ium***
Dat.	magn***īs***	magn***īs***	magn***īs***	omn***ibus***	omn***ibus***	omn***ibus***
Acc.	magn***ōs***	magn***ās***	magn***a***	omn***ēs***	omn***ēs***	omn***ia***
Abl.	magn***īs***	magn***īs***	magn***īs***	omn***ibus***	omn***ibus***	omn***ibus***
Voc.	magn***ī***	magn***ae***	magn***a***	omn***ēs***	omn***ēs***	omn***ia***

You should now have thoroughly learned all of the forms above and on the previous page.

3rd Declension Adjectives of One Termination

Most 3rd declension adjectives have two different endings in the nominative singular, one that is used when the adjective modifies masculine or feminine nouns (e.g. **omn*is* ager, omn*is* vīlla**) and a second ending that is used when the adjective modifies neuter nouns (**omn*e* sepulcrum**).

Some 3rd declension adjectives use the same form in the nominative when the adjective modifies masculine, feminine, *or* neuter nouns, as **immemor,** *forgetful*, and **ingēns,** *huge*. Thus, we can say **ingēns ager** (masculine), **ingēns vīlla** (feminine), and **ingēns sepulcrum** (neuter). Adjectives of this sort are called *adjectives of one termination.* The nominative and genitive are given in vocabulary entries for this type of adjective: **immemor, immemoris,** and **ingēns, ingentis.** The base is found by dropping the ***-is*** ending from the genitive singular, and to this base are added the same endings as for **omnis.** As always, the neuter nominative and accusative are the same in the singular and in the plural.

Exercise 22b

Write out a full set of the forms of **immemor.**

BUILDING THE MEANING
The Dative Case

1. The sentence below illustrates a basic pattern with which you have been familiar since Chapter 4:

   S DO TV
   Cornēlius fābulam nārrāvit.
   Cornelius told the story.

   You will often find sentences of this type with a subject (S), direct object (DO), and a transitive verb (TV) expanded with a word or phrase in the *dative case* that will modify the verb. In the sentence below the word in the dative case tells *to whom* the story was told:

   S DO IO TV
   Cornēlius fābulam **uxōrī** nārrāvit. (22:11–12)

   The word in the dative case, **uxōrī**, is called the *indirect object* (IO). Words or phrases in the dative case functioning as indirect objects will often be found with verbs of *giving*, *showing*, and *telling*. They answer the question "to whom...?"

   Note that sentences with indirect objects can often be translated two ways in English. For example, the sentence above can be translated:

   Cornelius told the story ***to his wife***. or *Cornelius told* ***his wife*** *the story.*

2. Note also that sometimes a word or phrase in the dative case can best be translated *for...* instead of *to...*:

   Servī meī bonam cēnam **vōbīs** parāre possunt. (19:2–3)
   My slaves are able to prepare a good dinner ***for you***.

3. The dative case may also be found in sentences in which the verb is intransitive and does not have a direct object:

   Aulus **Septimō** clāmāvit. (21:8–9)
   Aulus shouted ***to Septimus***.

   Aulus in somnō **eī** appāruit. (21:4)
   Aulus appeared ***to him*** *in (his) sleep.*

4. The intransitive verb **appropinquāre,** *to approach*, is sometimes used with the preposition **ad** + acc.:

   Mox **ad caupōnam** appropinquābant.
   Soon they were coming near ***to the inn****/approaching* ***the inn.***

   It may also be used with a word or phrase in the dative case:

   Iam **urbī** appropinquābant. (22:12)
   Already they were coming near ***to the city****/approaching* ***the city***.

5. You have also seen the dative case used with the impersonal verbal phrase **necesse est**, *it is necessary*, and the impersonal verb **licet**, *it is allowed*, with infinitives as their subjects:

   Cūr **mihi** quoque necesse est ad urbem redīre? (8:13–14)
   Why is to return to the city necessary ***for me*** *too?*
   Why is it necessary ***for me*** *too to return to the city?*

   "Licetne **nōbīs**," inquit Marcus, "hīc cēnāre?" (20:7)
   "Is to eat here allowed ***for us****?" said Marcus.*
   "Is it allowed ***for us****," said Marcus, "to eat here?"*
   "May ***we*** *eat here?" said Marcus.*

Exercise 22c

Reword the sentence **Cornēlius fābulam uxōrī nārrāvit** to show that Cornelius told the story to each of the following in turn: Septimus, Flāvia, puellae, mīles, puerī, raedārius, senātōrēs, caupō, viātōrēs.

Exercise 22d

In each sentence identify the word or phrase in the dative case and the reason for its use. Then read the sentence aloud and translate it:

1. Patruus pecūniam puerīs dat.
2. Ancilla invīta caupōnī scelestō cibum trādit.
3. Omnia patrī meō semper dīcō.
4. Nihil lēgātō prīncipis dīxit.
5. Cornēlius epistulam ad Titum mīsit et omnia eī explicāvit.
6. Marcus, "Tacē, Sexte!" inquit. "Nōbīs nōn licet hīc clāmāre."
7. In somnīs Aulus amīcō Septimō appāruit.
8. Dum Cornēliī urbī appropinquābant, Titus omnia eīs parābat.
9. Apollodōrus Cornēliīs cubicula mōnstrat. **mōnstrō, -āre, -āvī, -ātus,** *to show*
10. Servī alium lectum Aurēliae parāvērunt.

Exercise 22e

Give the Latin for:

1. Suddenly a soldier appeared to them.
2. "May I stay awake and hear the soldier's story?" asked Marcus.
3. It was necessary for Aurelia and Cornelia to go to bed, for they were tired.
4. Sextus told the soldier's story to Cornelia.
5. They were approaching the tomb of Caecilia Metella.

Nouns: Dative or Ablative?

You will have noticed that the dative and ablative cases often have identical endings, e.g., **servō, puellīs, mīlitibus**. How are you to tell which case is used in a particular sentence? The Latin will usually provide clues to help you decide correctly:

a. Is the noun preceded by a preposition? If it is, the noun will be in the ablative case because no preposition governs the dative case.

b. If there is no preposition, does the noun refer to a *person*? If it does, it will normally be in the dative because nouns referring to persons are usually governed by a preposition if they are in the ablative. If the noun refers to a *thing*, it is more likely to be ablative than dative (exception: a word in the dative case with the verb **appropinquāre** often refers to a thing).

Consider the following sentences, noting the clues provided by each word and group of words as you meet them:

1. **Canem nostrum puerō dedit.**
   The words **canem nostrum** are obviously accusative. When we reach **puerō**, knowing that **puer** refers to a person, we can say that it must be in the dative case because it would be governed by a preposition if it were in the ablative case. A Roman reading as far as **puerō** would have known before he reached the verb that someone was transferring "our dog" in some way or other "to the boy."

2. **Puerō canem nostrum dedimus.**
   The fact that **puerō** comes first in the sentence does not alter the reasoning. Since it refers to a person and is not governed by a preposition, it must be in the dative case and, again, some transfer is taking place.

3. **Canem nostrum baculō verberat.**
   When we come to **baculō**, knowing that **baculum** refers to a thing, we can be sure because of the sense that it is in the ablative case. A Roman would have understood as soon as he reached **baculō** that someone was "doing" something to our dog *with* a stick.

4. **Baculō canem nostrum verberat.**
   Again, the fact that **baculō** appears as the first word makes no difference. We again know that **baculō** must be in the ablative case because it refers to a thing, and when we come to **canem** we know that someone is "doing" something to our dog *with* a stick.

Remember that some 3rd declension nouns end in ***-ō*** in the nominative singular, e.g., **caupō**. By knowing that such nouns belong to the 3rd declension, you will not be tempted to think that the ***-ō*** indicates dative case.

Exercise 22f

Look carefully for the types of clues mentioned in the preceding discussion to help you with the words in boldface that could be dative or ablative in form. Identify each as dative or ablative and then translate the entire sentence:

1. Septimus omnia dē Aulō mortuō **cīvibus** explicāvit.
2. Mihi necesse est **equīs meīs** cibum dare.
3. Marcus **rāmō** lupum repellit.
4. Sextus **raedāriō** clāmāvit, "Tenē equōs! Cavē fossam!"
5. Raedārius **habēnīs** equōs dēvertēbat.
6. Cūr tū **ancillīs** lībertātem nōn dedistī?
7. Raedārius habēnās **manibus** sūmpsit.
8. Nōs bonam cēnam **hospitibus** parāvimus, domine.
9. **Puerīs** quoque cibum date!
10. Ego in animō habeō corpus et stercus **plaustrō** ē caupōnā removēre.
11. Mediā nocte Aulus in somnō **amīcō suō** appāruit.
12. **Rūsticīs** necesse erat bovēs tardōs **clāmōribus** et **baculīs** incitāre.
13. Mercātōrēs togās et tunicās **cīvibus** mōnstrant.

mercātor, mercātōris, m., *merchant*

The tomb of Caecilia Metella is situated on the Appian Way. The crenelations on the top of the rotunda are a medieval addition.

Exercise 22g

Here is the inscription from the tomb of Caecilia Metella on the Appian Way. Which words in the inscription are in the dative case, and which are in the genitive?

CAECILIAE
Q·CRETICI·F
METELLAE·CRASSI

Caeciliae
Q(uīntī) Crēticī f(īliae)
Metellae Crassī

(the tomb dedicated) to Caecilia Metella, daughter of Quintus (Caecilius Metellus) Creticus, (wife) of Crassus

FRONTIER LIFE I

ROME AND NORTHERN EUROPE

When we think of the Roman conquest of parts of northwestern Europe and the subsequent spread of Roman civilization to these areas, we most often visualize the Roman general Julius Caesar and his army subjugating what is now France, called **Gallia** by the Romans, from 58 to 51 B.C. and invading Britain in 55 and 54 B.C. Or we think of Agricola, legate of the Twentieth Legion in Britain (A.D. 71–73), who, when governor of Britain (A.D. 78–83), led Roman troops as far as the Scottish Highlands, where the Caledonii lived (Agricola was mentioned in "Eavesdropping" on pages 178–179).

These images of the northward expansion of Roman power and control are quite correct, but there were men, other than these commanders, who brought about the Romanization of the native peoples in these areas. Perhaps these men had greater influence than their commanders because they had closer contact with the ordinary people. These men were the **mīlitēs legiōnāriī**, the ordinary foot soldiers of the legions. What follows is an imaginary account of how a common soldier might have helped to bring about the Romanization process somewhere in **Gallia** or **Germānia** shortly after the Roman conquest of those areas.

Vercingetorix before Caesar, 52 B.C.

"Vercingetorix before Caesar, 52 B.C.," oil on canvas, Henri-Paul Motte, Musée Crozatier, Le Puy en Velay, France

Our soldier, whom we will call Lucius, is a man in the Twentieth Legion (**Legiō XX Valeria**). This legion was transferred from Illyricum to the site of the modern Cologne (called **Āra Ubiōrum**, "Altar of the Ubii," by the Romans) on the Rhine River (**Rhēnus**), a site inhabited by a German tribe known as the Ubii and protected since 38 B.C. by a Roman army camp. The legion was transferred there to help defend the Roman frontier shortly after the destruction of three Roman legions by the Germans in the Teutoburg Forest in A.D. 9 during the reign of the first emperor, Augustus (emperor 27 B.C.– A.D. 14). Lucius falls in love with Helge, an Ubian girl. A number of years before, Helge's family had been given land by Marcus Vipsanius Agrippa, when he moved the Ubii at their request from the eastern to the western bank of the Rhine in 38 B.C.

When Lucius learns that Helge is carrying his child, he arranges to marry her, although Roman law stipulated that any marriage contracted by a Roman soldier below the rank of centurion was invalid. However, many of the legionaries held marriage ceremonies with local women who lived in the area near the **castra** or legionary camp. Thus, before his bunkmates (**contubernālēs**), Lucius placed a small gold ring on the third finger of Helge's left hand, and she, prompted by Lucius, recited the traditional marriage

Roman Army Camp

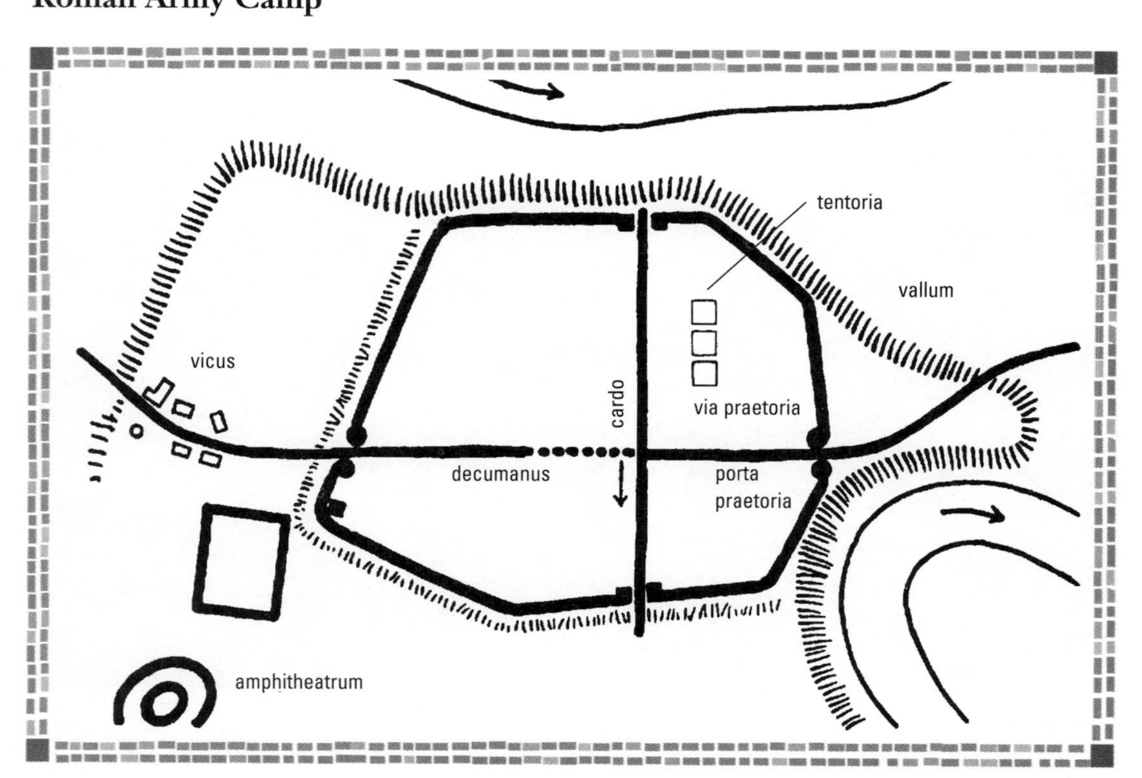

vow, **Ubi tū Gaius, ego Gaia**, "When/Where you are Gaius, I am Gaia." Although the girl knew only a few words of Latin, she understood that this stocky and swarthy man was now her "husband."

Before the marriage ceremony, Lucius and his comrades had built a small hut for Helge. However, instead of building the hut in any open space that suited them, as the Germans did in their villages, the men carefully selected a location in accordance with the plan of streets established by surveyors (**agrimēnsōrēs**) when the Roman settlement of Ara Ubiorum began to be transformed into an outpost town about 12 B.C. There were two main streets, the north-south axis or **cardō**, and the **decumānus**, the east-west axis, oriented to the sunrise on September 23, the birthday of Augustus Caesar. This plan provided locations for a **forum**, which included a marketplace with shops, a **tabulārium** for the keeping of records, a theater, temples with altars not only to the Roman gods but also to Helge's gods such as the Three Mothers, and houses for the town's inhabitants. This foresight and planning were very different from the haphazard way Helge's people built their settlements, and the girl felt new respect and admiration for her husband's people, the Romans.

WORD STUDY VI

English Words from the Fourth Principal Part of Latin Verbs

The stem of the fourth principal part of a Latin verb may be the source of other Latin words and of English derivatives. This stem is found by dropping the ***-us*** or the ***-ūrus*** from the end of the fourth principal part, e.g., the stem of **vīsus** is **vīs-**. Here are some common types of words formed from the stem of the fourth principal part:

1. No suffix.
   The stem may form an English word with no change:
   invent (**inventus**) fact (**factus**)

2. Silent *-e*.
   An English word may be formed by adding silent *-e* to the stem:
   narrate (**nārrātus**) finite (**fīnītus**)

3. Suffix ***-or***.
   When added to the stem of the fourth principal part, the Latin suffix ***-or*** creates a 3rd declension, masculine noun, which means *one who does* the action of the verb. These nouns are often borrowed into English with no change in spelling, although there is sometimes a change in meaning:

	Latin Noun & Meaning	English Word
nārrātus (nārrāre)	**nārrātor, nārrātōris,** m, *story-teller*	narrator
spectātus (spectāre)	**spectātor, spectātōris,** m, *onlooker, observer*	spectator
āctus (agere)	**āctor, āctōris,** m, *driver, doer, actor*	actor

4. Suffix ***-iō***.
   The Latin suffix ***-iō***, when added to the stem of the fourth principal part, forms a 3rd declension, feminine noun, which means the *act of, state of,* or *result of* the action of the verb. The genitive singular of these nouns ends in ***-iōnis***, and the base has **-iōn-**, which is the source of English words ending in *-sion* and *-tion*. The meaning of the English word is similar or identical to that of the Latin noun, which takes its meaning from the Latin verb:

	Latin Noun & Meaning	English Word
vīsus (vidēre)	**vīsiō, vīsiōnis,** f., *act of reviewing*	vision
nārrātus (nārrāre)	**nārrātiō, nārrātiōnis,** f., *act of telling (a story)*	narration

Note that whether the English word ends in *-sion* or *-tion* depends on whether the word from which it is derived ends in ***-sus*** or ***-tus***.

Exercise 1

Using the above information, give a 3rd declension Latin noun and an English derivative for each of the following. Check in a Latin dictionary to verify the existence of each noun and compare its meaning with that of its English derivative:

1. audītus (audīre)
2. cautus (cavēre)
3. exclāmātus (exclāmāre)
4. factus (facere)
5. mānsūrus (manēre)
6. missus (mittere)
7. petītus (petere)
8. positus (pōnere)

Exercise 2

Give the meaning of each English word below. Then give the fourth principal part, the infinitive, and the meaning of the verb from which the English word is derived. You may have to find some of the fourth principal parts in the Vocabulary at the back of this book:

1. apparition
2. cogitate
3. diction
4. habitation
5. inventor
6. motor
7. session
8. state
9. tacit

Latin Expressions in English

Latin phrases and expressions are often used in English. Some are very familiar, such as **et cetera** (etc.), *and the rest*. Others are more specialized, such as **ipso facto**, *by the fact itself*, a legal expression used to describe an assumption that has obvious truth, e.g., "A slave, ipso facto, had no right to vote."

While Latin expressions may sometimes be used in English as mere affectations, there are occasions when they are very effective in summarizing an idea succinctly. For example, the term ***de facto*** *segregation* refers to a long history of racial segregation that occurred *in fact*, even though no legal measures were taken to achieve it. **De jure** segregation, on the other hand, was achieved *by law*. These two Latin phrases capsulize these notions in a minimum of words, thereby making communication more efficient.

Exercise 3

Look up the following Latin expressions in an English dictionary. Use each expression in a sentence that illustrates its special use in English:

1. ad hoc
2. ad infinitum
3. modus operandi
4. non sequitur
5. per capita
6. per se
7. quid pro quo
8. sine qua non
9. status quo

CHAPTER 23

AT THE PORTA CAPENA

Intereā Titus, patruus Marcī et Cornēliae, eōs prope Portam Capēnam exspectābat. Cīvēs, mercātōrēs, servī per portam ībant atque hūc illūc currēbant. Titus tamen in lectīcā sedēbat. Ubi Cornēliōs cōnspexit, ē lectīcā dēscendit. Ē raedā dēscendērunt Cornēliī. Interdiū enim raedās intrā urbem agere Rōmānīs nōn licēbat.

Stupuit Sextus ubi multitūdinem cīvium, servōrum turbam vīdit. Undique erat strepitus plaustrōrum, undique clāmor mercātōrum, viātōrum, raedāriōrum. 5

Titus Cornēlium et Aurēliam et līberōs maximō cum gaudiō salūtāvit. "Quam laetus," inquit, "vōs omnēs excipiō! Nōnne estis itinere dēfessī?"

"Valdē dēfessī," respondit Cornēlius. "Mihi necesse est celeriter ad Cūriam īre, sed prīmum Aurēliam et Cornēliam domum dūcam." 10

"Ita vērō!" inquit Titus. "Ecce! Lectīcāriī, quōs vōbīs condūxī, vōs domum ferent. Ego puerōs cūrābō. Multa et mīra vidēbunt puerī, atque ego omnia eīs explicābō."

(continued)

2 **hūc illūc,** adv. *this way and that*
3 **lectīca, -ae,** f., *litter*
4 **interdiū** adv., *during the day*
5 **stupeō, -ēre, -uī,** *to be amazed, gape*
turba, -ae, f., *crowd, mob*
undique adv., *on all sides*
6 **strepitus**, *noise, clattering*
7 **maximus, -a, -um**, *greatest, very great*
gaudium, -ī, n., *joy*
9 **Cūria, -ae,** f., *Senate House*
10 **prīmum**, adv., *first*
domum, *homeward, home*
dūcam, *I will take*
11 **ferent**, *(they) will carry*
12 **cūrābō**, *I will take care of*
multa et mīra, *many wonderful things*
mīrus, -a, -um, *wonderful, marvelous*
vidēbunt, *(they) will see*

2 **currō, currere, cucurrī, cursūrus,** *to run*
3 **dēscendō, dēscendere, dēscendī, dēscēnsūrus,** *to come, go down/climb down*
4 **agō, agere, ēgī, āctus,** *to do, drive*
11 **condūcō, condūcere, condūxī, conductus,** *to hire*

Exercise 23a

Respondē Latīnē:

1. Quis Cornēliōs exspectābat?
2. Quī hūc illūc currēbant per portam?
3. Ubi sedēbat Titus?
4. Cūr Cornēliī ē raedā dēscendērunt?
5. Quid Sextus prope portam vīdit?
6. Quid Sextus prope portam audīvit?
7. Quōmodo Titus Cornēliōs salūtāvit?
8. Quō necesse est Cornēliō īre?
9. Quis lectīcāriōs condūxit?
10. Quis puerīs multa et mīra explicābit?

Itaque per viās urbis lectīcāriī patrem, mātrem, fīliam celeriter domum tulērunt. Postquam eō advēnērunt, Aurēlia et Cornēlia, itinere dēfessae, sē quiētī dedērunt. Cornēlius tamen sē lāvit, aliam togam virīlem induit, iterum in lectīcā cōnsēdit. 15

"Ad Cūriam celeriter!" inquit.

14 **eō** adv., *there, to that place*
sē quiētī dare, *to rest*
  quiēs, quiētis, f., *rest*
15 **virīlis, -is, -e,** *of manhood*

14 **adveniō, advenīre, advēnī, adventūrus,** *to reach, arrive (at)*
15 **induō, induere, induī, indūtus,** *to put on*
cōnsīdō, cōnsīdere, cōnsēdī, *to sit down*

Respondē Latīnē:

1. Quō lectīcāriī Cornēlium, Aurēliam, Cornēliam tulērunt?
2. Quid Aurēlia et Cornēlia ibi fēcērunt?
3. Quid fēcit Cornēlius postquam domum advēnit?

BUILDING THE MEANING

Adjectives as Substantives

In the sentence in line 12 of the story, **Multa et mīra vidēbunt puerī, atque ego omnia eīs explicābō,** the words **multa, mīra,** and **omnia** are adjectives, but they are here used with no nouns for them to modify. The adjectives themselves are used as *substantives*, i.e., as words that function as nouns.

The neuter gender and plural number of these particular substantives (**multa, mīra,** and **omnia**) imply the idea of *things*, and you may therefore translate *many and wonderful things* and *all things.* Note that Latin uses a conjunction between **multa** and **mīra,** while we would say merely "many wonderful things." Note also that we normally say "everything" instead of "all things," the literal translation of **omnia**.

You have also seen adjectives in the masculine or feminine used as substantives, e.g., **Cūnctī in caupōnam intrāvērunt** (19:1). Masculine adjectives so used, as here, refer to people in general, and **cūnctī** may be translated *everybody*. You have seen **omnēs** used in this way a number of times. A feminine adjective would refer to women, e.g., **bonae,** *good women.* We often use adjectives as substantives in English as well, e.g., "the good," "the brave," "the wise."

FORMS

Verbs: Future Tense I

Look at these sentences:

Ego omnia eīs **explicābō.**	***I will explain*** *everything to them.*
Multa et mīra **vidēbunt** puerī.	*The boys* ***will see*** *many wonderful things.*
Ego Cornēliam domum **dūcam.**	***I will take*** *Cornelia home.*
Brevī tempore ad Portam Capēnam **adveniēmus.**	*In a short time* ***we will arrive*** *at the Porta Capena.*

The words in boldface are examples of the *future tense*. The endings of the future tense are shown in the table below:

		1st and 2nd Conjugations	3rd and 4th Conjugations
Singular	1	*-bō*	*-am*
	2	*-bis*	*-ēs*
	3	*-bit*	*-et*
Plural	1	*-bimus*	*-ēmus*
	2	*-bitis*	*-ētis*
	3	*-bunt*	*-ent*

Note that in the future tense the endings of verbs in the 3rd and 4th conjugations are quite different from the endings of verbs in the 1st and 2nd conjugations.

Note also that the *-e-* of the ending in the 3rd and 4th conjugations is short before final ***-t*** and ***-nt***.

Note in the chart below that the letter *i* precedes the endings ***-am, -ēs, -et,*** etc., in 3rd conjugation ***-iō*** verbs (**iaciam, iaciēs, iaciet,** etc.) and in 4th conjugation verbs (**audiam, audiēs, audiet,** etc.).

		1st Conjugation	2nd Conjugation	3rd Conjugation		4th Conjugation
Infinitive		par*ā́re*	hab*ḗre*	mítt*ere*	iác*ere* (*-iō*)	aud*ī́re*
Singular	1	parā́*bō*	habḗ*bō*	mítt*am*	iáci*am*	aúdi*am*
	2	parā́*bis*	habḗ*bis*	mítt*ēs*	iáci*ēs*	aúdi*ēs*
	3	parā́*bit*	habḗ*bit*	mítt*et*	iáci*et*	aúdi*et*
Plural	1	parā́*bimus*	habḗ*bimus*	mitt*ḗmus*	iaci*ḗmus*	audi*ḗmus*
	2	parā́*bitis*	habḗ*bitis*	mitt*ḗtis*	iaci*ḗtis*	audi*ḗtis*
	3	parā́*bunt*	habḗ*bunt*	mítt*ent*	iáci*ent*	aúdi*ent*

Be sure to learn these forms thoroughly.

Exercise 23b

Read aloud, identify all verbs in the future tense, and translate:

1. Titus nōs prope Portam Capēnam exspectābit; omnēs maximō cum gaudiō salūtābit.
2. Hodiē magna sepulcra Rōmānōrum praeclārōrum vīdimus; crās Cūriam et alia aedificia Rōmāna vidēbimus.
3. Fortasse patruus noster nōs ad Cūriam dūcet.
4. Cornēliī omnēs sē parant; brevī tempore ad urbem iter facient.
5. Multa et mīra vident puerī; lectīcāriī eōs mox domum portābunt.
6. Cornēlius ē raedā dēscendet, nam raedam intrā urbem agere nōn licet.
7. Quam diū in urbe manēbis, pater?
8. Bene dormiētis, puerī. Longum enim iter hodiē fēcistis.
9. Cornēlia, itinere longō dēfessa, sē quiētī dabit.
10. Puerī multa rogābunt dē aedificiīs quae in urbis viīs vidēbunt.

faciō, facere, fēcī, factus, *to make, do*

maneō, manēre, mānsī, mānsus, *to remain, stay, wait for*

Exercise 23c

Using story 23, its verb list, and the charts of the future tense as guides, give the Latin for:

1. Will you run home, boys?
2. We will sit near the Porta Capena.
3. When will the Cornelii climb down out of the carriage?
4. Cornelius, will you drive your carriage inside the city during the day?
5. Who will hire the litter-bearers?
6. Litter-bearers, will you carry us home?
7. Where will Cornelius wash himself?
8. What will you put on, Cornelius?
9. We will all sit down in two litters.

Detail of the reconstructed general view of the Forum Romanum and the Imperial Fora, early third century A.D. Clockwise from the upper left-hand corner: Temple of Concord, Arch of Septimius Severus, Curia Julia, Basilica Aemilia, Temple of Antonius and Faustina, Regia (Temple of the Divine Julius in front of it), Temple of Castor (roof only), and Basilica Julia.
From The Ancient City *by Peter Connolly*

BUILDING THE MEANING

Present or Future Tense?

Look at these sentences:

Cornēlius multōs servōs hab***et.***	*Cornelius* ***has*** *many slaves.*
Scelestōs servōs ad vīllam rūsticam mitt***et.***	*He* ***will send*** *the wicked slaves to the country house and farm.*
Hodiē in caupōnā man***ēmus***.	*Today we* ***remain*** *in the inn.*
Crās Rōmam adveni***ēmus***.	*Tomorrow we* ***will reach*** *Rome.*

It is important to know to which conjugation a verb belongs in order to determine its tense.

The endings ***-ēs, -et, -ēmus, -ētis, -ent*** can denote the present tense of verbs of the 2nd conjugation or the future tense of verbs of the 3rd and 4th conjugations. If there is an *i* before the *e*, the verb will be the future tense of a 3rd conjugation ***-iō*** verb or the future tense of a 4th conjugation verb.

Exercise 23d

Following the examples, identify the remainder of the verb forms below:

Verb	Conjugation	Tense	Meaning
habent	2	present	they have
mittent	3	future	they will send
vident			
iubent			
ascendent			
admovent			
timent			
dūcent			
rīdent			
facient			

Exercise 23e

Look carefully at the verbs in the following sentences. Decide the conjugation number first (this will help you to get the tense right) and then read aloud and translate:

1. Puerī Eucleidem nōn vident sed vōcem eius audient.
2. Vidēsne senātōrēs in viīs? Quandō Cornēlius veniet?
3. Servī celeriter current, nam Cornēlium timent.
4. Sextus māne surget; in animō habet exīre.
5. Ego et Cornēlia tacēmus; patrem timēmus.

Exercise 23f

Take parts, read aloud, and translate:

Intereā Eucleidēs et puerī cum Titō extrā Portam Capēnam stābant.

TITUS: Salvēte, puerī! Quid in itinere vīdistis? Vīdistisne rūsticōs in agrīs? Agrōsne colēbant?

SEXTUS: Rūsticōs vīdimus. Agrōs nōn colēbant, sed sub arboribus quiēscēbant. At caupōnam vīdimus; nostra raeda in fossā haerēbat et nōbīs necesse erat in caupōnā pernoctāre. 5

MARCUS: Ita vērō! Gaudēbam quod pater meus in illā caupōnā pernoctāre cōnstituit. Caupō erat vir Graecus, amīcus Eucleidis.

SEXTUS: Ego quoque gaudēbam, nam mīles bonam fābulam nōbīs nārrāvit. In illā fābulā caupō quīdam hospitem necāvit. Tālēs fābulās amō. Sed quid nunc faciēmus? Ego volō Circum Maximum vīsitāre. Ecce! Nōnne Circum Maximum suprā mūrōs urbis exstantem vidēre possum? 10

MARCUS: Ita vērō! Est Circus Maximus. Nōn procul abest.

TITUS: Nōn possumus omnia hodiē vidēre. Crās satis temporis habēbimus.

SEXTUS: Sed quid est illud aedificium? Nōnne pontem ingentem suprā portam videō? 15

MARCUS: Nōn pontem hīc vidēs, ō stulte! Est aquaeductus, Aqua Marcia. Per illum aquaeductum Rōmānī aquam in urbem ferunt. Cavē imbrem, Sexte!

SEXTUS: Sed nōn pluit.

TITUS: Semper hīc pluit, Sexte. Rīmōsa enim est Aqua Marcia.

1 **extrā**, prep. + acc., *outside*
4 **at**, conj., *but*
10 **tālis, -is, -e**, *such*
11 **Circus Maximus**, *the Circus Maximus (a stadium in Rome)*
12 **suprā**, prep. + acc., *above*
mūrus, -ī, m., *wall*
exstantem, *standing out, towering*
14 **satis temporis**, *enough of time, enough time*
15 **pōns, pontis,** gen. pl., **pontium,** m., *bridge*
16 **stultus, -a, -um**, *stupid, foolish*
17 **Cavē imbrem!** *Watch out for the rain!*
imber, imbris, gen. pl., **imbrium** m., *rain*
19 **rīmōsus, -a, -um**, *full of cracks, leaky*

3 **colō, colere, coluī, cultus,** *to cultivate*
4 **quiēscō, quiēscere, quiēvī, quiētūrus**, *to rest, keep quiet*
7 **cōnstituō, cōnstituere, cōnstituī, cōnstitūtus**, *to decide*
18 **pluit, pluere, pluit**, usually found only in 3rd person singular, *it rains, is raining*

Exercise 23g

In the passage above, locate in sequence all verbs in the imperfect tense and all verbs in the future tense.

Forms

Verbs: Future Tense II

The following are the future tenses of the irregular verbs you have met:

Infinitive			ésse	pósse	vélle	nṓlle	férre	ī́re
Number and Person	Singular	1	ér***ō***	pót***erō***	vól***am***	nṓl***am***	fér***am***	ī́***bō***
		2	éri***s***	pót***eris***	vól***ēs***	nṓl***ēs***	fér***ēs***	ī́***bis***
		3	éri***t***	pót***erit***	vól***et***	nṓl***et***	fér***et***	ī́***bit***
	Plural	1	éri***mus***	pot***érimus***	vol***ḗmus***	nōl***ḗmus***	fer***ḗmus***	ī́***bimus***
		2	éri***tis***	pot***éritis***	vol***ḗtis***	nōl***ḗtis***	fer***ḗtis***	ī́***bitis***
		3	éru***nt***	pót***erunt***	vól***ent***	nṓl***ent***	fér***ent***	ī́***bunt***

Note that **velle, nōlle, ferre,** and **īre** have future tense endings like those of regular verbs. Note also where long vowels occur in the endings of these verbs. The tenses of the compounds of irregular verbs are formed in the same way as those of the uncompounded verbs, e.g., the future tense of **exeō** is **exībō**.

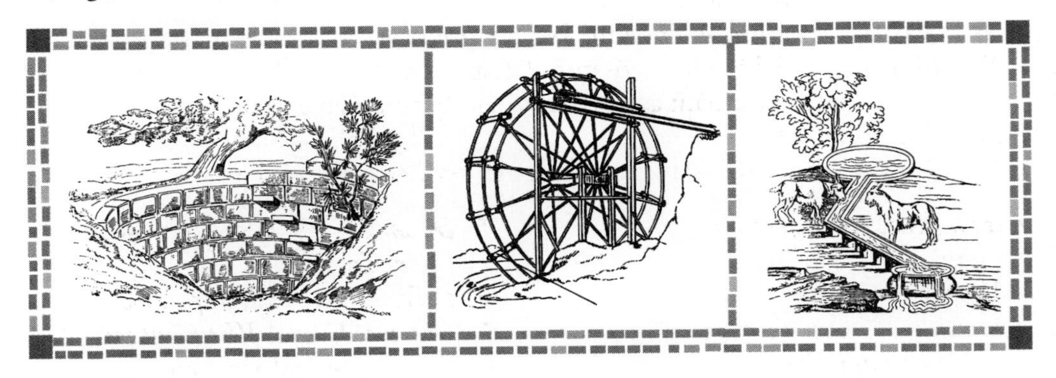

Exercise 23h

Read aloud, identify all verbs in the future tense, and translate:

1. Ībisne ad Cūriam, pater? Ita vērō! Ad Cūriam celeriter ībō.
2. Quandō domum redībis, pater? Nesciō.
3. Fortasse Cornēlius domum redīre brevī tempore poterit.
4. Eucleidēs et puerī in urbem māne exiērunt.
5. Necesse erat diū in urbe manēre.
6. Nocte vehicula magna onera in urbem ferent.
7. Puerī Circum Maximum crās vidēre volent.
8. Ubi līberī māne erunt? Tū līberōs nōn vidēbis, nam domō mox exībunt.
9. Sī equī strēnuē labōrābunt, raedam ē fossā extrahere poterunt.

(continued)

10. Sī pluet, ad silvam ambulāre nōlam.
11. Ferēsne cistam meam in caupōnam? Minimē! Tū ipse eam fer!
12. Redībitisne ad vīllam rūsticam? Fortasse redīre poterimus.
13. Volētisne crās ad Circum Maximum īre? Ita vērō! Crās illūc īre volēmus.
14. "Ego īre nōlam," inquit Aurēlia.
15. Post cēnam puerī cubitum īre nōlēbant.

Note that in sentences 9 and 10 the verbs in the clauses introduced by **sī** are in the future tense. English, however, requires the present tense here.

domō, *out of the house* **illūc,** adv., *there, to that place*

redeō, redīre, rediī or **redīvī, reditūrus,** irreg., *to return, go back*
exeō, exīre, exiī or **exīvī, exitūrus,** irreg. *to go out*

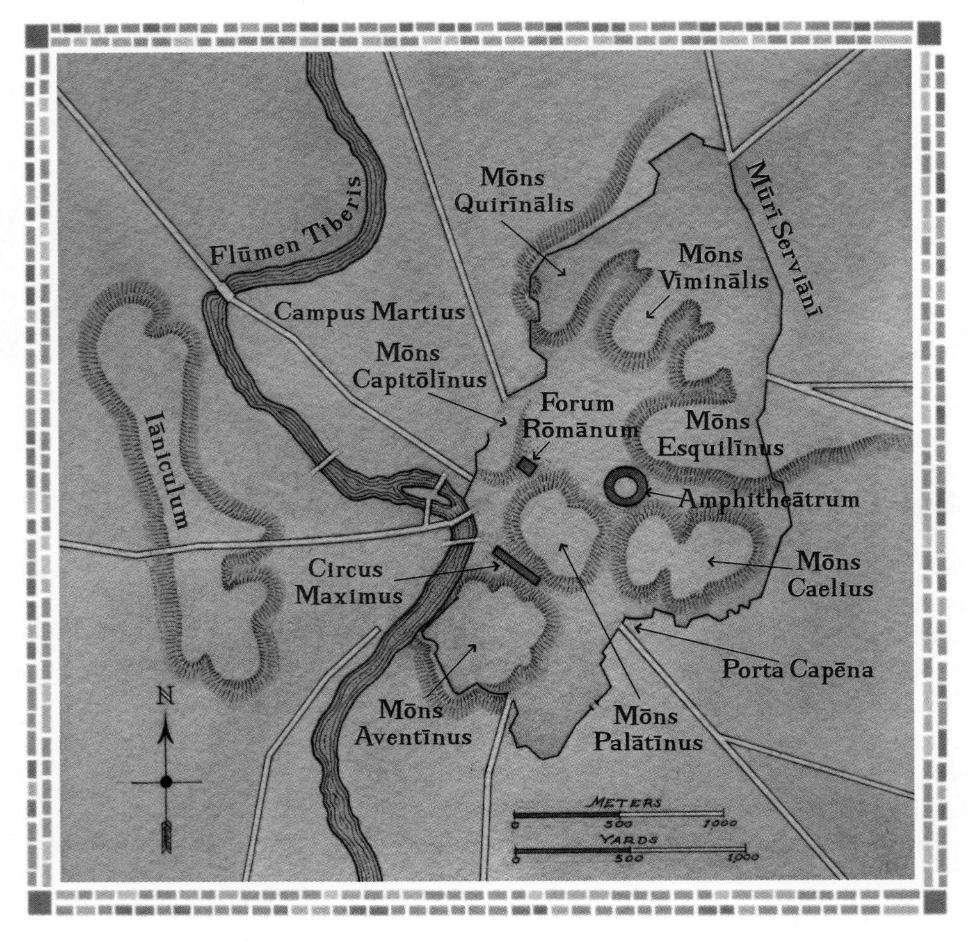

The Seven Hills of Rome

AQUEDUCTS

One feature of the city that the Cornelii would notice as they approached Rome was the evidence of the Romans' passion for water. Abundant water for baths and fountains and pools was a vital necessity to the Roman, so that water was brought in by the aqueducts whose arches strode into Rome from all directions. By A.D. 80, nine aqueducts were in use, carrying water across the plain to Rome from sources up to fifty-six miles or ninety kilometers distant.

The drawing on p. 209 shows the arches supporting the water-channel and a cross-section of the channel itself. To maintain the downhill flow, experts recommended a fall of six inches or fifteen centimeters in every ninety-eight feet or thirty meters. Tunnels, with inspection shafts built into them, were driven through those hills that were impossible to by-pass. Sometimes, by using the principle that water rises to its own level, a U-shaped arrangement of the tunnel allowed an uphill flow.

The first aqueduct, named the Aqua Appia after its builder Appius Claudius, was built in 312 B.C. and ran underground for much of its route in order to speed its construction and to hide its presence from Rome's enemies. Its waters supported the growth

A Roman aqueduct in southern France, called the Pont du Gard

Routes of the Roman Aqueducts

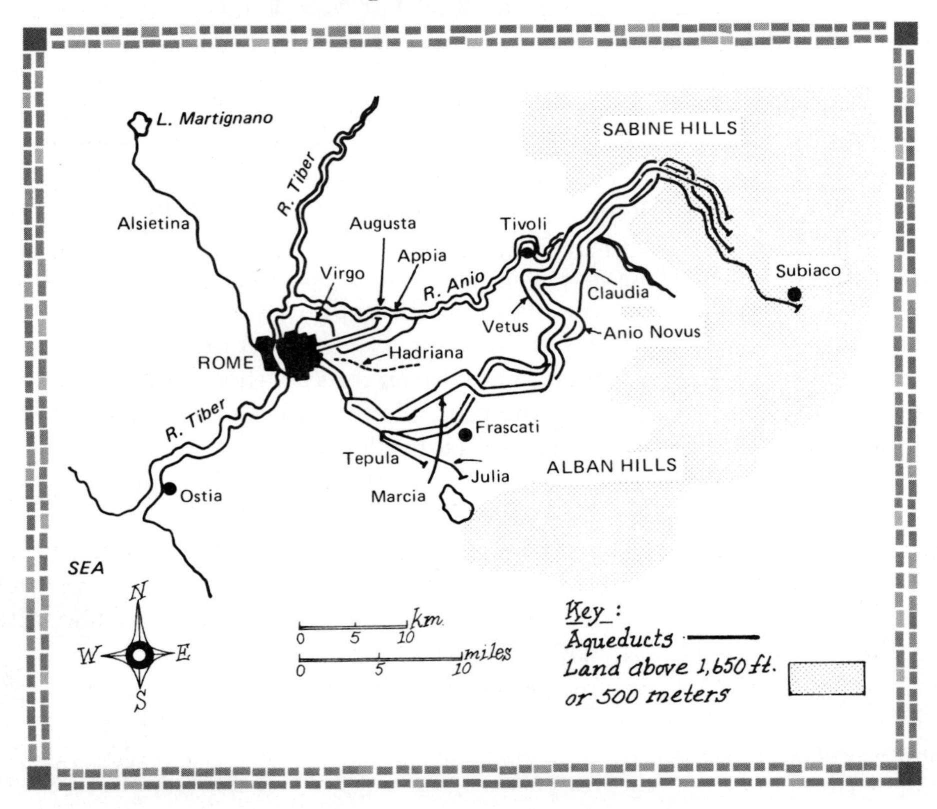

in Rome's population during the fourth century B.C. Appius' pride in its construction was commemorated in his epitaph, which lists this accomplishment on a par with his victories in war.

Later aqueducts had to supply water to the more hilly and elevated districts of Rome. Since the Romans used a gravity system to propel the flow of water, sources higher in the Sabine and Alban Hills had to be found.

The Romans then hit on the idea of using arches to support the water-channel. The arches turned out to be beautiful structures in themselves, but the Romans had adopted them for quite different reasons. They stood up better to earthquakes, always a hazard in Italy; the wind could blow through them, where a solid wall would invite disaster; and they could be easily repaired, as workmen could take the building materials from one side to the other.

Admiring comments about the aqueducts abound from native and foreigner alike. "Just as impressive," says one writer, "as the pyramids, but how much more useful!" Not only so, but we also have an astonishing book, *De aquis urbis Romae,* by Frontinus, Superintendent of Aqueducts, written about A.D. 97, describing the system in detail and the difficulties of organizing and maintaining it. He reports that, through bribery of watermen, supplies were sometimes diverted into private estates and never reached Rome at all. Householders in Rome itself often succeeded in bribing inspectors (who were, after all, slaves) to replace a narrow pipe by one of wider bore, while they continued to pay at the old rate!

The emperor appointed the Superintendent of Aqueducts, who, with his staff, had responsibility for maintaining and cleaning the whole vast system. Concern for the health of the immense population of Rome made the emperors keenly aware of the importance of maintaining a supply of clean water. In his official statement of his accomplishments, Augustus took justifiable pride in his improvement of the water supply of Rome:

> In many places I rebuilt the channels of the aqueducts that had collapsed due to old age, and the aqueduct which is called the Marcia I doubled in quantity, by means of a new source flowing into its channel.
>
> Augustus, *Accomplishments* 20

According to the latest available figures, the daily consumption of water in a large city today is about 120 gallons or 455 liters per person. According to Frontinus, in his day the Roman aqueducts could deliver over 264 million gallons or one billion liters in twenty-four hours, providing a daily allowance of about 240 gallons or 900 liters per person! The aqueducts leaked dreadfully, as the Cornelii found at the Porta Capena, and what with water thieves and corrupt inspectors, all this water did not actually reach Rome. For all that, the Roman citizen still had a lot of water at his disposal. Did he use it all? The answer is "Yes," because as one Roman writer put it, "The waters, having provided the city with the life-giving element, passed on into the sewers." The Roman, you see, hardly ever turned the tap off. For him, running water was quite literally running water!

Sketch of the Pont du Gard showing the water channel

ADDITIONAL READING:
The Romans Speak for Themselves: Book I: "The Aqueducts of Ancient Rome," pages 65–74.

Always Tomorrow

Simulac Titus et puerī et Eucleidēs urbem per Portam Capēnam intrāvērunt, clāmāvit Sextus, "Quid nōs prīmum faciēmus? Quō ībimus? Vīsitābimusne— ?"

"Quō tū nōs dūcēs, patrue?" interpellāvit Marcus. "Vidēbimusne Cūriam et Forum? Sextus multa dē Rōmā lēgit et audīvit et nunc, patrue, omnia vidēre vult."

Titus, "Tacēte! Tacēte!" inquit. "Forum crās vīsitābimus. Crās, Eucleidēs, tibi licēbit 5 puerōs eō dūcere. Tum erit satis temporis. Hodiē tamen, puerī, vōs domum per urbem dūcam et omnia in itinere vōbīs dēmōnstrābō."

Iam advēnerant ad Circum Maximum, quī nōn procul aberat. Stupuit Sextus ubi mōlem Circī Maximī vīdit. Marcus quoque stupuit, quamquam Circum anteā vīderat. Stupuit Titus, attonitus nōn mōle, sed silentiō Circī. 10

"Ēheu! Ēheu!" inquit Titus. "Hodiē Circus est clausus. Tribus diēbus tamen prīnceps ipse, Titus Flāvius Vespasiānus, lūdōs magnificōs faciet."

"Nōnne tū nōs eō dūcēs?" rogāvit Marcus.

"Ēheu! Ego nōn poterō vōs dūcere," inquit Titus. "Fortasse Eucleidēs vōs dūcet."

(continued)

1 **simulac,** conj., *as soon as*
8 **advēnerant**, *they had arrived*
9 **mōlēs, mōlis,** gen. pl., **mōlium**, f., *mass, huge bulk*
vīderat, *he had seen*
10 **attonitus, -a, -um**, *astonished, astounded*
11 **clausus, -a, -um**, *shut, closed*
12 **lūdī, -ōrum**, m. pl., *games*

4 **legō, legere, lēgī, lēctus**, *to read*
5 **licet, licēre, licuit** + dat., usually found only in 3rd person singular and infinitive, *it is allowed*

Exercise 24a
Respondē Latīnē:

1. Quis puerōs crās ad Forum dūcet?
2. Vīderatne Sextus anteā Circum Maximum?
3. Eratne Titus attonitus mōle Circī?
4. Cūr Circum hodiē puerī nōn intrant?
5. Quid faciet prīnceps tribus diēbus?
6. Dūcetne Titus puerōs ad lūdōs?

"Minimē!" respondit Sextus. "Librōs, nōn lūdōs amat Eucleidēs." 15

"Agite, puerī!" interpellāvit Titus. "Nunc circumībimus Montem Palātīnum et Forum intrābimus ad arcum Tiberiī. Ibi fortasse patrī tuō occurrēmus, Marce. Mox senātōrēs ē Cūriā exībunt."

Itaque Circum relīquērunt et Palātīnum circumiērunt. Titus in itinere mōnstrāvit puerīs mīra aedificia quae prīncipēs in Palātīnō aedificāverant. Tandem ad arcum Tiberiī 20 advēnērunt, iam labōre et aestū dēfessī.

"Hic est arcus," inquit Titus, "quem— "

"Omnia vidēre poteritis crās," interpellāvit Cornēlius, quī eō ipsō tempore ad arcum ē Cūriā advēnerat. "Cum ad Forum crās redieritis, Eucleidēs omnia vōbīs explicābit. Iam sērō est. Agite! Iam domum ībimus." 25

15 **liber, librī,** m., *book*
16 **Mōns Palātīnus, Montis Palātīnī,** m., *the Palatine Hill*
17 **arcus,** *arch*
20 **aedificō, -āre, -āvī, -ātus,** *to build*
21 **aestū,** *from the heat*
22 **quem,** acc., *which*
24 **redieritis,** *you will have returned, you return*

16 **circumeō, circumīre, circumiī** or **circumīvī, circumitus,** irreg., *to go around*
17 **occurrō, occurrere, occurrī, occursūrus** + dat., *to meet, encounter*

Respondē Latīnē:

1. Quid amat Eucleidēs?
2. Quī mīra aedificia in Palātīnō aedificāverant?
3. Quis puerīs prope arcum Tiberiī occurrit?
4. Quō Cornēlius puerōs hodiē dūcet?

BUILDING THE MEANING

Dative with Intransitive Compound Verbs

Look at the following sentence:

Ibi fortasse **patrī tuō** occurrēmus. (24:17) *Perhaps we will meet* ***your father*** *there.*

The verb **occurrere** is a compound verb, that is, it consists of the intransitive verb **currere** plus the prefix **ob-** *against*, which becomes **oc-** by assimilation to the initial consonant of the verb. The compound verb is still intransitive, and its meaning (*to run against, to meet*) is completed not by a direct object in the accusative case but by a word or phrase in the *dative case*, here **patrī tuō**.

You have also seen the intransitive compound verb **appropinquāre** (= the prefix **ad-** + **propinquāre**) used with the dative:

Iam **urbī** appropinquābant. (22:12)
Already they were coming near ***to the city****/approaching* ***the city****.*

Sentences with compound verbs and the dative such as these give us a fourth basic pattern of Latin sentences, in addition to the three basic patterns that you learned in Book I-A.

Ablative of Cause

You have met words or phrases in the ablative case assigning blame for something that has happened or stating the cause of someone's being in a certain state:

Tuā culpā raeda est in fossā. (14:7)
Because of your fault *the carriage is in the ditch.*
It's your fault that the carriage is in the ditch.

magnā īrā commōtus (14:17)	*moved* ***because of/with great anger***
itinere dēfessī (23:8)	*tired* ***because of/from the journey***

labōre et **aestū** dēfessī (24:21)
tired ***because of/from their exertion*** *and* ***the heat***

This is called the *ablative of cause*; note that no preposition is used in Latin.

FORMS

Verbs: Pluperfect Tense

Look at this sentence:

Stupuit quoque Marcus, quamquam Circum anteā **vīderat.** (24:9)
Marcus too was amazed, although he ***had seen*** *the Circus before.*

The verb in the subordinate clause in this sentence is in the *pluperfect tense*. A verb in the pluperfect tense describes an action that was completed *before* some other action in the past took place. Thus, Marcus had seen the Circus *before* the occasion when he saw it in our story.

Verbs in the pluperfect tense can nearly always be translated with *had*... in English.

The endings of the pluperfect tense are the same for *all* Latin verbs. They are identical to the imperfect tense of **esse**:

	1	***-eram***		1	***-erāmus***
Singular	2	***-erās***	Plural	2	***-erātis***
	3	***-erat***		3	***-erant***

These endings are added to the perfect stem, which is found by dropping the **-ī** from the end of the third principal part, e.g., **relīquī**, stem **relīqu-**.

	1	relīqu***eram***		1	relīqu***erāmus***
Singular	2	relīqu***erās***	Plural	2	relīqu***erātis***
	3	relīqu***erat***		3	relīqu***erant***

Exercise 24b

Read aloud and translate. Identify each pluperfect verb and explain how the action it describes was completed before some other action took place:

1. Eucleidēs puerōs ad urbem māne dūxerat et omnia eīs dēmōnstrābat.
2. Aurēlia laeta erat quod servī cēnam bonam iam parāverant.
3. Hodiē librum diū legēbam quem mihi heri dederās.
4. Dēfessus eram quod multās epistulās iam scrīpseram.
5. Vix domum advēnerant puerī, cum Eucleidēs in hortum intrāvit.

scrībō, scrībere, scrīpsī, scrīptus, *to write* **vix**, adv., *scarcely*

Exercise 24c

Substitute the corresponding pluperfect form for each verb in parentheses (all present tense), read the sentence aloud, and translate:

1. Tantum sonitum numquam anteā (audīmus) ______.
2. Marcus laetus erat quod patrī prope Cūriam (occurrit) ______.
3. Via erat plēna hominum quī ad urbem (veniunt) ______.
4. Lectīcāriī, quī Cornēlium per urbis viās (ferunt) ______, extrā Cūriam eum exspectābant.
5. Titus, quod Circum (invenit) ______ clausum, puerōs domum dūcēbat.
6. Sextus, ubi ad urbem advēnit, laetus erat quod numquam anteā in urbe Rōmā (est) ______.
7. Arcus, quem Tiberius (aedificat) ______, erat ingēns.
8. Senātōrēs iam ē Cūriā (exeunt) ______, cum puerī ad Forum advēnērunt.
9. Marcus multa aedificia quae iam (videt) ______, iterum vīsitābat.
10. Sextus, quod multa dē Rōmā (audit) ______ et (legit) ______, omnia vidēre volēbat.

tantus, -a, -um, *so great, such a big*

FRONTIER LIFE II

NORTH AFRICA

Cornelius has been recalled to Rome due to urgent messages the emperor and consuls have received from the governor of the province of Africa (who is appointed by the Senate) and the prefect (administrator) of Numidia (see map, page 244). One of the fierce nomadic tribes of North Africa, the Nasamones, has made several attacks on two of the colonies lately established in that province of Africa. The agricultural territory given to these colonies was seized from the Nasamones, who were consequently restricted to pasturing their flocks on poorer ground. Because these colonies contributed to the large supply of grain sent from Africa to Rome for free distribution to its inhabitants, the emperor asked the consuls to summon an extraordinary session of the Senate to consider what should be done to end the raids.

Cornelius' opinions and advice will be of particular interest to the emperor and Senate in their deliberations. At age seventeen Cornelius began his political career by serving as military tribune in the army stationed in Numidia and came to know some young men who are now leaders of the Nasamones. His subsequent experience in government offices has given him a good understanding of the potential danger posed by these raids. His first post after the army was on the Board of Twenty (**Vīgintīvirī**), where he and two others were placed in charge of the state mint. At age twenty-seven, elected as one of forty quaestors, he was in charge of the grain supply at Rome's port city, Ostia. As an ex-quaestor, Cornelius automatically became a member of the Senate and has attended its meetings regularly. At age thirty-two he was elected curule aedile and was in charge of regulating the grain supply at Rome. Two years ago as the officer in charge of lawsuits involving foreigners (**praetor peregrīnus**) he adjudicated law suits of non-Roman citizens; because of his prior stay in Africa, he specialized in suits of non-Roman citizens of Africa. His friends in the Senate think he will be elected consul in a few years and that the Senate will probably appoint him governor of Africa after his year in that office.

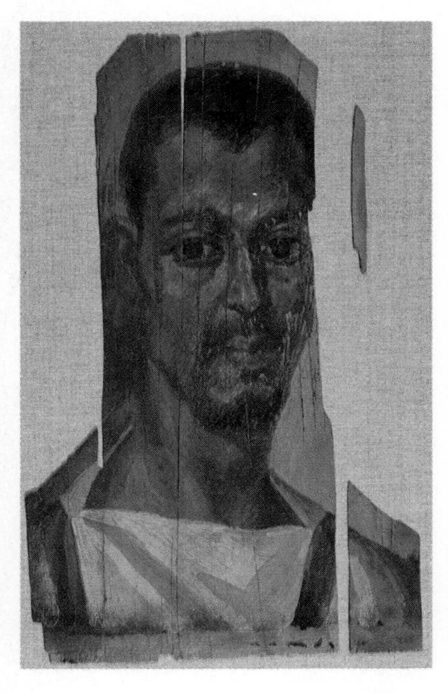

"Funerary Portrait of a Man," encaustic painting on linen, The Cleveland Museum of Art, John L. Severence Fund; "Portrait from Faiyum," wood and wax, Louvre, Paris, France

264–241 B.C. AND 218–201 B.C.

THE FIRST AND SECOND PUNIC WARS

As we learned in the essay on North Africa on p. 215, Cornelius was recalled to Rome to take part in senatorial deliberations over attacks by native tribesmen on recently founded Roman colonies in Africa. Rome's involvement with North Africa already spanned hundreds of years—going back as far, in fact, as the Punic Wars of the third and second centuries B.C.

Rome, the great land power of Italy, engaged Carthage, the great sea power of North Africa, in a long struggle for control of Sicily and the western Mediterranean Sea that lasted through three wars and spanned more than a century (264–146 B.C.) A strong navy protected the flourishing commercial center of Carthage, colonized as an outpost centuries earlier by the Phoenicians, whom the Romans called **Pūnicī**. In the First Punic War (264–241 B.C.), the Romans were quick to realize that if they wanted to win they too must take to the sea. Roman marines shocked the Carthaginians when they dropped gangways with sharp metal points on one end, called "crows" (**corvī**), onto their decks; these held the enemy ships fast while the Romans boarded them with their superior soldiers. The birth of the Roman fleet ultimately led to a Roman victory.

"Hannibal Swearing Eternal Enmity to Rome," oil on canvas, Jacopo Amigoni, Agnew & Sons, London, England

Just as significant was the hatred between the two nations that the war produced. Roman legend confidently reports that Hannibal Barca, when he was a boy of nine years old, stood before an altar with his father, Hamilcar, and swore his undying hatred of the Romans. When Hannibal was twenty-six, troops loyal to Hamilcar, who had been slain in battle in Spain, were quick to pledge allegiance to Hannibal. Determined to fulfill his father's dreams of revenge on the Roman conquerors and of a new Carthaginian empire, Hannibal set out for Italy to ignite the Second Punic War (218–201 B.C.).

With an army of Carthaginians and mercenaries, Hannibal left Spain, crossed the Pyrenees, proceeded up the coast of France, and arrived at the great barrier into northern Italy, the Alps. Thirty-seven elephants, including Hannibal's pet, Syrus, were the most memorable members of the forces that Hannibal led up the Alps.

Fending off the attacks of mountain tribesmen, battling against snow and cold and slippery paths, the fiercely loyal troops reached a promontory high in the Alps where Hannibal, pointing to the vista of Italy far below his troops, proclaimed: "Now you are crossing not only the walls of Italy, but those of Rome." When a rockslide blocked their way down, Hannibal ordered his men to build fires that heated the rocks; according to the Roman historian Livy, the rocks split apart when sour wine was poured on them, clearing a path that the Carthaginian army descended, elephants and all.

Employing clever tactics, Hannibal dealt the Romans crushing defeats as he swept southward through Italy. The worst occurred at Lake Trasimene, where mist rising off the water prevented the Romans from realizing that they were heading into an ambush until the trap had already been sprung. At Cannae, a year later, Hannibal led the center of his line in a planned retreat, luring the Romans into a trap again. Hannibal's cavalry

The Second Punic War, 218–201 B.C.

closed in from the flanks and dealt a crippling blow to the Roman army.

Hannibal did not have a large enough force at his command to march on the city of Rome, however. He waited, expecting that Rome's Italian allies would revolt and come over to his side. They did not. For years Hannibal and the wary Romans played cat and mouse. In 207, Hasdrubal, Hannibal's brother, crossed the Alps with a relief force but was intercepted by the Romans—a disaster Hannibal learned about when a Roman cavalryman tossed Hasdrubal's head into his camp.

Publius Cornelius Scipio, the Roman commander, after victories over Carthaginian forces in Spain, returned to Italy and convinced the Roman Senate to send him to Africa with a Roman army. Scipio achieved so much success there that Hannibal, after fifteen years of fighting in Italy, was summoned to return home and defend Carthage. On the plain of Zama, Scipio, employing Hannibalic tactics against his foe, claimed the decisive victory of the war. Scipio received the title (**cognōmen**) **Africānus.** Hannibal, Rome's most memorable enemy, was forced into exile.

FORMS

Verbs: Future Perfect Tense

Look at this sentence:

> "Cum ad Forum crās **redieritis**, Eucleidēs omnia vōbīs explicābit." (24:24)
> *"When **you return/will have returned** to the Forum tomorrow, Eucleides will explain everything to you."*

The verb in the subordinate clause in this sentence is in the *future perfect tense*. A verb in the future perfect tense describes an action that will have been completed *before* some other action in future time begins. Thus, the boys will have returned to the Forum *before* Eucleides will explain everything to them. Note that Latin verbs in the future perfect tense are often best translated by the present tense in English as in the example above, *When you return*... The literal translation is *When you will have returned*....

	1	***-erō***		1	***-erimus***
Singular	2	***-eris***	Plural	2	***-eritis***
	3	***-erit***		3	***-erint***

The endings of the future perfect tense are the same for *all* Latin verbs. They are identical to the future tense of **esse,** except for the 3rd person plural:

These endings are added to the perfect stem, which is found by dropping the ***-ī*** from the end of the third principal part, e.g., **redeō, redīre, rediī,** perfect stem **redi-.**

1	redí***erō***	1	redi***érimus***
2	redí***eris***	2	redi***éritis***
3	redí***erit***	3	redí***erint***

Exercise 24d

Read aloud and translate:

1. Sī baculum coniēceris, canēs ferōciter lātrābunt.
2. Cum ad Portam Capēnam advēnerimus, ē raedā dēscendēmus.
3. Sī equī raedam ē fossā extrāxerint, Cornēliī ad urbem iter facere poterunt.
4. Nisi caupō alium lectum in cubiculum mōverit, Aurēlia ibi dormīre nōlet.
5. Crās puerī, cum surrēxerint, strepitum plaustrōrum audient.
6. Eucleidēs et puerī, ubi Circum relīquērunt et Palātīnum circumiērunt, Forum intrāvērunt.
7. Cum ad arcum Tiberiī advēnerint, Cornēliō occurrent.
8. Crās puerī dēfessī erunt, sī omnia aedificia in forō vīsitāverint.
9. Aurēlia et Cornēlia, cum domum advēnerint, sē quiētī dabunt.
10. Aurēlia et Cornēlia, cum ē lectīs surrēxerint, lānam trahent.

moveō, movēre, mōvī, mōtus, *to move*

Exercise 24e

Using the sentences in Exercise 24d and the charts of pluperfect and future perfect forms as guides, give the Latin for:

1. The boys had already thrown the stick.
2. We had already arrived at the Porta Capena.
3. The horses had not yet dragged the carriage out of the ditch.
4. Unless you move/will have moved another bed into the bedroom, we will not be willing to sleep here.
5. Tomorrow when you get up/will have gotten up, Sextus, you will hear the noise of wagons.
6. Eucleides and the boys had already left the Circus and had gone around the Palatine.
7. When we arrive/will have arrived at the arch of Tiberius, we will meet Cornelius.
8. Yesterday the boys had visited all the buildings in the forum. At night they were tired from their exertion/labor, and the heat.
9. Aurelia and Cornelia had already rested.
10. What will you do when you get up/will have gotten up, Aurelia and Cornelia?

FRONTIER LIFE III

CULTURAL ASSIMILATION

In "Rome and Northern Europe" on pp. 193–195, you were introduced to the Ubian girl Helge and her Roman legionary husband Lucius. Their story continues here.

One day, shortly before Helge's child was born, an officer of the *Legio XX Valeria* came to Helge's hut and saw that she was weaving a colorful tartan for her husband. The men of the legion needed new tunics and cloaks, and the officer decided that the legionaries' women (**focāriae**) could weave and make tunics and cloaks for the legion. When Helge finished the tartan, she then wove cloth for legionary tunics and cloaks. Afterward, whenever she and the other Ubian legionary wives saw their men wearing the tunics and cloaks they had made, she and her friends felt pride in their work.

Helge bore a son, and when he was nine days old Lucius, the proud father, gave the baby his name and placed a **bulla** containing good luck charms around the child's neck in accordance with the Roman custom. Because Helge was not the daughter of a Roman citizen, little Lucius did not inherit Roman citizenship from his father. However, Lucius, the legionary, knew that his son would be given citizenship when discharged after twenty-five years of service as an auxiliary. Helge knew that Roman citizenship brought certain privileges: exemption from taxation, the right to run for public office, and rights of appeal in cases of litigation in the Roman court.

As little Lucius grew from child to young man, the Romanization process continued. Lucius grew up speaking both Latin and the language of his mother's people. When the boy was seven years old, his father enrolled him in a school run by a Greek freedman. Helge learned that while the customs of her people allowed only the priests to know how to read and write, the Romans permitted literacy to everyone.

The population of the Roman settlement increased, and to meet its needs the men of the *Legio XX Valeria* and the *Legio I Germanica* built an underground aqueduct to bring water to the city from springs in the nearby hills. The legionaries also built a headquarters (**praetōrium**) for the Roman governor of Lower Germany and a wall to enclose and protect the inhabitants. In addition, a road and a dock alongside the Rhine were built.

The years passed and Helge and Lucius were now the parents of four children. In addition to the first son, a daughter and two other sons had been born to them. Their first son joined the auxiliaries and looked forward to receiving the coveted Roman citizenship. Although years earlier Helga had been reluctant to accept Roman ways, she now had grown to appreciate the advantages of Roman civilization, especially after she and a merchant were involved in a dispute over a price and the matter was settled in the court before a Roman magistrate (**praetor**) with both sides satisfied, instead of by a fight in which someone might have been killed. When she went shopping, she used Roman coin, which was acceptable to all the tradesmen instead of the complicated system of barter used by her own people and the clans on the other side of the Rhine.

The weaving craft of Northern Europe developed into a magnificent tapestry art form that often commemorated myths of antiquity.

"Paris Pursued by Menelaus and Saved by Venus," tapestry by Pierre and François Van der Borght from the Atelier Bruxellais, Musée Jacquemart-André, Paris, France

Finally, Lucius received his honorable discharge (**missiō honesta**) from the legion, and, using his mustering-out pay of 3000 sesterces, he opened up a small tavern where he and his old comrades and other legionaries met to drink, spin tales of past campaigns, and play at **latrunculī** (a game like chess). His two younger sons also joined the auxiliaries and along with their older brother participated in the invasion of Britain in A.D. 43.

And so we see how a common foot soldier peaceably helped spread Roman civilization and its benefits. Not all of Rome's conquests were military! The most enduring aspects of its civilization—its laws, its customs, and its architectural and engineering accomplishments—are still embodied in our present-day civilization.

ROMAN LIFE XII

MEMORIAL INSCRIPTION

The following inscription on a tombstone found in Colchester, England, commemorates a centurion of the *Legio XX Valeria*, named Marcus Favonius Facilis:

M·FAVON·M·F·POL·FACI
LIS>LEG XX VERECVND
VS·ET·NOVICIUS·LIB·POSV
ERUNT·H·S·E

M(arcus) Favōn(ius), M(arcī) f(īlius) Pol(liā)(tribū), Facilis (centuriō) leg(iōnis) XX. Verēcund-
us et Novīcius līb(ertī) posu-
ērunt. H(īc) s(itus) e(st).

Marcus Favonius Facilis, son of Titus, of the Pollia tribe, centurion of the Twentieth legion. Verecundus and Novicius his freedmen set up this tomb. Here he lies buried.

Still standing today, the Arch of Titus in Rome has inspired artists for centuries.
"View of Rome," watercolor and ink on paper, John Vanderlyn, N.Y. State Senate House, Albany

REVIEW V: CHAPTERS 22–24

Exercise Va: Dative Case

Supply Latin words to match the English cues. Be sure to give the right endings. Read each sentence aloud and translate it:

1. Sextus fābulam dē caupōne scelestō _______ nārrābat. (to Cornelius)
2. Eucleidēs mandāta _______ et _______ dabat. (to the slaves) (to the slave-women)
3. Dum Cornēlius fābulam _______ nārrābat, _______ appropinquābant. (to his wife) (the city)
4. Interdiū raedās intrā urbem agere _______ nōn licēbat. (to *or* for the Romans)
5. "_______ necesse est ad Cūriam īre." (For me)
6. Titus respondet, "_______ lectīcāriōs condūxī." (For you, *pl.*)
7. "Ego multa et mīra _______ et _______ explicābō," inquit Titus. (to you, *sing.*) (to Sextus)
8. "_______ in caupōnā pernoctāre necesse erat," inquit Sextus. (for us)
9. Crās Forum vīsitāre _______ licēbit. (to *or* for the boys)
10. Hodiē māne _______ dormīre licet. (to *or* for Cornelia)
11. Cornēlius ē Cūriā mox exībit. _______ Marcus et Sextus occurrent. (Him)
12. Titus mīra aedificia _______ mōnstrāvit. (to the boys)
13. Crās multa alia aedificia _______ mōnstrābit. (to them)

Exercise Vb: Future, Pluperfect, and Future Perfect Tenses

Identify the tenses of the verbs, read aloud, and translate:

1. "Sī ego ad Cūriam sērō advēnerō, senātōrēs īrātī erunt," cōgitābat Cornēlius.
2. Sextus numquam aedificia tam magnifica vīderat.
3. Crās Eucleidēs puerōs ad Forum dūcet.
4. Ībisne cum puerīs, Cornēlia?
5. Crās puerī in Forō aderunt et aedificia vidēbunt.
6. Cornēlius fābulam dē caupōne scelestō nārrātam nōn audīverat.
7. "Sī fābulam mīlitis audīverimus, pater, statim cubitum ībimus," inquit Marcus.
8. Crās Cornēlius fābulam Aurēliae nārrāre poterit.
9. Nēmō caupōnam Apollodōrī anteā reprehenderat.
10. Cum pater manūs lāverit et aliam togam induerit, ad Cūriam statim ībit.

tam, adv., *so, such*

Exercise Vc: Verb Forms

Give the requested forms of the following verbs in the present, imperfect, future, perfect, pluperfect, and future perfect tenses:

	Present	Imperfect	Future	Perfect	Pluperfect	Future Perfect
1. circumīre (3rd pl.)						
2. dēscendere (2nd sing.)						
3. ferre (2nd pl.)						
4. dare (1st pl.)						
5. esse (3rd sing.)						
6. respondēre (1st sing.)						
7. surgere (3rd pl.)						
8. cōgitāre (2nd sing.)						
9. conicere (1st sing.)						
10. venīre (1st pl.)						

Exercise Vd: Reading Comprehension

Read the following passage and answer the questions below with full sentences in Latin:

ROME'S FIERCEST ENEMY

Ubi Hannibal puer novem annōrum erat, pater eius, nōmine Hamilcar, ad Hispāniam multīs cum mīlitibus nāvigāre parābat. Multīs ante annīs Rōmānī Hamilcarem in bellō vīcerant; ab Carthāginiēnsibus īnsulās Siciliam et Sardiniam cēperant. Nunc in animō habēbat Hamilcar ad Hispāniam trānsīre et ibi imperium novum condere. In Āfricā manēre nōlēbat puer Hannibal, itaque patrī appropinquāvit.

"Pater, pater!" clāmāvit Hannibal. "Dūc mē tēcum ad Hispāniam! Nōlī mē in Āfricā cum puerīs relinquere!"

"Sed tū puer es," respondit pater, quī eō ipsō tempore ōmina ad āram cōnsulere parābat. "Virī Carthāginiēnsēs, nōn puerī, hostēs Rōmānīs sunt."

"Puer nōn sum," inquit Hannibal. "Sī tū hostis Rōmānīs es, ego quoque Rōmānīs hostis sum."

"Sī ita cōgitās," inquit Hamilcar, "necesse tibi erit id iūre iūrandō affirmāre." Manum fīliī in capite victimae posuit.

Hannibal, "Ego semper hostis Rōmānīs erō," inquit. "Semper contrā Rōmānōs pugnābō. Nōn quiēscam nisi urbem Rōmam cēperō."

Itaque Hamilcar sēcum ad Hispāniam fīlium Hannibalem dūxit. Multīs post annīs, ubi Hannibal dux Carthāginiēnsium erat, ingentem exercitum contrā Rōmānōs dūxit; multa et mīra perfēcit. Contrā Rōmānōs diū pugnāvit et eōs multīs in proeliīs vīcit. Numquam habuērunt Rōmānī hostem ferōciōrem.

1 **annus, -ī**, m., *year*
2 **Hispānia, -ae**, f., *Spain*
nāvigō, -āre, -āvī, -ātūrus, *to sail*
multīs ante annīs, *many years before*
3 **bellum, -ī**, n., *war*
Carthāginiēnsēs, Carthāginiēnsium, m. pl., *the Carthaginians*
īnsula, -ae, f., *island*
5 **imperium, -ī**, n., *empire*
9 **ōmen, ōminis**, n., *omen*
āra, -ae, f., *altar*
12 **hostis, hostis**, gen. pl., **hostium**, m., *enemy*
13 **id**, *it*
iūre iūrandō affirmāre, *to affirm by swearing an oath*
14 **caput, capitis**, n., *head*
victima, -ae, f., *sacrificial victim*
15 **contrā**, prep. + acc., *against*
16 **pugnō, -āre, -āvī, -ātūrus**, *to fight*
17 **multīs post annīs**, *many years later*
18 **exercitus**, *army*
20 **proelium, -ī**, n., *battle*
ferōciōrem, *fiercer*

3 **vincō, vincere, vīcī, victus**, *to conquer*
4 **trānseō, trānsīre, trānsiī** or **trānsīvī, trānsitus**, irreg., *to go across*
5 **condō, condere, condidī, conditus**, *to found*
19 **perficiō, perficere, perfēcī, perfectus**, *to accomplish*

1. How old was Hannibal when his father prepared to sail to Spain?
2. What had the Romans done many years before?
3. What did Hamilcar intend to do?
4. What did Hannibal not want to do?
5. Why did Hamilcar want to leave Hannibal in Africa?
6. What did Hannibal want to be?
7. Where did Hamilcar place Hannibal's hand?
8. Hannibal will never rest unless he does what?
9. How did Hannibal go about trying to fulfill his oath?
10. Did the Romans ever have a fiercer enemy?

Roman battle ship

Exercise Ve

1. In lines 1–6 of the passage above, identify two verbs in the pluperfect tense and explain why this tense is used in each instance.
2. In lines 13–16 of the passage above, identify five verbs in the future and future perfect tenses, and explain why the tense is used in each instance.

CHAPTER 25

FIRST MORNING IN ROME

Iam diēs erat. Magnus erat clāmor in urbe. Servī ad Forum magnō tumultū onera ferēbant. Undique clāmor et strepitus! Sed nihil clāmōris, nihil strepitūs ad Marcum pervēnit. In lectō stertēbat, nam dēfessus erat. Sextus quoque in lectō manēbat sed dormīre nōn poterat. Clāmōribus et strepitū excitātus, iam cōgitābat dē omnibus rēbus quās Titus heri nārrāverat. "Quid hodiē vidēbimus? Cornēliusne nōs in Forum dūcet? 5
Ego certē Forum et Cūriam et senātōrēs vidēre volō."

Intereā Eucleidēs, quī prīmā lūce exierat, iam domum redierat. Statim cubiculum puerōrum petīvit et, "Eho, puerī!" inquit. "Cūr nōndum surrēxistis? Abhinc duās hōrās ego surrēxī. Quod novum librum emere volēbam, in Argīlētum māne dēscendī ad tabernam quandam ubi in postibus nōmina multōrum poētārum vidēre potes. 10
Catullus, Flaccus—"

At puerī celeriter interpellāvērunt quod Eucleidēs, ut bene sciēbant, semper aliquid novī docēre volēbat. "Quid in viīs vīdistī?"

Eucleidēs, "Nihil," inquit, "nisi miserum hominem lapidibus oppressum. Bovēs lapidēs quadrātōs in plaustrō trahēbant ad novum aedificium quod Caesar prope 15
Domum Auream cōnficit. Illud aedificium est ingēns amphitheātrum et mox prīnceps lūdōs ibi faciet. Sī bonī puerī fueritis, fortasse ad lūdōs ībitis."

1 **tumultus,** *uproar, commotion*
4 **excitātus, -a, -um,** *wakened, aroused*
dē omnibus rēbus, *about everything*
8 **Eho!** *Hey!*
abhinc duās hōrās, *two hours ago*
abhinc, adv., *ago, previously*
10 **ad tabernam quandam,** *to a certain shop*
taberna, -ae, f., *shop*
postis, postis, gen. pl., **postium,** m., *door-post*
poēta, -ae, m., *poet*
12 **aliquid,** *something*
14 **lapis, lapidis,** m., *stone*
oppressus, -a, -um, *crushed*
15 **quadrātus, -a, -um,** *squared*
quod, *which*
16 **Domus Aurea,** *(Nero's) Golden House*

3 **perveniō, pervenīre, pervēnī, perventūrus,** *to arrive (at), reach*
stertō, stertere, stertuī, *to snore*
15 **trahō, trahere, trāxī, tractus,** *to drag, pull*
16 **cōnficiō, cōnficere, cōnfēcī, cōnfectus,** *to finish*

Exercise 25a

Respondē Latīnē:

1. Cūr Sextus dormīre nōn poterat?
2. Quid Sextus facere et vidēre vult?
3. Cūr Eucleidēs in Argīlētum dēscendit?
4. Quid in postibus tabernae vīdit?
5. Quid Eucleidēs in viīs vīdit?
6. Quid prīnceps mox faciet?

FORMS

Nouns: 4th and 5th Declensions

Most Latin nouns belong to the 1st, 2nd, or 3rd declensions. There are two other declensions, to which a few nouns belong. Most 4th declension nouns are masculine, and most 5th declension nouns are feminine. Note, however, that **diēs** is usually masculine. Be sure to learn these forms thoroughly.

Number Case	4th Declension	5th Declension	
Singular			
Nominative	arc***us***	di***ēs***	r***ēs***
Genitive	arc***ūs***	di***ēī***	r***eī***
Dative	arc***uī***	di***ēī***	r***eī***
Accusative	arc***um***	di***em***	r***em***
Ablative	arc***ū***	di***ē***	r***ē***
Vocative	arc***us***	di***ēs***	r***ēs***
Plural			
Nominative	arc***ūs***	di***ēs***	r***ēs***
Genitive	arc***uum***	di***ērum***	r***ērum***
Dative	arc***ibus***	di***ēbus***	r***ēbus***
Accusative	arc***ūs***	di***ēs***	r***ēs***
Ablative	arc***ibus***	di***ēbus***	r***ēbus***
Vocative	arc***ūs***	di***ēs***	r***ēs***

Nouns of the 4th and 5th declensions will appear in vocabularies as follows:

4th Declension

aestus, -ūs, m., *heat*
aquaeductus, -ūs, m., *aqueduct*
arcus, -ūs, m., *arch*
complexus, -ūs, m., *embrace*
domus, -ūs, f., *house*
manus, -ūs, f., *hand*
rīsus, -ūs, m., *smile, laugh*
senātus, -ūs, m., *Senate*
sonitus, -ūs, m., *sound*
strepitus, -ūs, m., *noise, clattering*
tumultus, -ūs, m., *uproar, commotion*

5th Declension

diēs, diēī, m., *day*
rēs, reī, f., *thing, matter, situation*

Exercise 25b

Identify the case and number of each of the following nouns (give all possibilities):

1. sonitūs
2. diēbus
3. arcum
4. arcuum
5. diēs
6. senātuī
7. reī
8. diērum
9. rem
10. sonituum
11. rīsū
12. aestus
13. tumultibus
14. rēs
15. domus

ante meridiem, *before noon*
post meridiem, *after noon*
per diem, *a daily allowance for expenses*
in medias res, *into the middle of things*
in situ, *in its original place*

Exercise 25c

Read aloud and translate. Identify the case and number of each 4th and 5th declension noun:

1. Mediā nocte tumultum magnum audīvī. Quae erat causa huius tumultūs? Magnō cum strepitū bovēs plaustra per viās trahēbant. Prīmum strepitus procul aberat; deinde in viā nostrā erat tumultus.
   causa, -ae, f., *reason* **huius,** *of this*
   absum, abesse, āfuī, āfutūrus, irreg., *to be away, be absent, be distant*

2. Multās rēs manibus nostrīs facimus. Eucleidēs manū stilum tenēbat, nam puerōs scrībere docēbat. Puerī arborēs manibus et pedibus anteā ascenderant. Manūs igitur eōrum sordidae erant. Eucleidēs eōs iussit manūs statim lavāre.
   stilus, -ī, m., *pen* **eōrum,** *of them, their*

3. Multōs diēs in vīllā manēbāmus. Vēnit tamen diēs reditūs. Necesse erat iter trium diērum facere quod ad urbem celerrimē redīre volēbāmus. Eō diē discessimus. Duōs diēs per Viam Appiam iter faciēbāmus. Tertiō diē Rōmam pervēnimus.
   reditus, -ūs, m., *return* **eō diē,** *on that day* **tertius, -a, -um,** *third*

4. Titus rem mīram nōbīs nārrāvit. Servus, quī nocte per viās urbis ambulābat, subitō fūgit perterritus. Quae erat causa huius reī? In viā occurrerat canī quī, ut ipse dīxit, tria capita habēbat. Dē tālibus rēbus in librīs saepe legimus sed numquam tālem rem ipsī vīdimus. Dē hāc rē omnēs cīvēs multās fābulās nārrant.
   fugiō, fugere, fūgī, fugitūrus, *to flee* **caput, capitis,** n., *head*

BUILDING THE MEANING

The Partitive Genitive or Genitive of the Whole

Look at the following sentence:

> Eucleides semper **aliquid novī** docēre volēbat. (25:12–13)
> *Eucleides always wanted to teach* ***something new.***

The Latin words in boldface literally mean *something of the new*. The word **novī** is an adjective in the neuter genitive singular used as a substantive (see page 66). A better English translation is simply *something new*.

The word in the genitive case refers to a larger whole (*the new*) of which only a part (**aliquid,** *something*) is under consideration. This is called the *partitive genitive* or *genitive of the whole*.

Here are other examples that you have seen in the stories:

> Nihil **malī.** (21:7)
> *Nothing* ***of a bad thing.*** *= There is nothing wrong.*

> satis **temporis** (24:6)
> *enough* ***of time*** *= enough* time

> nihil **clāmōris,** nihil **strepitūs** (25:2)
> *nothing* ***of shouting****, nothing* ***of noise*** *= no shouting, no noise*

ROMAN LIFE XIII

ROME

IMPRESSIONS OF ROME

What nation is so far distant, Caesar, or so barbarous that it does not have a representative at the games here in your city? Here come farmers from the Balkans, natives of South Russia nurtured on horse's blood, people from the banks of the Nile, as well as those from the Atlantic's farthest shores. Here too are Arabs, men from Southern Turkey, German tribesmen, and Ethiopians—all so different in dress and in appearance. Their speech too sounds all different; yet it is all one when you are hailed, Caesar, as the true father of our country.

Martial, *De spectaculis* III

Contemporary American artist's vision of the streets of Rome
"Roman Street Scene," watercolor and ink on paper, Derrick Quarles, private collection

This terra-cotta plaque from the bustling port and commercial center of Ostia shows a shopfront with (far left) the shopkeeper and a customer haggling over the price of a hare; fresh-killed poultry hanging from a rack; an aged customer buying fruit from the shopkeeper's wife; hutches containing hares beneath the counter; and two monkeys on the counter to attract the attention of passers-by.
Museo Ostiense, Ostia Antica

Caecilius, in your own eyes you are a polished gentleman, but take my word for it, you are not. What are you then? A clown! You are like the hawker from across the Tiber who trades pale brimstone matches for broken glass or the man who sells to the idle bystanders soggy pea-pudding; like the keeper and trainer of snakes or the cheap slaves of the salt-sellers; like the hoarse-voiced seller of smoking sausages with his hot trays or a third-class street poet.

Martial, *Epigrams* I.41

If duty calls, the crowd gives way and the rich man is borne along rapidly over their heads by stout Liburnian bearers. On the way he will read, write, or sleep, for with the windows shut the litter induces sleep. Even so, he will get there before us. Though we hurry, the sea of humanity in front hinders us, and the great throng following jostles our backs. One man strikes us with his elbow, another with a hard pole; one knocks a beam against our heads, another a barrel. Our legs are plastered with mud, we are trampled on all sides by great feet, a soldier's hob-nailed boot crushes my toe. Newly patched togas are torn. A tall fir tree sways as the wagon rumbles on. Other carts carry pine trees, a nodding menace over the heads of the crowd. If the cart carrying Ligurian stone tilts forward and pours its overturned pile on the crowds, what remains of their bodies?

Juvenal, *Satires* III.239

THE STREETS OF ROME

Roman houses were neither named nor numbered. Hence the very complicated instructions given to those wishing to reach a certain "address":

> Every time you meet me, Lupercus, you ask, "May I send a slave to fetch your book of poems? I'll return it as soon as I've read it." Lupercus, it's not worth troubling your slave. It's a long journey to the Pear Tree, and I live up three flights of steep stairs. You can find what you want closer to home. No doubt you often go down to the Argiletum. There's a shop opposite Caesar's Forum with both door-posts covered with advertisements so that you can in a moment read the names of all the poets. Look for me there.
>
> Martial, *Epigrams* I.117

Domitian, who followed Titus as Emperor of Rome, issued an edict forbidding shopkeepers to display their wares on the streets. This, according to Martial, was a vast improvement:

> The aggressive shopkeepers had taken the whole city away from us and never kept to the limits of their thresholds. But you, Domitian, ordered our narrowed streets to expand and what had been but a path has now become a street. No longer do they chain wine bottles to the pillars in front of their shops, and no longer are officials forced to walk in the middle of the mud. No longer does the barber blindly draw his razor in a dense crowd, and no longer do the greasy fast-food shops take up the whole street. The barbers, bartenders, cooks, and butchers now keep to their own thresholds. Now Rome is a city again, whereas before it was just one big shop.
>
> Martial, *Epigrams* VII.61

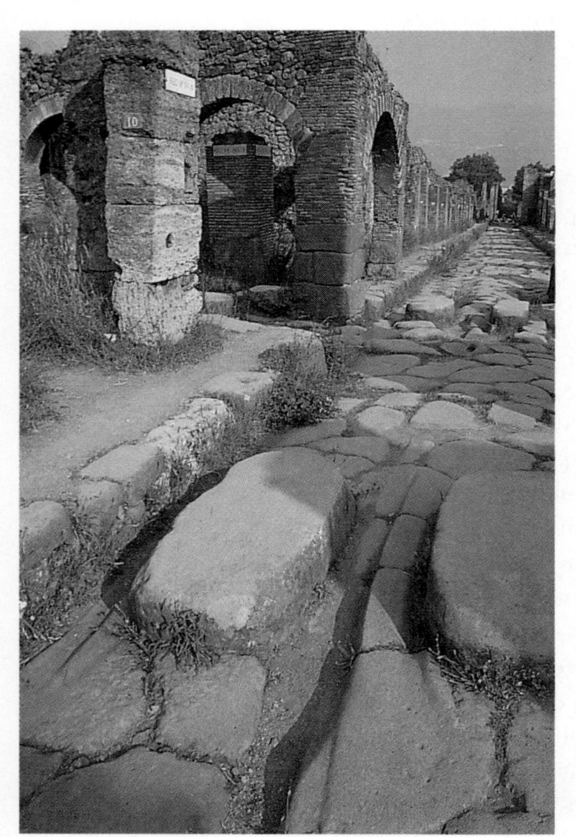

Streets had raised stepping stones that allowed pedestrians to cross when the street was flooded with rainwater.

Shopping malls are as old as Rome. Here, art lovers admire wares on display in an elaborate portico setting. Notice the many pedestrians on the upper level.

"Roman Art Lover," oil on canvas, Sir Lawrence Alma-Tadema, Milwaukee Art Center, Wisconsin

COLUMNS AND PORTICOS

The column was one of the main features of Roman architecture. Sometimes a single column was used to support a statue; more often, columns were used to support the roofs or to form the entrance-porches of temples and other buildings.

From the idea of the porch, there developed the portico or long covered walk, which afforded the citizens protection from sun and dust, while allowing them to enjoy the fresh air. In the shelter of the portico various activities took place. The Portico of Minucius was used as a corn-exchange; in another a vegetable market was held. In the porticos philosophers lectured, poets recited, schoolmasters held their classes, lawyers met their clients, entertainers performed, snacks were sold, and business deals were concluded. In fact, porticos became so common that it was eventually possible to walk from one end of the city to the other without coming out into the open at all!

According to one writer, porticos covered more than a quarter of the total area of the Campus Martius, the number of columns supporting them being about 2,000. Halls built in the shelter of these housed wall-maps of Rome and the Roman world, exhibitions of wonders from the Far East, natural marvels such as a snake 23 yards or 21 meters long, and, in the Portico of Philippus, a display of wigs and the latest in ladies' hairstyles.

ADDITIONAL READING:

The Romans Speak for Themselves: Book I: "Finding One's Way in Ancient Rome," pages 75–81.

Exercise 25d

Take parts, read aloud, and translate:

SEXTUS: Quam dēfessus sum, Marce! Nam hodiē māne dormīre nōn poteram. Tantus clāmor in viīs erat.
MARCUS: Quālem clāmōrem audīvistī? Ego certē nihil clāmōris audīvī.
SEXTUS: Quid? Nōnne audīvistī illōs canēs in viīs lātrantēs? Multās hōrās lātrābant. Numquam audīvī tantum strepitum. Audīvī etiam clāmōrem multōrum hominum quī per viās currēbant. 5
MARCUS: Quid clāmābant?
SEXTUS: Id audīre nōn poteram, nam omnēs simul clāmābant. Certē tamen īrātī erant. Erat quoque strepitus plaustrōrum. Nōs in urbe heri plaustra nōn vīdimus. Unde vēnērunt plaustra? 10
MARCUS: Interdiū nōn licet plaustra intrā urbem agere. Nocte igitur necesse est labōrāre. Servī in urbem ferēbant cibum, vīnum, lapidēs—
SEXTUS: Cūr lapidēs in urbem tulērunt?
MARCUS: Caesar ingēns amphitheātrum in urbe cōnficit.
SEXTUS: Nōs illud aedificium vīdimus? 15
MARCUS: Heri illud cōnspexistī, ubi ad Forum cum patre meō dēscendēbāmus. Heri nōn satis temporis erat id īnspicere quod pater domum festīnābat. Sed mox amphitheātrum iterum vīsitābimus atque id īnspiciēmus. Fortasse Eucleidēs nōs dūcet.
SEXTUS: Dum hoc mihi dīcis, multī hominēs in domum vēnērunt. Quī sunt? 20
MARCUS: Nōnne heri in urbe vīdistī multōs cīvēs post senātōrem sequentēs? Hic erat patrōnus, illī erant clientēs. Pater meus est patrōnus multōrum cīvium. Tū audīvistī clientēs domum intrantēs.
SEXTUS: Ēheu! Eucleidēs quoque intrāvit!

12 **vīnum, -ī,** n., *wine*
21 **sequentēs,** *following*
hic, *this, the latter*
22 **illī,** *those, the former*

Patrōnī were wealthy men who gave food or money to their dependents (**clientēs**). The **clientēs** came to the patron's home early in the morning to receive this dole and then escorted him to the Forum and performed other services for him. Here is Juvenal's satirical comment:

> Now the meager dole sits on the outer edge of the threshold of the patron's house to be snatched up by the clients in their togas. But first the patron inspects each face, fearing that someone might come and claim his due under a false name. Once he recognizes you, you'll get your share.
>
> Juvenal, *Satires* I.95–99

ROMAN LIFE XIV

EUCLEIDES THE TOUR GUIDE

Marcus had always visualized himself showing Sextus around the city of Rome, but he should have realized that Cornelius would never allow Sextus and himself to wander around Rome unsupervised. If neither Cornelius nor Titus was free to act as guide, Eucleides was bound to be their companion. He certainly knew a lot; the trouble was, there was no stopping him.

"Rome," Eucleides was now saying in that pedagogical tone of his, "is built on seven hills, the most famous being the Capitoline and the Palatine. By now, of course, it has far outstripped these petty limits. Augustus divided it into fourteen regions, which are in turn subdivided into 265 **vīcī** or wards. At the last census the population numbered 1,284,602, living in 1,797 **domūs** and 46,602 **īnsulae**."

"I can't see any islands!" complained Sextus, in all seriousness.

"**Īnsulae**," explained Eucleides, "are those apartment buildings, some of them five stories high."

"And the **Īnsula Feliculae** is the biggest in the world," said Marcus.

"There are," said Eucleides, "64 miles of streets, using your Roman measurements."

"Not very wide, are they?" commented Sextus.

"The maximum width according to *The Twelve Tables* can be only 17 feet."

"And some of them are not even paved!" cried Sextus, peering along the dark tunnel they were now traversing between the **īnsulae**.

Īnsula

"Watch out!" yelled Marcus, pulling Sextus and Eucleides close to the wall to dodge a deluge of slops from a third-floor window.

"We'll have the law on you for that!" shouted Marcus up at the unseen law-breaker. But Eucleides, not anxious to linger bandying threats, hustled the boys off through the labyrinth of shadowy alleys.

Suddenly they emerged into the blinding sun of the open Forum.

"This," said Eucleides impressively, pointing to a massive column, "is the center of the universe, the *Golden Milestone*. Erected by Augustus, it bears upon it in letters of gilt bronze the distances to all the cities of the Empire."

But it was not the *Golden Milestone* the boys were looking at, nor was it the splendor of the temple of Jupiter Optimus Maximus on the Capitoline Hill behind them. They were gazing into the **Forum Rōmānum,** which glittered with marble and bronze and gold. Senators and businessmen with their slaves were hurrying in and out of the **basilicae** that flanked the Forum. The noise was deafening. Cries of sausage-sellers and pastry-vendors mingled with the uproar of every language under heaven. White toga and tunic jostled with colorful foreign garb of all kinds.

Eucleides, sensing their preoccupation, was just pursing his lips to launch into a lecture on the Forum; but Marcus and Sextus were off, scampering along the **Via Sacra**.

"Come and tell us what's going on here!" they shouted, running to the far end of the Forum where their attention had been caught by the feverish activity of an army of masons engaged, amidst mountains of rubble and building stone, in some mammoth task of demolition or construction—it was hard to tell which.

"The Emperor Nero—" began Eucleides breathlessly as he caught up with them.

"I know," said Marcus. "He's the one that set Rome on fire for fun."

"The Emperor Nero," Eucleides repeated, "on the space cleared of unsightly hovels by a quite accidental fire, built the wonderful **Domus Aurea**."

"And they're still working at it by the look of it!" said Sextus, grinning.

"No, you idiot!" said Marcus. "Vespasian and Titus pulled down parts of Nero's folly and are putting up things for the citizens of Rome to enjoy, baths, for instance, and—"

"And that terrific statue over there?" pointed Sextus.

"That was a statue of Nero himself," Marcus went on, "but Vespasian put rays around its head and made it into a statue of the sun-god."

"It is 118 feet high," began Eucleides, but his hearers were gone again, toward an immense building nearing completion.

"What's this?" they asked, as an exhausted Eucleides caught up with them.

"This is the **Amphitheātrum Flāvium**," he gasped. "The Emperor Titus is to dedicate it soon."

ADDITIONAL READING:

The Romans Speak for Themselves: Book I: "Domus Aurea Neronis," pages 82–88.

Plan of the Roman Forum

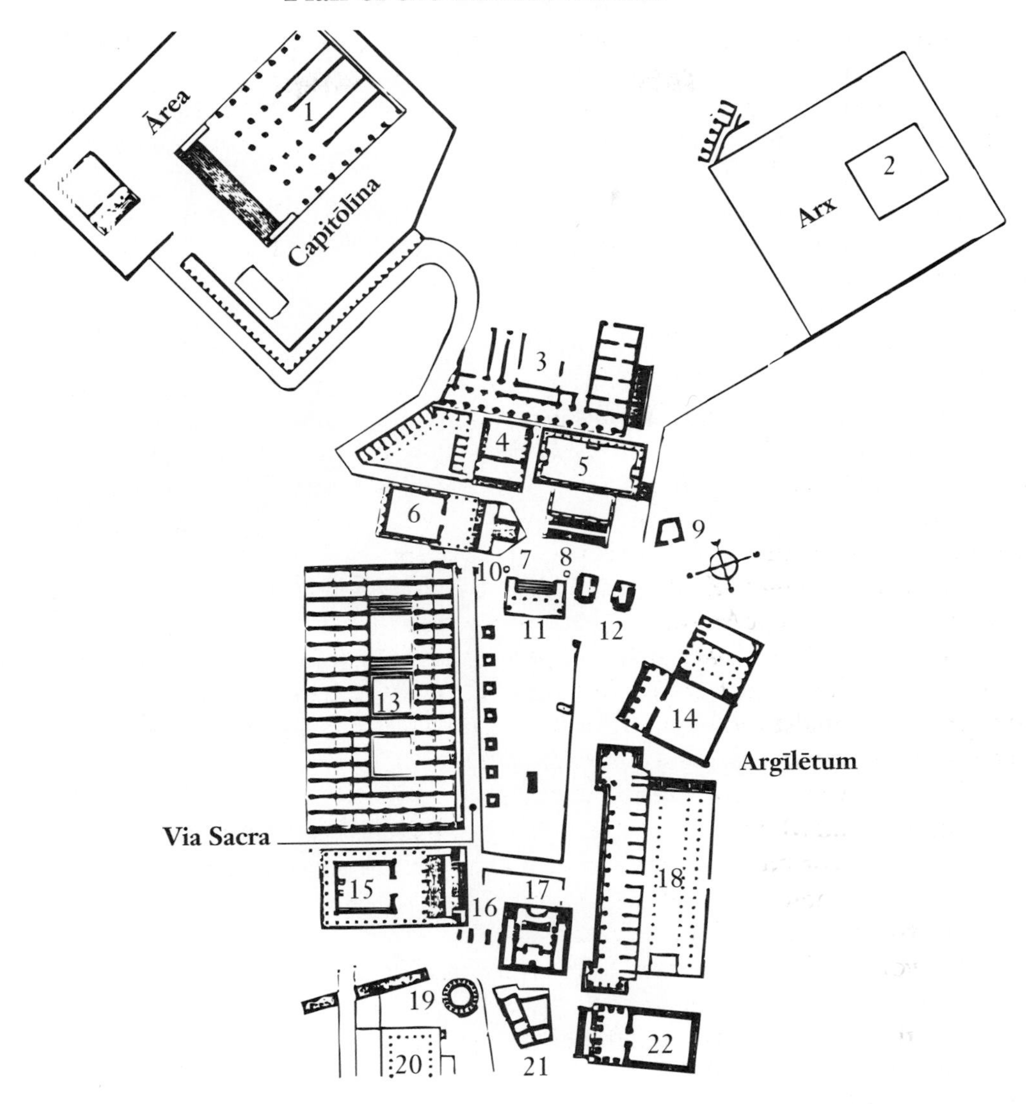

1 Templum Iovis Optimī Maximī Capitōlīnī
2 Templum Iūnōnis Monētae
3 Tabulārium
4 Templum Vespāsiānī
5 Templum Concordiae
6 Templum Saturnī
7 Mīliārium Aureum
8 Umbilīcus Urbis
9 Carcer
10 Arcus Tiberiī
11 Rōstra
12 Arcus Sevērī
13 Basilica Iūlia
14 Cūria Iūlia
15 Templum Castoris
16 Arcus Augustī
17 Templum Dīvī Iūliī
18 Basilica Aemilia
19 Templum Vestae
20 Ātrium Vestae
21 Rēgia
22 Templum Antōniī et Faustīnae

A GRIM LESSON

Eucleidēs et puerī iam domum redierant. Post cēnam Cornēlius et Marcus et Sextus in ātriō sedēbant.

"Quid hodiē vīdistis, puerī?" inquit Cornēlius.

"Nihil nisi aedificia antīqua," respondit Marcus. "Nōs in urbem exīre volumus sōlī. Cūr nōn licet?"

Cui Cornēlius, "Est perīculōsum sine custōde exīre in viās huius urbis. Sunt multī hominēs scelestī quī bona cīvium arripiunt. Nōnnumquam hī hominēs cīvēs ipsōs necant. Vōbīs igitur nōn licet sine custōde exīre. Iam sērō est. Nunc necesse est vōbīs cubitum īre. Nōlīte cessāre sed īte statim!"

Puerī, labōre diēī dēfessī, simulac cubitum iērunt, obdormīvērunt.

Postrīdiē māne Marcus in lectō suō iacēbat et dē Circō Maximō ita cōgitābat: "Quandō Circum Maximum vīsitābimus? Cūr pater meus nōs exīre vetat? Heri nūllōs hominēs scelestōs in urbe vīdī. Interdiū certē praedōnēs nōbīs nōn nocēbunt. Meum patrem, quod est senātor Rōmānus, praedōnēs timent. Nihil perīculī est."

Brevī tempore, ut Marcō vidēbātur, puerī ad Circum ībant. Mox mōlem ingentem Circī Maximī Marcus cōnspexit.

"Ecce!" clāmāvit Marcus. "Est Circus. Cum intrāverimus, tandem aurīgās ipsōs spectābimus."

Subitō tamen in viam sē praecipitāvērunt trēs hominēs.

"Cavē illōs hominēs!" clāmāvit Sextus. "Illī certē nōs in domūs vīcīnās trahent et ibi nōs necābunt."

Sed frūstrā, nam Marcus, metū commōtus, postquam Sextum audīvit clāmantem, ad terram cecidit et iacēbat in lutō immōbilis.

(continued)

2 **ātrium, -ī**, n., *atrium, main room*
4 **nisi**, conj., *unless, except*
6 **sine**, prep. + abl., *without*
custōs, custōdis, m., *guard*
7 **bona, bonōrum**, n. pl., *goods, possessions*
nōnnumquam, adv., *sometimes*
11 **postrīdiē**, adv., *on the following day*
iaceō, -ēre, -uī, -itūrus, *to lie, be lying down*
13 **praedō, praedōnis**, m., *robber*
noceō, -ēre, -uī, -itūrus + dat., *to do harm (to), harm*
15 **ut Marcō vidēbātur**, *as it seemed to Marcus, as Marcus thought*
22 **metus, -ūs**, m., *fear*
23 **terra, -ae**, f., *earth, ground*
lutum, -ī, n., *mud*

7 **arripiō, arripere, arripuī, arreptus**, *to grab hold of, snatch, seize*
12 **vetō, vetāre, vetuī, vetitus**, *to forbid*

Exercise 26a Respondē Latīnē:

1. Cūr nōn licet puerīs exīre in urbem sōlīs?
2. Quōcum puerīs licet exīre in urbem?
Quōcum...? *With whom*...?
3. Quō ībant puerī?
4. Quī sē in viam praecipitāvērunt?

"Eho!" clāmāvit ūnus ē praedōnibus. "Quō abīs, parvule? Quid est nōmen tuum? Nōnne tū filius es senātōris? Nōnne nōmen tuum est Marcus Cornēlius?" 25

Cui Marcus, "Quid vultis, scelestī? Nihil pecūniae habeō. Nōlīte mē verberāre! Sī mihi nocueritis, pater meus certē vōs pūniet."

Sed interpellāvit praedō, "Tacē, puer! Tū es captīvus noster neque ad patrem redībis. Nēmō nunc poterit tē servāre. Ipse enim tē necābō."

Tum praedō gladium strīnxit. Sextus stabat perterritus et, "Fer auxilium!" clāmāvit. 30 "Fer auxilium!" Sed nēmō clāmōrem audīvit. Nēmō auxilium tulit. Marcus oculōs clausit et mortem exspectābat.

Nihil accidit. Oculōs aperuit. In lectō erat suō. Somnium modo fuerat. Hodiē tamen domī manēre cōnstituit Marcus. Exīre nōluit.

24 **parvulus, -a, -um,** *small, little*
29 **servō, -āre, -āvī, -ātus,** *to save*
30 **gladius, -ī,** m., *sword*
31 **oculus, -ī,** m., *eye*
34 **domī,** *at home*

30 **stringō, stringere, strīnxī, strictus,** *to draw*
31 **claudō, claudere, clausī, clausus,** *to shut*
33 **accidit, accidere, accidit,** *(it) happens*
aperiō, aperīre, aperuī, apertus, *to open*

Respondē Latīnē:

1. Quid fēcit Marcus postquam Sextum clāmantem audīvit?
2. Cūr praedō gladium strīnxit?
3. Quis vēnit ubi Sextus clāmāvit?

FORMS

Demonstrative Adjectives and Pronouns: *Hic* and *Ille*

Look at the following sentences:

Ille tabellārius equōs vehementer incitāvit.	***That*** *courier fiercely whipped the horses on.*
Quis in **illō** aedificiō habitat?	*Who lives in* ***that*** *building?*
Hī canēs lātrant modo.	***These*** *dogs are only barking.*
Est perīculōsum in viās **huius** urbis exīre.	*It is dangerous to go out into the streets of* ***this*** *city.*
Sextus, **hīs** clāmōribus et **hōc** strepitū excitātus, dormīre nōn poterat.	*Roused by* ***these*** *shouts and* ***this*** *noise, Sextus could not sleep.*

You will see from the above examples that both **hic** and **ille** are used adjectivally with nouns to point out someone or something. **Hic** points to someone or something near at hand or near in time, while **ille** points to someone or something further away or distant in time or space. These are called *demonstrative adjectives*, from the Latin verb **dēmōnstrō, dēmōnstrāre,** *to point out, show*.

Here is a table showing all the cases of **hic** (*this, these*) and **ille** (*that, those*) in masculine, feminine, and neuter genders:

Number Case	Masc.	Fem.	Neut.	Masc.	Fem.	Neut.
Singular						
Nominative	hic	haec	hoc	ille	illa	illud
Genitive	huius	huius	huius	illīus	illīus	illīus
Dative	huic	huic	huic	illī	illī	illī
Accusative	hunc	hanc	hoc	illum	illam	illud
Ablative	hōc	hāc	hōc	illō	illā	illō
Plural						
Nominative	hī	hae	haec	illī	illae	illa
Genitive	hōrum	hārum	hōrum	illōrum	illārum	illōrum
Dative	hīs	hīs	hīs	illīs	illīs	illīs
Accusative	hōs	hās	haec	illōs	illās	illa
Ablative	hīs	hīs	hīs	illīs	illīs	illīs

The Latin sentences above show these demonstrative words being used as *adjectives* modifying nouns; they may also be used without nouns as *pronouns* meaning *he, she, it, this, that,* etc.:

> **Ille**, postquam **haec** audīvit, ē caupōnā sē praecipitāvit.
> ***He**, after he heard **this** (lit., **these things**), rushed out of the inn.*
>
> Postquam **hoc** fecit,... *After he did **this**,...*
>
> Marcus patrem, "Quid est **illud**?" rogāvit. *Marcus asked his father, "What is **that**?"*
>
> "Cavē illōs hominēs!" clāmāvit Sextus. "**Illī** certē nōs in domūs vīcīnās trahent et ibi nōs necābunt." (26:20–21)
> *"Be careful of those men!" shouted Sextus. "**They** will certainly drag us into the neighboring houses and kill us there."*

Sometimes **hic** refers to a nearer noun and means *the latter*, while **ille** refers to a farther noun and means *the former*:

> Nōnne heri in urbe vīdistī multōs cīvēs post senātōrem sequentēs? **Hic** erat patrōnus, **illī** erant clientēs. (25d:21–22)
> *Didn't you see yesterday in the city many citizens following behind a senator? **The latter** (literally, **this one**, i.e., the one last mentioned) was a patron, **the former** (literally, **those men**, i.e., the ones first mentioned) were clients.*

Be careful to distinguish **hic**, the adjective or pronoun, from the adverb **hīc**, *here*:

> Quid tū **hīc**? (9:8) *What (are) you (doing) **here**?*

Exercise 26b

Read aloud and translate:

1. Hic puer in hāc viā, ille in illā habitat.
2. Illa puella in hāc vīllā habitat; hī puerī in illā habitant.
3. Sī in hāc caupōnā pernoctābimus, hic caupō nōbīs certē nocēbit.
4. Illī praedōnēs illōs viātōrēs sub illīs arboribus petunt.
5. Quandō illī haec onera in vīllam portābunt?
6. Nōlī illud plaustrum in hanc urbem interdiū agere!
7. Huic puerō multa dabimus, illī nihil.
8. Hīs rūsticīs licēbit agrōs huius vīllae rūsticae colere.
9. Huic senātōrī ad Cūriam in lectīcā redīre necesse erat.
10. Illī aedificiō appropinquāre perīculōsum est, nam scelestī hominēs ibi habitant.
11. Ūnus ex hīs praedōnibus aliquid illī servō dīcēbat.

Exercise 26c

Choose the proper form of **hic** or **ille** to modify the noun in italics, and then read the sentence aloud and translate:

1. Cornēliī in ________ *vīllā* habitant.
2. "Spectāte ________ *arcum*, puerī!" clāmāvit Eucleidēs.
3. Ōlim ________ *puellae* in agrīs ambulābant.
4. Vīlicus cibum ________ *servō* nōn dabit.
5. "Vīdistīne ________ *aedificium*, Marce?" inquit Sextus.
6. Raeda ________ *mercātōris* prope tabernam manet.
7. Māne ________ *canēs* ferōciter lātrābant.
8. Bona ________ *rūsticōrum* in raedā erant.
9. Ūnus ex ________ *praedōnibus* gladium strīnxit.
10. Nōbīs ________ *arborēs* ascendere nōn licet.
11. ________ *rem* explicāre nōn possum.
12. ________ *strepitus* Marcum nōn excitāvit.

Exercise 26d

Using story 26 and the charts of demonstrative adjectives as guides, give the Latin for:

1. It is not dangerous to go out into the streets of that city.
2. Those wicked men seized the goods of these citizens.
3. Yesterday I saw this wicked man in that city.
4. Sextus had never seen this huge mass of the Circus Maximus.
5. Marcus will never give money to that robber.

Exercise 26e Take parts, read aloud, and translate:

AURELIA'S CONCERN FOR SEXTUS

Quīnta hōra est. Domī in tablīnō Gaius Cornēlius strēnuē labōrat sōlus. Iam ā Cūriā rediit et nunc ōrātiōnem scrībit, quam crās apud senātum habēbit. Aurēlia iānuae tablīnī appropinquat et tacitē intrat, nam coniugem vexāre nōn vult.

AURĒLIA: Salvē, Gaī! Esne occupātus?
CORNĒLIUS: Ita vērō! Paulisper tamen colloquium tēcum habēre possum. Quid agis, uxor? 5
AURĒLIA: Sollicita dē Sextō sum, coniūnx.
CORNĒLIUS: Dē Sextō? Cūr? Quid ille puer molestus iam fēcit?
AURĒLIA: Nihil malī fēcit Sextus. Sollicita sum quod hic puer numquam anteā in urbe tantā adfuit. Puerī in urbe sine custōde exīre 10 nōn dēbent. Necesse est igitur et Marcō et Sextō custōdem habēre.
CORNĒLIUS: Titus frāter meus custōs cum illīs ībit. Eucleidēs quoque Sextum custōdiet. Ille enim puerōs ad lūdum dūcet.
AURĒLIA: Frātrī Titō nōn cōnfīdō, et Sextus Eucleidem numquam audiet. Nam Eucleidēs numquam tacet. 15
CORNĒLIUS: (*īrātus*) Sī Sextus custōdem nōn audīverit, ego ipse eum pūniam!
AURĒLIA: Minimē, Gaī. Sextus nōn est puer scelestus. Est, ut bene scīs, puer strēnuus. Mātrem tamen propter ēruptiōnem Montis Vesuviī nōn iam habet Sextus. Certē eam valdē dēsīderat. Dēbēmus Sextum dīligenter cūrāre. 20
CORNĒLIUS: Ita vērō! Estō! Ubi nōn in Cūriā sum, ego ipse puerōs custōdiam. Aliter aut patruus Titus aut Eucleidēs verbōsus eōs cūrābit.
AURĒLIA: Grātiās tibi agō, coniūnx!
CORNĒLIUS: Nunc, sī vīs, abī! Sōlus esse volō. Mihi necesse est hanc ōrātiōnem cōnficere. 25

1 **quīntus, -a, -um,** *fifth*
tablīnum, -ī, n., *study*
2 **ōrātiō, ōrātiōnis,** f., *oration, speech*
quam...habēbit, *which he will deliver*
apud, prep. + acc., *in front of, before*
3 **coniūnx, coniugis,** *m./f., husband, wife*
5 **colloquium, -ī,** n., *conversation*
11 **dēbeō, -ēre, -uī, -itūrus** + infin., *ought*
13 **lūdus, -ī,** m., *school*
18 **propter,** prep. + acc., *on account of, because of*
Mōns Vesuvius, Montis Vesuviī, m., *Mount Vesuvius*
19 **dēsīderō, -āre, -āvī, -ātus,** *to long for, miss*
22 **aliter,** adv., *otherwise*
aut...aut..., conj., *either...or...*
23 **Grātiās tibi agō!** *I thank you! Thank you!*
24 **sī vīs,** *if you wish, please*

10 **adsum, adesse, adfuī, adfutūrus,** irreg., *to be present*
14 **cōnfīdō, cōnfīdere** + dat., *to give trust (to), trust*

ROME BECOMES A WORLD LEADER

Rome, the victor over Carthage, became an international power, the ruler of the western Mediterranean. Winning the war with Hannibal gave Rome secure control over Sicily, Spain, and Sardinia. Then, after subduing the Gauls in northern Italy, the Romans looked toward the East. Starting with Macedonia, the former ally of Carthage, Rome gradually took control of Greece and the Greek states in Asia Minor. In order to maintain a balance of power, the Romans established a permanent military presence all around the Mediterranean Sea.

The act that symbolized this age of control came in 146 B.C., when the consul Lucius Memmius demolished the city of Corinth and sold her inhabitants into slavery. In the same year, the Senate acceded to Marcus Cato's relentless pronouncement at the close of every speech he made to the Senate, **Carthāgō dēlenda est**, "Carthage must be destroyed." By razing that city, too, the Roman army ended the Third Punic War (149–146 B.C.). The Roman commander, Publius Cornelius Scipio Aemilianus Africanus, adoptive grandson of Hannibal's conqueror, had his troops sow the land with salt to assure its infertility and had them curse the site.

Rome Rules the Mediterranean

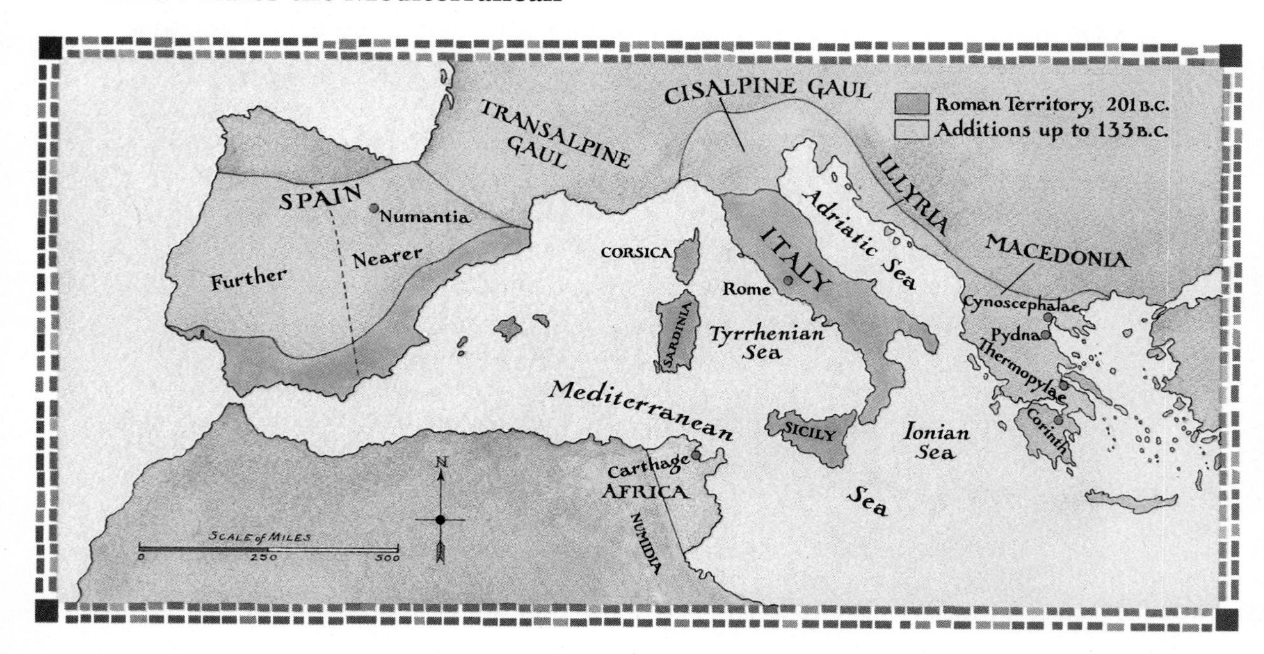

The Roman Senate emerged as the dominant power in the state during the years of conflict with Carthage and expansion into the eastern Mediterranean. Whereas new consuls, praetors, and other magistrates were elected every year, Senators were appointed for life. This stable, more permanent voice of authority directed both foreign and domestic policies and administered finances. The **nōbilēs**, descended from the old families of patrician and plebeian stock, formed a ruling aristocracy, whose ranks supplied most of the consuls and exerted most of the influence on the way the Roman government operated. The Roman Senate organized the newly acquired foreign territories into provinces (**prōvinciae**), whose governors, taken from the pool of former magistrates, were responsible to that same body.

The Italian economy changed when Roman senators spent their share of war-booty and profits from the provinces on the purchase of large estates (**lātifundia**), and under this system there developed a more organized, more profitable type of agriculture that utilized slave labor. The model Roman of earlier times, a citizen-soldier who farmed his own fields, was pushed off his land and into the city. Deriving sufficient wealth from their **lātifundia**, senators chose not to venture into the new realm of international trade; this lucrative opportunity was seized instead by a growing middle class, the equestrian order, members of which emerged as leaders of Roman commerce.

The Nine Muses were among the goddesses of Greek origin that were embraced by the Romans.

Roman sarcophagus showing frieze with the Nine Muses, Louvre, Paris, France

Graecia capta ferum victōrem cēpit, said the poet Horace: "Captive Greece captivated her uncivilized conqueror." Roman life had already been changing during the century before Rome destroyed Corinth and Carthage, as the Romans had gotten to know the Greeks, their language, and their literature, partly through contact with the Greek cities of southern Italy and Sicily.

Both the family-based Roman worship of rustic spirits, who watched over farms, flocks, and storeroom, and the formal state religion began to incorporate Greek rituals, and the Roman gods became associated with the Greek Olympians, who were more human in appearance and personality. At the same time, the Stoic philosophy preached by many Greeks at this time, which offered an intellectual basis for a strong moral code, was welcomed by leading Romans.

Greece also taught Rome the value of literature. Livius Andronicus adapted a Greek play for the Roman stage in 240 B.C., the year after the First Punic War. Gnaeus Naevius composed the *Bellum Punicum*, an epic poem in which he combined the history of the

Scipio depicted by Poussin

"The Continence of Scipio," oil on canvas, Nicolas Poussin, Pushkin Museum, Moscow, Russia

First Punic War with the myth of Queen Dido of Carthage and Aeneas, the Trojan hero and forefather of Rome. In another epic, the *Annales*, Quintus Ennius recounted the glorious history of Rome from its beginnings to his own day. More firmly based on Greek content and form were the comic plays of Plautus and Terence, in which Latin-speaking Italian characters with Greek names romped through Greek plots.

Marcus Cato, fiercely advocating that Romans retain the old standards of Italian independence, wrote the *Origines*, a Roman history book for his son, and the *De agricultura*, advice for Roman landholders. He lamented the appearance of Greek statues in Roman homes and condemned the new interest in barbers and Greek cooks.

Many more Romans, such as Scipio Aemilianus, rather enjoyed the new luxuries, became patrons of the arts, and welcomed the civilizing influence of Greek teachers, writers, and philosophers. Once Rome learned Greek literature and ideas, she evolved into a Hellenized civilization best labeled Greco-Roman. Roman culture and control of earlier days had both outgrown Italy.

CHAPTER 27

A VISIT TO THE RACES

Chariot-racing (**lūdī circēnsēs**) was perhaps the most popular spectacle in ancient Rome. It was held in the **Circus Maximus**, a huge open-air stadium in the valley between the Palatine and the Aventine hills. It could hold about 200,000 spectators, seated in tiers around the race track (**curriculum**).

It has been estimated that at one time some 90 holidays (**fēriae**) were given over to games at public expense. On these days the citizens were "celebrating a holiday" (**fēriātī**).

A barrier (**spīna**) ran down the center of the course, and the chariots (**quadrīgae**), each pulled by four horses, had to complete seven laps, about five miles or eight kilometers in all. Fouling was permitted, and collisions were frequent, especially at the turning posts (**mētae**). A race began when the Emperor (**Caesar)** or presiding official gave the signal (**signum**) by dropping a white cloth (**mappa**).

The charioteers, some of whom won great popularity and very high salaries, were employed by four companies (**factiōnēs**), each with its own color—the "Reds" (**russātī**), the "Whites" (**albātī**), the "Greens" (**prasinī**), and the "Blues" (**venetī**). Rival groups of spectators were accustomed to show their support (**favēre**) for each color vociferously.

One charioteer we hear about, Gaius Apuleius Diocles, drove chariots for the Red Stable for twenty-four years, ran 4,257 starts, and won 1,462 victories.

No wonder Marcus, Cornelia, and Sextus are eager to go to the races! As we return to our story, three days after the Cornelii arrived in Rome, Sextus is sitting alone when suddenly Marcus rushes in.

MARCUS: Sexte! Sexte! Hodiē nōbīs licet ad lūdōs circēnsēs īre. Eucleidēs mē et tē et Cornēliam ad Circum dūcet.

SEXTUS: Lūdōs circēnsēs amō. Sed nōnne Circus clausus erit?

MARCUS: Minimē! Circus nōn erit clausus, nam hodiē cīvēs omnēs fēriātī sunt. Viae erunt plēnae hominum. Virī, mulierēs, līberī Circum celerrimē petent. 5

SEXTUS: Sed cūr nōn nunc discēdimus? Ego sum iam parātus.

MARCUS: Simulac Cornēlia ē somnō surrēxerit, statim ībimus.

(Much to the boys' disgust, Cornelia was rather late in waking up from her siesta, but soon they were all ready to leave.)

EUCLEIDĒS: Agite! Iam tandem ad Circum īre tempus est. Estisne parātī, puerī? Esne parāta, Cornēlia? 10

(Eucleides takes Cornelia and the boys quickly through the streets; they can now hear the noise of the Circus crowds.)

EUCLEIDĒS: Iam ā Circō nōn procul absumus. Nōnne strepitum audītis? Ecce! Omnēs ad Circum festīnant. Brevī tempore nōs ipsī intrābimus. *(continued)* 15

5 **mulier, mulieris,** f., *woman*

(They enter the Circus.)

CORNĒLIA: Quam ingēns est turba hominum! Tōtus Circus est plēnus spectātōrum.

EUCLEIDĒS: Ita vērō! Semper multī spectātōrēs in Circō sunt. Hīc cōnsīdēmus?

MARCUS: Minimē! Prope curriculum sedēre necesse est quod ibi omnia vidēre poterimus. 20

EUCLEIDĒS: At prope curriculum sedēre perīculōsum est. Pater vester multa dē perīculō dīxit.

MARCUS: Nihil perīculī est, nam Titus, patruus meus, cum amīcīs prope curriculum sedēre solet.

SEXTUS: Ecce! Caesar ipse iam surrēxit; signum dare parat. Ego russātīs favēbō. 25

MARCUS: Ego albātīs.

CORNĒLIA: Ego venetīs.

MARCUS: Ecce! Mappa! Signum est!

CORNĒLIA: Quam ferōciter equōs verberant illī aurīgae! Quam celeriter equōs agunt! Quam temerāriī sunt! Nōnne mortem timent? 30

SEXTUS: Ecce! Russātus meus certē victor erit, nam equōs magnā arte agit.

25 **faveō, favēre, fāvī, fautūrus** + dat., *to give favor (to), support*

(continued)

Chariot race in the Circus

"The Campana Relief: A Chariot Race in the Circus," The British Museum, London, England

MARCUS:	Ō mē miserum! Aurīga meus equōs dēvertit. Cavē mētam! Cavē mētam! Esne sēmisomnus, fatue? Cūr mētam nōn vītāvistī?	
CORNĒLIA:	Ēheu! Ille aurīga cecidit. Humī iacet. Estne mortuus?	
SEXTUS:	Minimē! Minimē! Ecce! Animum recuperāvit. Iam surgit.	35
CORNĒLIA:	Audīvistisne clāmōrēs hōrum spectātōrum? Magnā vōce nōmina aurīgārum et equōrum semper clāmant! Undique ingēns est strepitus! Tantum strepitum ego numquam audīvī.	
MARCUS:	Russātī vīcērunt, sed mox etiam albātī vincent. Glōria albātōrum erit immortālis!	40
EUCLEIDĒS:	Hoc fortasse accidet, sed Caligula ipse, ut dīcunt, prasinōs amābat.	

(continued)

32 **dēvertō, dēvertere, dēvertī, dēversus,** *to turn aside*
34 **humī,** *on the ground*
39 **vincō, vincere, vīcī, victus,** *to conquer, win*

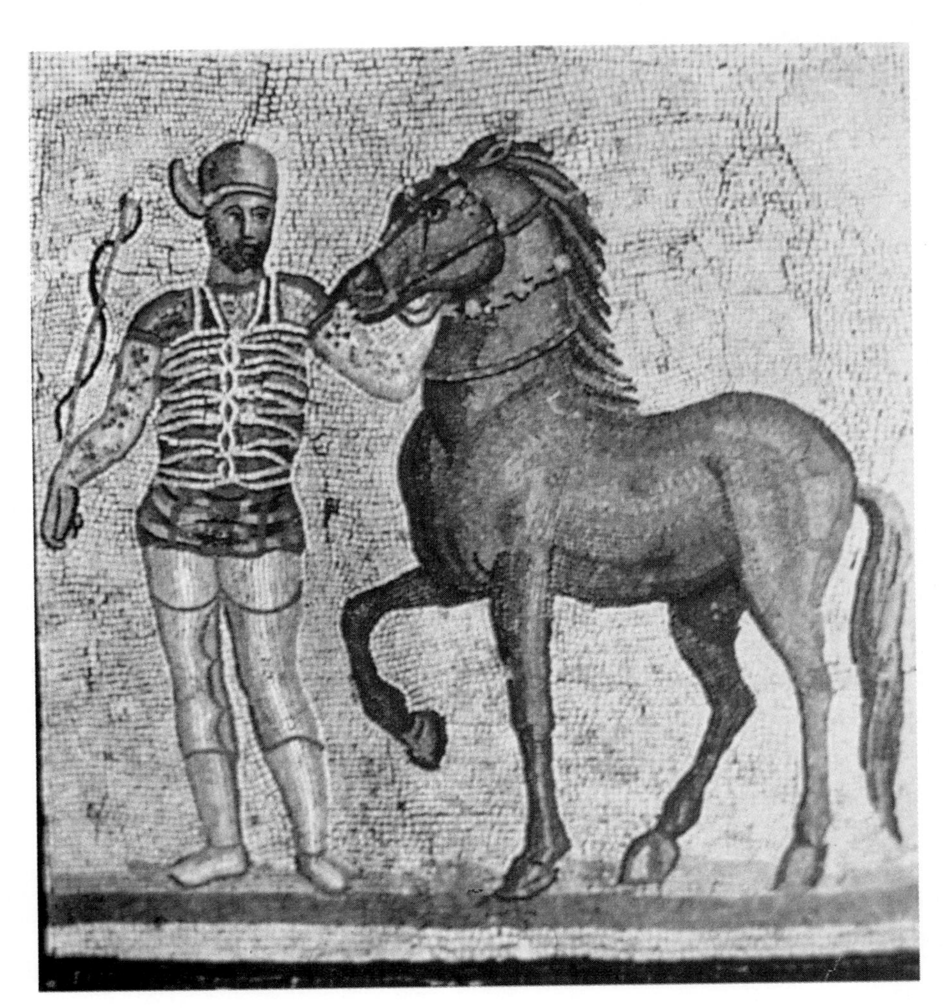

Charioteer's clothing

(They watch a few more races, but it is not Marcus' lucky day. Eucleides becomes a little anxious as it grows later. He had been caught once before in a crush at the gates.)

EUCLEIDĒS: Iam sērō est. Nunc domum redībimus.

SEXTUS: Nōndum tempus est domum redīre. Ecce! Aurīgae habēnās sūmpsērunt et signum exspectant. 45

EUCLEIDĒS: Nisi mox discēdēmus, turbam ingentem vītāre nōn poterimus. Agite! Domum!

Chariot racing

ADDITIONAL READING:

The Romans Speak for Themselves: Book I: "Finding a Date in Ancient Rome or Why Some Men Went to the Chariot Races," pages 89–98; "Pliny's Views on the Chariot Races," pages 93–98.

BUILDING THE MEANING

Dative with Special Intransitive Verbs

Look at the following sentences:

Sī **mihi** nocueritis, pater meus certē vōs pūniet. (26:26–27)
If you do harm ***to me****, my father will certainly punish you.*
If you harm ***me****, my father will certainly punish you.*

Frātrī Titō nōn cōnfīdō. (26e:14)
I do not give trust ***to (my) brother Titus.***
I do not trust ***(my) brother Titus.***

Ego **russātīs** favēbō. (27:25)
I will give favor ***to the reds.***
I will favor/support ***the reds.***

The verbs **nocēre,** *to do harm (to),* **cōnfīdere,** *to give trust (to),* and **favēre,** *to give favor (to),* are intransitive and so do not take direct objects in the accusative case. Their meaning is completed by a word or phrase in the dative case. The meaning of the dative case in this type of sentence can be clearly seen in the literal translations of the sentences above: *If you do harm* ***to me****, I do not give trust* ***to (my) brother Titus,*** and *I will give favor* ***to the reds***. In translating into idiomatic English, we usually use a direct object, as in the alternative translations above.

These sentences are similar in pattern to those discussed on p. 212, "Dative with Intransitive Compound Verbs," and may be grouped with those as a basic pattern of Latin sentences.

FORMS

Pronouns: Personal

Look at these sentences:

Prīnceps **mē** vidēre vult. — *The emperor wants to see* ***me.***
Eīs dōnum dedistī. — *You gave* ***them*** *a present.*
Tēcum ībit. — *He will go with* ***you.***

The words **ego,** *I,* **tū,** *you* (singular), and **is, ea, id,** *he, she, it,* and **nōs** *we,* **vōs,** *you* (plural), and **eī, eae, ea,** *they,* are called *personal pronouns* because they show what person is involved in the action. Here is a complete chart:

Case	1st.	2nd	3rd Masc.	3rd Fem.	3rd Neut.
Singular					
Nominative	ego	tū	is	ea	id
Genitive	meī	tuī	eius	eius	eius
Dative	mihi	tibi	eī	eī	eī
Accusative	mē	tē	eum	eam	id
Ablative	mē	tē	eō	eā	eō
Plural					
Nominative	nōs	vōs	eī	eae	ea
Genitive	nostrī nostrum	vestrī vestrum	eōrum	eārum	eōrum
Dative	nōbīs	vōbīs	eīs	eīs	eīs
Accusative	nōs	vōs	eōs	eās	ea
Ablative	nōbīs	vōbīs	eīs	eīs	eīs

For **nōs** and **vōs**, two genitive forms are found, as shown in the chart. Their use is limited, as is the use of the genitives of **ego** and **tū**, and you will not meet any of these genitives until later in your study of Latin. They are *not* used to indicate possession (see below, "Adjectives: Possessive").

Notice how the preposition **cum** is attached to the end of **tē** in the third example above. So also you will find **mēcum, nōbīscum,** and **vōbīscum** (but **cum** is not used in this way with **eō, eā, eō,** or **eīs**).

Exercise 27a

Select, read aloud, and translate:

1.	Necesse erat _______ prope curriculum sedēre.	eius/nōbīs
2.	Eucleidēs _______ dēmōnstrābat circum et aurīgās.	ego/mē/mihi
3.	Nōn vult, Sexte, Cornēlia prope _______ sedēre.	tū/tibi/tē
4.	Sextus saepe _______ vexat.	eī/eam/eius
5.	Cornēlius clāmābat et servī vōcem _______ audīvērunt.	eius/eum/eōrum

Pronouns: Reflexive

Look at these sentences:

> **Mē** in piscīnā vīdī.
> *I saw **myself** in the fishpond.*
>
> Ubi cecidistis, **vōbīs** nocuistis.
> *When you fell, you hurt **yourselves**.*

The words in boldface are being used as reflexive pronouns. A pronoun is reflexive when it refers to the subject of the sentence, as **mē** in the first sentence refers to the understood 1st person subject of the verb **vīdī**, just as in the translation *myself* refers to *I*.

While the genitive, dative, accusative, and ablative forms of the regular 1st and 2nd person pronouns may be used reflexively, as in the examples above, there are special forms for the 3rd person reflexive pronoun, as in the following sentences:

> Puellae, ubi cecidērunt, **sibi** nocuērunt.
> *The girls hurt **themselves** when they fell.*
>
> Marcus **sē** in piscīnā cōnspexit.
> *Marcus caught sight of **himself** in the fishpond.*

In the first example, **sibi** refers to **puellae**, just as in the translation *themselves* refers to "the girls."

Here is the complete set of forms of the 3rd person reflexive pronoun:

Genitive	suī
Dative	sibi
Accusative	sē
Ablative	sē

There is no nominative form. The same forms (**suī, sibi, sē,** and **sē**) are used for singular and plural and for masculine, feminine, and neuter, so this pronoun can mean *himself, herself, oneself, itself,* or *themselves.* For example, **sibi** can mean *to/for himself, to/for herself, to/for oneself, to/for itself,* or *to/for themselves.*

Exercise 27b

Select, read aloud, and translate:

1. Aurēlia _______ in aquā cōnspexit.	sibi/sē/suī
2. "Ego _______ in aquā cōnspexī," inquit Aurēlia.	sē/mē/sibi
3. Canēs ē iānuā caupōnae _______ praecipitant.	mē/sibi/sē
4. Nocuistīne _______, ubi cecidistī?	tē/tibi/sibi
5. Ego _______ nōn nocuī.	mihi/sibi/mē

Adjectives: Possessive

In your reading you will not find the genitive of the 1st and 2nd person pronouns or of the reflexive pronouns used to indicate possession. Rather, you will find a *possessive adjective*:

Librum **tuum** legō.
*I am reading **your** book.*

Librum **meum** legō.
*I am reading **my (own)** book.*

The possessive adjectives, corresponding to the personal and reflexive pronouns, are 1st and 2nd declension adjectives, as follows:

meus, -a, -um	*my, my own, mine*
tuus, -a, -um	*your, your own, yours* (singular)
suus, -a, -um	*his own, her own, its own*
noster, nostra, nostrum	*our, our own, ours*
vester, vestra, vestrum	*your, your own, yours* (plural)
suus, -a, -um	*their own*

Notice that just as the pronoun **sē** is used for both singular and plural, so also the adjective **suus, -a, -um** can be singular or plural and mean *his own, her own,* or *their own.*

Exercise 27c

Select, read aloud, and translate:

1.	Ad lūdōs circēnsēs cum amīcīs _______ ībitis.	vestrī/vestrīs/vestrōs
2.	Omnēs spectātōrēs factiōnī _______ favent.	suae/suīs/suum
3.	In somniō _______ appāruērunt praedōnēs scelestī.	meīs/meī/meō
4.	In vīllā _______ sunt multī servī.	nostrī/nostra/nostrā
5.	Puellae domī cum amīcīs _______ manēbant.	suae/suīs/suō

factiō, factiōnis, f., *company (of charioteers)*

Note carefully the distinction in use between the reflexive adjective **suus, -a, -um,** *his own, her own, their own,* and the genitives of the 3rd person pronoun, namely, **eius,** *of him = his,* or *of her = her,* and **eōrum**, **eārum**, *of them = their:*

Marcus librum **suum** habet.
*Marcus has **his own** book.*

Puellae librōs **suōs** habent.
*The girls have **their own** books.*

Marcus librum **eius** habet.
*Marcus has **his** (e.g., Sextus') book.*

Puellae librōs **eōrum** habent.
*The girls have **their** (e.g., the boys') books.*

Exercise 27d

Using the dialogue at the beginning of this chapter and the information on special intransitive verbs, pronouns, and adjectives as guides, give the Latin for the following. Be sure to use pronouns for the emphatic words in italics:

1. As soon as *she* has gotten up, we will go.
2. *We* want to sit near the race track.
3. *I* favor the whites. Do *you* favor them?
4. Look at the blue! *I* favor him.
5. Is your blue winning?
6. My white fell down. Did he hurt himself?
7. *He* is safe, but he harmed his own horses.
8. The horses of your blue are safe.
9. My charioteer did not harm his own horses.
10. It is time for us to return home.

Prefixes: Compound Verbs I

Compare the following sentences:

1. Equī raedam **trahunt**.
   *The horses **pull** the carriage.*
2. Servī lectum **ferēbant**.
   *The slaves **were carrying** the bed.*

1. Equī raedam **extrahunt**.
   *The horses **pull out** the carriage.*
2. Servī lectum **referēbant**.
   *The slaves **were carrying back** the bed.*

In the right-hand column a prefix has been added to the beginning of the verb to give it a more specific meaning. Verbs with prefixes attached to them are called *compound verbs*. Common prefixes are:

ab-, abs-, ā-, *away, from*
ad-, *toward, to*
circum-, *around*
con-, *along with, together*
(or simply to emphasize)
dē-, *down, down from*
dis-, dī-, *apart, in different directions*
ex-, ē-, *out, out of*
in-, *into, in, on*
inter-, *between*
per-, *through* (or simply to emphasize)
prae-, *in front, ahead*
praeter-, *past, beyond*
prō-, prōd-, *forward*
re-, red-, *back, again*
sub-, *under, below*
trāns-, trā-, *across*

Note that many of these are common prepositions.
Be sure to learn these prefixes thoroughly.

Exercise 27e

Read aloud and translate. Identify each compound verb and give the meaning of its prefix. You are to deduce the meanings of compound verbs that you have not met in the stories.

1. Pater līberōs ē vīllā ēdūxit et trāns viam trādūxit.
2. Cornēlius Eucleidem iussit līberōs abdūcere.
3. Eucleidēs līberōs ad hortum redūxit.
4. Servī togās et tunicās in cistās repōnunt.
5. Ubi ad Portam Capēnam veniunt, servī onera dēpōnunt.
6. Ubi plaustrum invēnit, stercus remōvit et corpus extrāxit.
7. Cornēliī Rōmam heri advēnērunt.
8. Homō per viam it. Mox viam trānsībit et ad vīllam redībit.
9. Ubi urbem intrāmus, necesse est Aquam Marciam subīre.
10. Puerī Circum relīquērunt et Palātīnum circumiērunt.
11. Nihil clāmōris, nihil strepitūs ad Marcum pervēnerat.
12. Puerōs, quod praecurrēbant, identidem revocābat Cornēlius.

ROMAN LIFE XV

INSCRIPTIONS CONCERNING CHARIOTEERS

HONORARY INSCRIPTION

P. Aelius, Marī Rogātī fīl(ius), Gutta Calpurniānus equīs hīs vīcī in factiōne venetā: Germinātōre n(igrō) Āf(rō) LXXXXII, Silvānō r(ūfō) Āf(rō) CV, Nitid(ō) gil(vō) Āf(rō) LII, Saxōne n(igrō) Āf(rō) LX, et vīcī praemia m(aiōra) $\overline{\text{L}}$ I, $\overline{\text{XL}}$ IX, $\overline{\text{XXX}}$ XVII.

I, Publius Aelius Gutta Calpurnianus, son of Marius Rogatus, won for the Blue stable with the following horses: Germinator, African black, 92 (times); Silvanus, African chestnut, 105 (times); Glossy, African sorrel, 52 (times); Saxon, African black, 60 (times); and I won major purses of 50,000 sesterces (1), of 40,000 sesterces (9), and of 30,000 sesterces (17).

SEPULCHRAL INSCRIPTION

D. M. Epaphrodītus agitātor f(actiōnis) r(ussātae), vīc(it) CLXXVIII, et ad purpureum līber(ātus) vīc(it) VIII. Beia Felicula f(ēcit) coniugī suō merentī.

To the deified spirits (of) Epaphroditus, driver for the Red stable; he won 178 (times), and after being manumitted to the Purples he won 8 (times). Beia Felicula made (this monument) for her deserving husband.

CURSES AGAINST CHARIOTEERS AND THEIR HORSES

Adiūrō tē, daemōn, quīcumque es et dēmandō tibi ex hāc hōrā ex hāc diē ex hōc mōmentō, ut equōs Prasinī et Albī cruciēs occīdās, et agitātōrēs Clārum et Fēlīcem et Prīmulum et Rōmānum occīdās collīdās, neque spīritum illīs relinquās.

I adjure you, demon, whoever you are, and I ask of you from this hour, from this day, from this moment, that you torture and kill the horses of the Green and the White, and that you kill and smash their drivers Clarus and Felix and Primulus and Romanus, and leave no breath in them.

WORD STUDY VII

Prefixes

Knowledge of Latin prefixes will help not only with the meanings of Latin compound verbs but also with the meanings of many English words derived from them. For example, when the Latin simple verb **portāre** is combined with various prefixes, the resulting compound verbs provide English with several words, e.g.:

deport (from **dēportāre**)
export (from **exportāre**)
report (from **reportāre**)
transport (from **trānsportāre**)

Relying on your knowledge of prefixes, can you tell the meaning of each of the English words above?

Some English words are derived from the infinitive base of the Latin compound verb, e.g., *transport* (from **trānsportāre**). Others are derived from the stem of the fourth principal part, e.g., *transportation* (from **trānsportātus**). (For the suffix *-tion* see Word Study VI.)

Exercise 1

After each Latin simple verb below is a group of English verbs that are derived from Latin compounds of that simple verb. (The Latin compound verbs are in parentheses.) Give the meaning of each English verb:

dūcō, dūcere, dūxī, ductus, *to lead*

1. to conduct (**condūcere**)
2. to induct (**indūcere**)
3. to deduct (**dēdūcere**)
4. to reduce (**redūcere**)
5. to produce (**prōdūcere**)
6. to adduce (**addūcere**)

pōnō, pōnere, posuī, positus, *to put*

1. to propose (**prōpōnere**)
2. to dispose (**dispōnere**)
3. to expose (**expōnere**)
4. to depose (**dēpōnere**)
5. to transpose (**trānspōnere**)
6. to deposit (**dēpōnere**)

cēdō, cēdere, cessī, cessūrus, *to go*

1. to precede (**praecēdere**)
2. to recede (**recēdere**)
3. to intercede (**intercēdere**)

variant spelling:

4. to proceed (**prōcēdere**)
5. to exceed (**excēdere**)

Note that **cēdere** can also mean *to yield*. From this meaning come the following English derivatives:

6. to cede (**cēdere**)
7. concede (**concēdere**)

ferō, ferre, tulī, lātus, irreg., *to bring, carry, bear*

1. to refer (**referre**)
2. to infer (**īnferre**)
3. to defer (**dēferre**)
4. to transfer (**trānsferre**)
5. to confer (**cōnferre**)
6. to relate (**referre**)

Exercise 2

Give the infinitive of the Latin compound verb from which each of the following English nouns is derived. Use each English noun in a sentence that illustrates its meaning:

1. disposition
2. proponent
3. recess
4. inference
5. product
6. exposition
7. relation
8. procession
9. conference
10. precedent
11. translator
12. concession
13. deduction
14. referee
15. reference

Exercise 3

Each adjective in the pool below is derived from a Latin compound verb. Choose an adjective to fill each blank and give the Latin compound verb from which it is derived:

1. Eucleides provided an atmosphere for the boys that would lead them to learn. The atmosphere was ______ to learning.
2. Although the horses tried to pull the carriage out, their efforts brought forth no results. Their efforts were not ______.
3. Some masters treat their slaves with violence that goes beyond reasonable limits. Their use of violence is ______.
4. Davus was not unhappy, but he was not as happy as he might have been if he were not a slave. Davus enjoyed ______ happiness.
5. When Cornelius entered a shop, the merchant left the other customers and helped him immediately. Cornelius received ______ treatment.
6. After he considered all of the evidence, the overseer was certain which slave stole the money. The overseer used ______ reasoning to come to his conclusion.
7. When the emperor went by, all the citizens bowed respectfully. The emperor was greeted in a ______ manner.

relative	deferential	conducive
productive	excessive	preferential
deductive		

Latin Abbreviations in English

Many abbreviations used in English are actually abbreviations of Latin words. For example, the common abbreviations for morning and afternoon, A.M. and P.M., stand for the Latin phrases **ante merīdiem** (*before noon*) and **post merīdiem** (*after noon*).

Exercise 4

With the aid of an English dictionary, give the full Latin words for the following abbreviations and explain how each is used in English:

1. etc.
2. A.D.
3. P.S.
4. i.e.
5. e.g.
6. N.B.
7. ad lib
8. vs.
9. cf.
10. et al.
11. q.v.
12. Rx

Exercise 5

Replace the words in italics with abbreviations chosen from the list in Exercise 4 above:

1. The senators discussed the most critical problems first, *for example*, the revolt in Judea.
2. Titus was known for his ability to *speak at will* on almost any subject.
3. The eruption of Vesuvius occurred in *the year of our Lord* 79.
4. Titus pointed out the Curia, the Arch of Tiberius, *and the rest*, as they passed them.
5. The announcement of the chariot race read, "Reds *against* Blues."
6. Eucleides said that they would return early, *that is*, before the eleventh hour.
7. At the bottom of the letter Cornelius added an *afterthought*.
8. Cornelius had invited Titus, Messala, *and others*, to a dinner-party.
9. The abbreviation "B.C." is used to give dates before the birth of Christ. (*Compare* the abbreviation "A.D.")
10. A sign near the Porta Capena read, "*Note well*: It is forbidden to drive wagons or carriages within the city during the day."
11. "*Take this*" was written at the bottom of the doctor's prescription.
12. "*Which see*" is written after a word or topic that needs further explanation, and it directs the reader to find such explanation elsewhere in the book.

Find examples of Latin abbreviations in textbooks, newspapers, or magazines and bring them to class.

REVIEW VI: CHAPTERS 25–27

Exercise VIa: Demonstrative Adjectives

Select the correct form first of **hic, haec, hoc** and then of **ille, illa, illud** to modify each of the following nouns:

1. diem	(hōrum/hunc/hoc)	(illum/illōrum/illud)
2. arbore	(hōc/hae/hāc)	(illō/illā/illae)
3. lutum	(hoc/hunc/hōc)	(illum/illud/illō)
4. diēbus	(hās/hōs/hīs)	(illās/illīs/illōs)
5. fēminam	(hunc/hanc/hoc)	(illam/illum/illud)
6. terrās	(hōs/hāc/hās)	(illā/illōs/illās)
7. mandātō	(hōc/hoc/hāc)	(illā/illō/illud)
8. terra	(hae/hāc/haec)	(illā/illae/illa)
9. oculō	(hoc/huic/hic)	(illud/ille/illī)
10. arcuum	(hōrum/hārum/hunc)	(illārum/illōrum/illum)
11. somnia	(haec/hae/hanc)	(illā/illa/illam)
12. rīsū	(hāc/hī/hōc)	(illō/illā/illī)
13. vōcum	(hārum/hōrum/hunc)	(illārum/illum/illōrum)
14. diē	(hōc/hoc/haec)	(illud/illō/illa)
15. manūs	(huius/hōs/hī)	(illōs/illīus/illī)

Exercise VIb: Agreement of Adjectives and Nouns

From the pool of words below, choose an adjective to go with each noun in Exercise VIa above. Give the noun with the adjective in its proper form to modify the noun.

bonus, -a, -um	īrātus, -a, -um	parvulus, -a, -um
brevis, -is, -e	longus, -a, -um	pūrus, -a, -um
dēfessus, -a, -um	magnus, -a, -um	scelestus, -a, -um
prīmus, -a, -um	multī, -ae, -a	sēmisomnus, -a, -um
īnfirmus, -a, -um	novus, -a, -um	sordidus, -a, -um
ingēns, ingentis	omnis, -is, -e	vester, vestra, vestrum

Exercise VIc: Personal Pronouns

Give the correct form of the appropriate Latin pronoun to translate the English word or phrase in italics:

1. *I* heard nothing. What did *you* hear, Marcus?
2. *We* heard nothing because we were asleep, but the girls were awake. *They* heard the rumbling of wagons in the street.

3. He didn't see *me*, but I saw *him*.
4. He gave the book *to me*, not *to you*, Cornelia.
5. No, he gave it *to us*.
6. It is really *his* book.
7. But he gave it *to them*.
8. The girls are in the house. I saw *them* there.
9. Did you see *her*?
10. No, Marcus and Sextus, but I saw *you*.
11. The dog is yours, Marcus and Cornelia. Father gave it *to you*.

Exercise VId: Personal Pronouns, Reflexive Pronouns, and Possessive Adjectives

Select the correct form to translate the English word or phrase in italics:

1. I have *my* book. (mihi/meum/meī)
2. Did he give you *your* book, Marcus? (vestrum/tuum/tibi)
3. She hurt *herself* when she fell. (eī/sibi/eae)
4. She saw *herself* in the mirror. (sē/eam/eum)
5. Did you leave *your* books at school, girls? (vōs/vestrum/vestrōs)
6. Yes, we left *our* books there. (nostrōs/nōs/vestrōs)
7. He has *his own* book. (eius/suum/sē)
8. No, he doesn't. He has *her* book. (eius/suum/suam)
9. Do the boys all have *their own* books? (eōrum/suōs/sibi)
10. No, the boys took the girls' books by mistake. So now they have *their* books. (eārum/suōs/eōrum)

Exercise VIe: Verb Forms

Give the requested forms of the following verbs in the present, imperfect, future, perfect, pluperfect, and future perfect tenses:

	Present	Imperfect	Future	Perfect	Pluperfect	Future Perfect
1. vetāre (*1st pl.*)	______	______	______	______	______	______
2. aperīre (*3rd pl.*)	______	______	______	______	______	______
3. stertere (*2nd pl.*)	______	______	______	______	______	______
4. esse (*3rd sing.*)	______	______	______	______	______	______
5. emere (*3rd sing.*)	______	______	______	______	______	______
6. ferre (*2nd sing.*)	______	______	______	______	______	______
7. arripere (*1st sing.*)	______	______	______	______	______	______
8. docēre (*1st sing.*)	______	______	______	______	______	______
9. posse (*2nd sing.*)	______	______	______	______	______	______
10. velle (*1st pl.*)	______	______	______	______	______	______

Exercise VIf: Reading Comprehension

Read the following passage and answer the questions below with full sentences in Latin:

ROMAN INFLUENCE IN THE EAST: 168 B.C.

Ōlim, ubi Lūcius Aemilius Paulus et Pūblius Licinius cōnsulēs Rōmānī erant, cīvēs Alexandrīnī auxilium ā Rōmānīs petīvērunt. Obsidēbat enim urbem Alexandrīam magnō exercitū Antiochus, rēx Syriae. Hic rēx superbus erat et, quod rēgnum suum augēre in animō habēbat, Aegyptiōs vincere volēbat. Rōmānī Aegyptiīs favēbant, sed exercitum ad Aegyptum mittere nōn poterant. Erat tamen senātor quīdam cōnsulāris, Gaius Popilius Laenās nōmine, quī eō ipsō tempore iter in illīs partibus faciēbat. Hunc senātōrem ad Aegyptum mīsit senātus Rōmānus quod auxilium Aegyptiīs offerre voluit. 5

Antiochus, ubi Popilius advēnit, ad eum nūntiōs mīsit, nam hunc senātōrem cōnsulere volēbat. Vēnit rēx Syriae ad congressum vestibus magnificīs indūtus cum magnā multitūdine mīlitum. Vēnit Popilius sōlus, togā praetextā indūtus, cum duodecim modo līctōribus. Rēgī appropinquāvit et statim dīxit: "Necesse est mihi ad senātum respōnsum tuum, Antioche, referre. Quid ā Rōmānīs petis, bellum aut pācem?" 10

Stupuit Antiochus et sēcum cogitābat: "Cūr ille Rōmānus mē nōn timet? Nūllum exercitum habet, sed neque commōtus neque sollicitus est." Antiochus ipse vērō commōtus et sollicitus erat et Popiliō igitur respondit, "Necesse est dē hāc rē cum amīcīs meīs cōnsulere." 15

Habēbat in manū Popilius baculum quod omnēs lēgātī Rōmānī sēcum ferre solēbant. Hōc baculō Popilius circulum in arēnā circum rēgem Syriae scrīpsit. "Antequam ē circulō exīs," rēgī dīxit, "mihi respōnsum dabis." Attonitus erat Antiochus. Popilium et imperium Rōmānum valdē timēbat. Dīxit: "Faciam id quod cēnset senātus Rōmānus." Ad mīlitēs rediit et exercitum ad Syriam statim redūxit. Tanta erat dignitās et auctōritās huius lēgātī et senātūs Rōmānī. 20

1 **cōnsul, cōnsulis,** m., *consul (one of the two chief annual magistrates of the Roman state)*
2 **Alexandrīnus, -a, -um,** *of Alexandria (a city in Egypt)*
3 **exercitus, -ūs,** m., *army*
rēx, rēgis, m., *king*
superbus, -a, -um, *arrogant, haughty*
4 **rēgnum, -ī,** n., *kingdom*
Aegyptiī, -ōrum, m. pl., *the Egyptians*
5 **Aegyptus, -ī,** f., *Egypt*
6 **cōnsulāris, -is, -e,** *having the status of an exconsul*
10 **congressus, -ūs,** m., *meeting*
vestis, vestis, gen. pl., **vestium,** f., *garment, clothes*
indūtus, -a, -um + abl., *dressed (in)*
12 **duodecim,** *twelve*
līctor, līctōris, m., *lictor (official attendant)*
13 **respōnsum, -ī,** n., *answer*
14 **bellum, -ī,** n., *war*
pāx, pācis, f., *peace*
17 **vērō,** adv., *truly*

20 **circulus, -ī,** m., *small circle*
arēna, -ae, f., *sand*
21 **antequam,** conj., *before*
22 **imperium, -ī,** n., *empire, power*
24 **dignitās, dignitātis,** f., *honor, status, dignity*
auctōritās, auctōritātis, f., *influence, prestige, authority*

2 **obsideō, obsidēre, obsēdī, obsessus,** *to besiege*
4 **augeō, augēre, auxī, auctus,** *to increase*
8 **offerō, offerre, obtulī, oblātus,** irreg., *to provide*
13 **referō, referre, rettulī, relātus,** irreg., *to bring back*
23 **cēnseō, cēnsēre, cēnsuī, cēnsus,** *to decree*

1. When did the citizens of Alexandria seek help from the Romans?
2. Who was besieging Alexandria?
3. Why did he want to conquer the Egyptians?
4. Whom did the Senate send to Egypt?
5. How did Antiochus come to his meeting with Popilius?
6. How did Popilius come?
7. Was Popilius afraid of Antiochus?
8. Was Antiochus afraid of Popilius?
9. What did Popilius do? What did he say?
10. How did Antiochus respond?

Exercise VIg: 4th and 5th Declension Nouns

1. In the first, second, and fourth paragraphs of the story above, locate four different 4th declension nouns.
2. In the third paragraph of the story, locate one 5th declension noun.

FORMS

The following charts show the forms of typical Latin nouns, adjectives, pronouns, and verbs in the cases and tenses presented in this book. As an aid in pronunciation, markings of long vowels and of accents are included.

I. Nouns

Number Case	1st Declension	2nd Declension				3rd Declension		
	Fem.	**Masc.**	**Masc.**	**Masc.**	**Neut.**	**Masc.**	**Fem.**	**Neut.**
Singular								
Nominative	puéll***a***	sérv***us***	púer	áger	bácul***um***	páter	vōx	nṓmen
Genitive	puéll***ae***	sérv***ī***	púer***ī***	ágr***ī***	bácul***ī***	pátr***is***	vṓc***is***	nṓmin***is***
Dative	puéll***ae***	sérv***ō***	púer***ō***	ágr***ō***	bácul***ō***	pátr***ī***	vṓc***ī***	nṓmin***ī***
Accusative	puéll***am***	sérv***um***	púer***um***	ágr***um***	bácul***um***	pátr***em***	vṓc***em***	nṓmen
Ablative	puéll***ā***	sérv***ō***	púer***ō***	ágr***ō***	bácul***ō***	pátr***e***	vṓc***e***	nṓmin***e***
Vocative	puéll***a***	sérv***e***	púer	áger	bácul***um***	páter	vōx	nṓmen
Plural								
Nominative	puéll***ae***	sérv***ī***	púer***ī***	ágr***ī***	bácul***a***	pátr***ēs***	vṓc***ēs***	nṓmin***a***
Genitive	puell***ā́rum***	serv***ṓrum***	puer***ṓrum***	agr***ṓrum***	bacul***ṓrum***	pátr***um***	vṓc***um***	nṓmin***um***
Dative	puéll***īs***	sérv***īs***	púer***īs***	ágr***īs***	bácul***īs***	pátr***ibus***	vṓc***ibus***	nōmín***ibus***
Accusative	puéll***ās***	sérv***ōs***	púer***ōs***	ágr***ōs***	bácul***a***	pátr***ēs***	vṓc***ēs***	nṓmin***a***
Ablative	puéll***īs***	sérv***īs***	púer***īs***	ágr***īs***	bácul***īs***	pátr***ibus***	vṓc***ibus***	nōmín***ibus***
Vocative	puéll***ae***	sérv***ī***	púer***ī***	ágr***ī***	bácul***a***	pátr***ēs***	vṓc***ēs***	nṓmin***a***

Number Case	4th Declension		5th Declension	
	Masc.	**Neut.**	**Masc.**	**Fem.**
Singular				
Nominative	árc***us***	gén***ū***	dí***ēs***	r***ēs***
Genitive	árc***ūs***	gén***ūs***	di***ḗī***	r***éī***
Dative	árc***uī***	gén***ū***	di***ḗī***	r***éī***
Accusative	árc***um***	gén***ū***	dí***em***	r***em***
Ablative	árc***ū***	gén***ū***	dí***ē***	r***ē***
Vocative	árc***us***	gén***ū***	dí***ēs***	r***ēs***
Plural				
Nominative	árc***ūs***	gén***ua***	dí***ēs***	r***ēs***
Genitive	árc***uum***	gén***uum***	di***ḗrum***	r***ḗrum***
Dative	árc***ibus***	gén***ibus***	di***ḗbus***	r***ḗbus***
Accusative	árc***ūs***	gén***ua***	dí***ēs***	r***ēs***
Ablative	árc***ibus***	gén***ibus***	di***ḗbus***	r***ḗbus***
Vocative	árc***ūs***	gén***ua***	dí***ēs***	r***ēs***

II. Adjectives

Number Case	1st and 2nd Declensions			3rd Declension		
	Masc.	Fem.	Neut.	Masc.	Fem.	Neut.
Singular						
Nominative	mágn**us**	mágn**a**	mágn**um**	ómn**is**	ómn**is**	ómn**e**
Genitive	mágn**ī**	mágn**ae**	mágn**ī**	ómn**is**	ómn**is**	ómn**is**
Dative	mágn**ō**	mágn**ae**	mágn**ō**	ómn**ī**	ómn**ī**	ómn**ī**
Accusative	mágn**um**	mágn**am**	mágn**um**	ómn**em**	ómn**em**	ómn**e**
Ablative	mágn**ō**	mágn**ā**	mágn**ō**	ómn**ī**	ómn**ī**	ómn**ī**
Vocative	mágn**e**	mágn**a**	mágn**um**	ómn**is**	ómn**is**	ómn**e**
Plural						
Nominative	mágn**ī**	mágn**ae**	mágn**a**	ómn**ēs**	ómn**ēs**	ómn**ia**
Genitive	magn**ṓrum**	magn**ā́rum**	magn**ṓrum**	ómn**ium**	ómn**ium**	ómn**ium**
Dative	mágn**īs**	mágn**īs**	mágn**īs**	ómn**ibus**	ómn**ibus**	ómn**ibus**
Accusative	mágn**ōs**	mágn**ās**	mágn**a**	ómn**ēs**	ómn**ēs**	ómn**ia**
Ablative	mágn**īs**	mágn**īs**	mágn**īs**	ómn**ibus**	ómn**ibus**	ómn**ibus**
Vocative	mágn**ī**	mágn**ae**	mágn**a**	ómn**ēs**	ómn**ēs**	ómn**ia**

III. Numbers

Case	Masc.	Fem.	Neut.
Nominative	ū́n**us**	ū́n**a**	ū́n**um**
Genitive	ūn**ī́us**	ūn**ī́us**	ūn**ī́us**
Dative	ū́n**ī**	ū́n**ī**	ū́n**ī**
Accusative	ū́n**um**	ū́n**am**	ū́n**um**
Ablative	ū́n**ō**	ū́n**ā**	ū́n**ō**

Case	Masc.	Fem.	Neut.	Masc.	Fem.	Neut.
Nominative	dú**o**	dú**ae**	dú**o**	tr**ēs**	tr**ēs**	tr**ía**
Genitive	du**ṓrum**	du**ā́rum**	du**ṓrum**	tr**íum**	tr**íum**	tr**íum**
Dative	du**ṓbus**	du**ā́bus**	du**ṓbus**	tr**íbus**	tr**íbus**	tr**íbus**
Accusative	dú**ōs**	dú**ās**	dú**o**	tr**ēs**	tr**ēs**	tr**ía**
Ablative	du**ṓbus**	du**ā́bus**	du**ṓbus**	tr**íbus**	tr**íbus**	tr**íbus**

IV. Personal Pronouns

Case	1st	2nd	3rd		
			Masc.	Fem.	Neut.
Singular					
Nominative	égo	tū	is	éa	id
Genitive	méī	túī	éius	éius	éius
Dative	míhi	tíbi	éī	éī	éī
Accusative	mē	tē	éum	éam	id
Ablative	mē	tē	éō	éā	éō
Plural					
Nominative	nōs	vōs	éī	éae	éa
Genitive	nóstrī nóstrum	véstrī véstrum	eṓrum	eā́rum	eṓrum
Dative	nṓbīs	vṓbīs	éīs	éīs	éīs
Accusative	nōs	vōs	éōs	éās	éa
Ablative	nṓbīs	vṓbīs	éīs	éīs	éīs

V. Reflexive Pronoun

	Singular	Plural
Nominative	—	—
Genitive	súī	súī
Dative	síbi	síbi
Accusative	sē	sē
Ablative	sē	sē

VI. Relative Pronoun

	Masc.	Fem.	Neut.
Singular			
Nominative	quī	quae	quod
Genitive	cúius	cúius	cúius
Dative	cui	cui	cui
Accusative	quem	quam	quod
Ablative	quō	quā	quō
Plural			
Nominative	quī	quae	quae
Genitive	quṓrum	quā́rum	quṓrum
Dative	quíbus	quíbus	quíbus
Accusative	quōs	quās	quae
Ablative	quíbus	quíbus	quíbus

VII. Interrogative Pronoun

Case	Singular			Plural		
	Masc.	Fem.	Neut.	Masc.	Fem.	Neut.
Nominative	quis	quis	quid	quī	quae	quae
Genitive	cúius	cúius	cúius	quṓrum	quā́rum	quṓrum
Dative	cui	cui	cui	quíbus	quíbus	quíbus
Accusative	quem	quem	quid	quōs	quās	quae
Ablative	quō	quō	quō	quíbus	quíbus	quíbus

VIII. Indefinite Adjective

Number Case	Masc.	Fem.	Neut.
Singular			
Nominative	quī́dam	quaédam	quóddam
Genitive	cuiúsdam	cuiúsdam	cuiúsdam
Dative	cúidam	cúidam	cúidam
Accusative	quéndam	quándam	quóddam
Ablative	quṓdam	quā́dam	quṓdam
Plural			
Nominative	quī́dam	quaédam	quaédam
Genitive	quōrúndam	quārúndam	quōrúndam
Dative	quibúsdam	quibúsdam	quibúsdam
Accusative	quṓsdam	quā́sdam	quaédam
Ablative	quibúsdam	quibúsdam	quibúsdam

IX. Demonstrative Adjectives and Pronouns

Number Case	Masc.	Fem.	Neut.	Masc.	Fem.	Neut.
Singular						
Nominative	hic	haec	hoc	ílle	ílla	íllud
Genitive	húius	húius	húius	illī́us	illī́us	illī́us
Dative	húic	húic	húic	íllī	íllī	íllī
Accusative	hunc	hanc	hoc	íllum	íllam	íllud
Ablative	hōc	hāc	hōc	íllō	íllā	íllō
Plural						
Nominative	hī	hae	haec	íllī	íllae	ílla
Genitive	hṓrum	hā́rum	hṓrum	illṓrum	illā́rum	illṓrum
Dative	hīs	hīs	hīs	íllīs	íllīs	íllīs
Accusative	hōs	hās	haec	íllōs	íllās	ílla
Ablative	hīs	hīs	hīs	íllīs	íllīs	íllīs

X. Regular Verbs

			1st Conjugation	2nd Conjugation	3rd Conjugation		4th Conjugation
	Infinitive		parā́re	habḗre	míttere	iácere (-iō)	audī́re
	Imperative		párā	hábē	mítte	iáce	aúdī
			parā́te	habḗte	míttite	iácite	audī́te
Present	Singular	1	párō	hábeō	míttō	iáciō	aúdiō
		2	párās	hábēs	míttis	iácis	aúdīs
		3	párat	hábet	míttit	iácit	aúdit
	Plural	1	parā́mus	habḗmus	míttimus	iácimus	audī́mus
		2	parā́tis	habḗtis	míttitis	iácitis	audī́tis
		3	párant	hábent	míttunt	iáciunt	aúdiunt
Imperfect	Singular	1	parā́bam	habḗbam	mittḗbam	iaciḗbam	audiḗbam
		2	parā́bās	habḗbās	mittḗbās	iaciḗbās	audiḗbās
		3	parā́bat	habḗbat	mittḗbat	iaciḗbat	audiḗbat
	Plural	1	parābā́mus	habēbā́mus	mittēbā́mus	iaciēbā́mus	audiēbā́mus
		2	parābā́tis	habēbā́tis	mittēbā́tis	iaciēbā́tis	audiēbā́tis
		3	parā́bant	habḗbant	mittḗbant	iaciḗbant	audiḗbant
Future	Singular	1	parā́bō	habḗbō	míttam	iáciam	aúdiam
		2	parā́bis	habēbis	míttēs	iáciēs	aúdiēs
		3	parā́bit	habḗbit	míttet	iáciet	aúdiet
	Plural	1	parā́bimus	habḗbimus	mittḗmus	iaciḗmus	audiḗmus
		2	parā́bitis	habḗbitis	mittḗtis	iaciḗtis	audiḗtis
		3	parā́bunt	habḗbunt	míttent	iácient	aúdient
Perfect	Singular	1	parā́vī	hábuī	mī́sī	iḗcī	audī́vī
		2	parāvístī	habuístī	mīsístī	iēcístī	audīvístī
		3	parā́vit	hábuit	mī́sit	iḗcit	audī́vit
	Plural	1	parā́vimus	habúimus	mī́simus	iḗcimus	audī́vimus
		2	parāvístis	habuístis	mīsístis	iēcístis	audīvístis
		3	parāvḗrunt	habuḗrunt	mīsḗrunt	iēcḗrunt	audīvḗrunt
Pluperfect	Singular	1	parā́veram	habúeram	mī́seram	iḗceram	audī́veram
		2	parā́verās	habúerās	mī́serās	iḗcerās	audī́verās
		3	parā́verat	habúerat	mī́serat	iḗcerat	audī́verat
	Plural	1	parāverā́mus	habuerā́mus	mīserā́mus	iēcerā́mus	audīverā́mus
		2	parāverā́tis	habuerā́tis	mīserā́tis	iēcerā́tis	audīverā́tis
		3	parā́verant	habúerant	mī́serant	iḗcerant	audī́verant
Future Perfect	Singular	1	parā́verō	habúerō	mī́serō	iḗcerō	audī́verō
		2	parā́veris	habúeris	mī́seris	iḗceris	audī́veris
		3	parā́verit	habúerit	mī́serit	iḗcerit	audī́verit
	Plural	1	parāvérimus	habuérimus	mīsérimus	iēcérimus	audīvérimus
		2	parāvéritis	habuéritis	mīséritis	iēcéritis	audīvéritis
		3	parā́verint	habúerint	mī́serint	iḗcerint	audī́verint

XI. Irregular Verbs

Infinitive			ésse	pósse	vélle
Imperative			es	—	—
			és***te***	—	—
Present	**Singular**	1	su***m***	pós***sum***	vól***ō***
		2	e***s***	pót***es***	vī***s***
		3	es***t***	pót***est***	vul***t***
	Plural	1	sú***mus***	pós***sumus***	vólu***mus***
		2	és***tis***	pot***éstis***	vúl***tis***
		3	su***nt***	pós***sunt***	vólu***nt***
Imperfect	**Singular**	1	éra***m***	pót***eram***	volḗ***bam***
		2	érā***s***	pót***erās***	volḗ***bās***
		3	éra***t***	pót***erat***	volḗ***bat***
	Plural	1	erā́***mus***	pot***erā́mus***	volē***bā́mus***
		2	erā́***tis***	pot***erā́tis***	volē***bā́tis***
		3	éra***nt***	pót***erant***	volḗ***bant***
Future	**Singular**	1	ér***ō***	pót***erō***	vól***am***
		2	éri***s***	pót***eris***	vól***ēs***
		3	éri***t***	pót***erit***	vól***et***
	Plural	1	éri***mus***	pot***érimus***	vol***ḗmus***
		2	éri***tis***	pot***éritis***	vol***ḗtis***
		3	éru***nt***	pót***erunt***	vól***ent***

Infinitive			nṓlle	férre	ī́re
Imperative			nṓl***ī***	fer	ī
			nōl***ī́te***	fér***te***	ī́***te***
Present	**Singular**	1	nṓl***ō***	fér***ō***	é***ō***
		2	nōn vī***s***	fer***s***	ī***s***
		3	nōn vul***t***	fer***t***	i***t***
	Plural	1	nṓlu***mus***	féri***mus***	ī́***mus***
		2	nōn vúl***tis***	fér***tis***	ī́***tis***
		3	nṓlu***nt***	féru***nt***	éu***nt***
Imperfect	**Singular**	1	nōlḗ***bam***	ferḗ***bam***	ī́***bam***
		2	nōlḗ***bās***	ferḗ***bās***	ī́***bās***
		3	nōlḗ***bat***	ferḗ***bat***	ī́***bat***
	Plural	1	nōlē***bā́mus***	ferē***bā́mus***	ī***bā́mus***
		2	nōlē***bā́tis***	ferē***bā́tis***	ī***bā́tis***
		3	nōlḗ***bant***	ferḗ***bant***	ī́***bant***
Future	**Singular**	1	nṓl***am***	fér***am***	ī́***bō***
		2	nṓl***ēs***	fér***ēs***	ī́***bis***
		3	nṓl***et***	fér***et***	ī́***bit***
	Plural	1	nōl***ḗmus***	fer***ḗmus***	ī́***bimus***
		2	nōl***ḗtis***	fer***ḗtis***	ī́***bitis***
		3	nṓl***ent***	fér***ent***	ī́***bunt***

Perfect, Pluperfect, and Future Perfect Tenses of Irregular Verbs

Full charts are not supplied for these forms because (except for the perfect of **eō**, for which see below) they are not irregular in any way. They are made in the same way as the perfect, pluperfect, and future perfect tenses of regular verbs, by adding the perfect, pluperfect, and future perfect endings to the perfect stem. The perfect stem is found by dropping the *-ī* from the third principal part. The first three principal parts of the irregular verbs are as follows (the perfect stem is underlined):

sum, esse, fu*ī*
possum, posse, potu*ī*
volō, velle, volu*ī*
nōlō, nōlle, nōlu*ī*
ferō, ferre, tul*ī*
eō, īre, i*ī* or īv*ī*

Examples:

Perfect: fuistī, voluērunt, tulimus
Pluperfect: fueram, potuerant, nōluerāmus
Future Perfect: fuerō, volueris, tulerimus

The perfect forms of **eō** made from the stem **i-** are as follows:

Singular: iī, īstī, iit
Plural: iimus, īstis, iērunt

Note that the stem vowel (**i-**) contracts with the *-i* of the endings ***-istī*** and ***-istis*** to give **ī-** (**īstī, īstis**).

The perfect forms of **eō** made from the stem **īv-** are regular, as follows:

Singular: īvī, īvistī, īvit
Plural: īvimus, īvistis, īvērunt

BUILDING THE MEANING

I. PARTS OF SPEECH

The following are seven basic parts of speech:

- nouns: names of persons, places, things, qualities, or acts (see Book I-A, page 4)
- pronouns: words that stand in place of nouns, e.g., *she* in place of *Cornelia* (see Book I-B, pages 119–121)
- adjectives: words that describe persons, places, things, qualities, or acts (see Book I-A, page 4)
- verbs: words that denote actions (e.g., *sits*) or existence (e.g., *is*) (see Book I-A, page 4)
- adverbs: words that modify verbs, adjectives, or other adverbs (see Book I-A, pages 100–101)
- prepositions: words such as *from*, *in*, and *at*, which introduce prepositional phrases (see Book I-A, page 64)
- conjunctions: words that link other words, phrases, or clauses (see Book I-B, pages 150–152)

II. BASIC PATTERNS OF LATIN SENTENCES

You have met Latin sentences with four basic patterns:

A. Subject and Intransitive Verb (see Book I-A, page 20)

Cornēlia **sedet.** (1:3) — *Cornelia* ***sits.***

This sentence has only a subject (S) and an intransitive verb (IV). **Cornēlia** is in the nominative case and is therefore the subject of the sentence.

The verb in the above sentence expresses an action that simply tells what the subject is doing. The action of the verb does not affect anyone or anything else. Verbs when so used are called intransitive verbs (IV).

The verb **est** in the following sentence is of the same type:

In pictūrā **est** puella. (1:1)
A girl ***is*** *in the picture.* — *There is a girl in the picture.*

B. Subject, Linking Verb, and Complement (see Book I-A, page 8)

Cornēlia **est** puella. (1:1) — *Cornelia* ***is*** *a girl.*

This sentence has a subject, **Cornēlia**, and a verb, **est**, as well as another word in the nominative case, **puella**. This word is linked to the subject by the verb **est**. The word **puella** is called a complement (C), because it completes the meaning of the sentence. **Est** is called a linking verb (LV) because it links the subject with the complement.

The linking verb in the following sentence links the subject with an adjective, which serves as a complement:

Cornēlia **est** laeta. (1:2–3) *Cornelia* ***is*** *happy.*

When the subject is plural, the verb and the complement are also plural:

Mārcus et Sextus **sunt** amīcī. (3:2–3) *Marcus and Sextus* ***are*** *friends.*

C. Subject, Direct Object, and Transitive Verb (see Book I-A, page 20)

Sextus Cornēliam **vexat.** (4:1) *Sextus* ***annoys*** *Cornelia.*

In this sentence there is a subject, a direct object (DO; see Book I-A, pages 20 and 40), and a verb. The direct object is in the accusative case, and it names the person or thing that receives the action of the verb. The verbs in such sentences are said to be transitive verbs (TV).

D. Subject, Dative, and Intransitive Verb (see Book I-B, pages 78 and 119)

1. Dative with Intransitive Compound Verbs (see Book I-B, page 78)

   Ibi fortasse patrī tuō **occurrēmus.** (24:17)
   Perhaps ***we will meet*** *your father there.*

   Iam urbī **appropinquābant.** (22:12)
   Already ***they were coming near*** *to the city.*
   Already ***they were approaching*** *the city.*

2. Dative with Special Intransitive Verbs (see Book I-B, page 119)

   Sī mihi **nocueritis,** pater meus certē vōs pūniet. (26:26–27)
   If ***you do harm*** *to me, my father will certainly punish you.*
   If ***you harm*** *me, my father will certainly punish you.*

   Frātrī Titō nōn **cōnfīdō**. (26e:14)
   I do *not give* ***trust*** *to (my) brother Titus.*
   I do *not* ***trust*** *(my) brother Titus.*

   Ego russātīs **favēbō.** (27:25)
   I will give favor *to the reds.*
   I will favor/support *the reds.*

III. SENTENCE TYPES

Every Latin sentence expresses a statement, a command, an exclamation, or a question.

A. The following are statements:

In pictūrā est puella. (1:1)
A girl is in the picture.

Flāvia scrībit. (1:5)
Flavia writes.

Sextus Cornēliam vexat. (4:1)
Sextus annoys Cornelia.

B. Sentences may express commands and have their verbs in the imperative (see Book I-A, page 74):

Dēscende, Sexte! (4:6)
Come down, *Sextus!*

Abīte, molestī! (3:8)
Go away, *pests!*

Negative commands are expressed with **nōlī** (singular) or **nōlīte** (plural) plus an infinitive (see Book I-A, page 74):

Nōlī servōs **excitāre!** (9:9)
Don't wake up *the slaves!*

C. A sentence may express an exclamation:

Quam celeriter appropinquat! (15:12)
How quickly it is approaching!

D. Statements can be turned into questions by placing an important word (often the verb) first and attaching the letters **-ne** to it (see Book I-A, page 13):

Puer ignāvus est.
The boy is cowardly.
(statement)

Est**ne** puer ignāvus? (5:4)
Is the boy cowardly?
(question)

Questions are introduced by the word **Nōnne...?** when the speaker clearly expects the answer "yes":

Nōnne cēnāre vultis? (19:2)
Surely *you want to eat,* ***don't you****?*

Questions are often introduced by interrogative words such as the following:

Cui...? *To whom...?* (sing.)
Cuius...? *Whose...?* (sing.)
Cūr...? *Why...?*
Quālis...? *What sort of...?*
Quandō...? *When...?*
Quem...? *Whom...?* (sing.)
Quī...? *Who...?* (pl.)
Quibus...? *To whom...?* (pl.)
Quid...? *What...?*
Quis...? *Who...?* (sing.)
Quō...? *Where...to?*
Quōcum...? *With whom...?* (sing.)
Quō īnstrūmentō...? *With what implement...? How...?*
Quōmodo...? *In what manner...? In what way...? How...?*
Quōs...? *Whom...?* (pl.)
Quot...? *How many...?*
Ubi...? *Where...?*
Unde...? *From where...?*

IV. MORE ABOUT VERBS

A. Tenses of Verbs

1. Verbs can be in the present tense, describing actions or situations in present time:

   a. in a simple statement of fact:

   Cornēliī Rōmam redīre **parant.**
   *The Cornelii **prepare** to return to Rome.*

   b. in a description of an ongoing action:

   Hodiē Cornēliī Rōmam redīre **parant.**
   *Today the Cornelii **are preparing** to return to Rome.*

   c. in a question:

   Auditne Dāvus clāmōrem?
   ***Does** Davus **hear** the shouting?*

   d. in an emphatic statement:

   Clāmōrem ***audit.***
   *He **does hear** the shouting.*

   e. in a denial:

   Clāmōrem nōn **audit.**
   *He **does** not **hear** the shouting.*

2. The imperfect tense (see Book I-A, pages 98 and 106–107) shows action in the past that was:

   a. going on for a time:

   Ego et Marcus **spectābāmus** cisium. (14:10)
   *Marcus and I **were watching** the carriage.*

   Cornēlia dormīre **volēbat.** (13:8)
   *Cornelia **wanted** to sleep.*

   b. repeated:

   Marcus **vexābat** Cornēliam. (13:7–8)
   *Marcus **kept annoying** Cornelia.*

   c. habitual or customary:

   Dāvus in Britanniā **habitābat.**
   *Davus **used to live** in Britain.*

   d. beginning to happen:

   Equōs ad raedam nostram **dēvertēbat.** (14:11)
   *He **began to turn** the horses **aside** in the direction of our carriage.*

3. The future tense indicates an action that will take place at some time subsequent to the present (see Book I-B, page 67):

   Brevī tempore ad Portam Capēnam **adveniēmus.** (22:26)
   *In a short time **we will arrive** at the Porta Capena.*

4. The perfect, pluperfect, and future perfect tenses are formed from the perfect stem, which is found by dropping the ***-ī*** from the third principal part of the verb, e.g., **parāvī**, perfect stem **parāv-**. These tenses describe completed actions.

5. The perfect tense refers to an action that happened or to something that someone did in past time (see Book I-B, page 16):

   Eō ipsō tempore ad iānuam caupōnae **appāruit** homō obēsus. (18:12)
   *At that very moment a fat man **appeared** at the door of the inn.*

   The perfect tense may also refer to an action that someone has completed as of present time (see Book I-B, page 17):

   Servī meī alium lectum tibi **parāvērunt.** (19:17–18)
   *My slaves **have prepared** another bed for you.*

6. The pluperfect tense describes an action that was completed before some other action in the past took place (see Book I-B, page 79):

   Titus in itinere mōnstrāvit puerīs mīra aedificia quae prīncipēs in Palātīnō **aedificāverant.** (24:19–20)
   *Along the way Titus showed the boys the wonderful buildings, which the emperors **had built** on the Palatine.*
   (The emperor had built the buildings *before* Titus showed them to the boys.)

7. The future perfect tense describes an action that will have been completed before some other action in future time begins (see Book I-B, page 84):

   Cum **intrāverimus,** tandem aurīgās ipsōs spectābimus. (26:17–18)
   *When we **enter/will have entered,** we will finally watch the charioteers themselves.*
   (The speakers will have entered the Circus Maximus *before* they will watch the charioteers.)

B. Infinitives

The infinitive is the form of the verb marked by "to..." in English (e.g., "to walk") and by the letters ***-re*** in Latin (e.g., **errāre, rīdēre,**

ascendere, and **dormīre**). You have seen three uses of the infinitive in Latin sentences:

1. The complementary infinitive (see Book I-A, page 26 and Book I-B, page 28):

   Sextus arborēs **ascendere** vult. *Sextus wants **to climb** trees.*

   Here the infinitive completes the meaning of the main verb. Other verbs and verbal phrases that are often completed with infinitives are: **nōlle, posse, parāre, solēre, timēre,** and **in animō habēre**.

2. The infinitive with impersonal verbal phrase and impersonal verbs:

   Nōbīs necesse est statim **discēdere.**(9:13)
   ***To leave** immediately is necessary for us.*
   *It is necessary for us **to leave** immediately.*

   Licetne nōbīs hīc **cēnare?** (20:7)
   *Is **to dine** here allowed for us?*
   *Is it allowed for us **to dine** here?*
   May we dine here?

   The verbal phrase **necesse est** and the verb **licet** are said to be impersonal, because we may translate them with the impersonal phrases *it is necessary* and *it is allowed*. In the Latin sentences, however, the infinitives are the grammatical subjects of the verbs.

3. The infinitive as subject of the verb **est** (see Book I-B, page 28):

   Etiam in caupōnā **pernoctāre** saepe est perīculōsum. (20:19)
   ***To spend the night** in an inn is also often dangerous.*
   *It is also often dangerous **to spend the night** in an inn.*

   Here **pernoctāre,** *to spend the night,* is the subject of the sentence, and **perīculōsum** is a complement after the linking verb. It is neuter in gender because the infinitive used as subject functions as a neuter verbal noun.

4. Accusative and infinitive (see Book I-A, page 72, and Book I-B, page 28):

   Aurēlia **Cornēliam** docet vīllam **cūrāre.** (6:11)
   *Aurelia teaches **Cornelia** (how) **to take care of** the country house.*

   Ancillam iubet aliās tunicās et stolās et pallās in cistam **pōnere.** (10:2)
   *She orders **the slave-woman to put** other tunics and stolas and pallas into a chest.*

   Cūr pater meus **nōs exīre** vetat? (26:12)
   *Why does my father forbid **us to go out?***

V. MODIFIERS

There are many ways in which the thought expressed by a sentence can be elaborated and made fuller and clearer. For example, various kinds of modifiers can be used. Any noun or verb in a sentence can have modifiers.

A. Modifiers of Nouns

1. Adjectives may be used to modify nouns. They must agree with the nouns they modify in gender, case, and number (see Book I-A, pages 34–35 and 120–121, and Book I-B, pages 5–6):

   Flāvia in vīllā **vīcīnā** habitat. (1:4)
   Flavia lives in a ***neighboring*** *country house.*

   Cum senātōre **Rōmānō** iter facit. (page 121, Book I-A)
   He travels with a ***Roman*** *senator.*

   Omnēs vīllās, **omnēs** agrōs, **omnēs** arborēs vident. (page 5, Book I-B)
   They see ***all*** *the country houses,* ***all*** *the fields,* ***all*** *the trees.*

2. Adjectives that modify the subject of the verb may sometimes best be translated as adverbs:

   Brevī tempore, ubi Marcus advenit, eum **laetae** excipiunt. (6:12–13)
   In a short time, when Marcus arrives, they welcome him ***happily.***

3. The Genitive Case

   a. You have also seen a word or phrase in the genitive case used as a modifier (see Book I-A, page 80), usually with another noun. The genitive case relates or attaches one noun or phrase to another:

      Dāvus ad portam **vīllae** stat. (11:17)
      Davus stands near the door ***of the country house.***

      The genitive case sometimes indicates possession:

      Vīlicus ipse vīllam **dominī** cūrat. (11:3)
      The overseer himself looks after the country house ***of the master.***

   b. Genitive with Adjectives

      You have also seen words or phrases in the genitive case used with adjectives, such as **plēnus** (see Book I-A, page 80):

      Brevī tempore ārea est plēna **servōrum** et **ancillārum.** (11:4)
      In a short time the space is full ***of slaves*** *and* ***slave-women.***

      A word or phrase in the genitive is usually used with adjectives of remembering and forgetting:

immemor **terrōris nocturnī** (22:3)
forgetful ***of his fear during the night***

c. Partitive Genitive or Genitive of the Whole

The genitive case may be used to indicate the whole of which something is a part (partitive genitive or genitive of the whole) (see Book I-B, page 95):

"Nihil **malī**," inquit. (21:7)
"Nothing ***of a bad thing,****" he said.*
"Nothing bad" or *"There is nothing wrong."*

Crās satis **temporis** habēbimus. (23f:14)
Tomorrow we will have enough ***(of) time.***

Nihil **pecūniae** habeō. (26:26)
I have nothing ***of money.***
I have no money.

Compare:

Magnus numerus **servōrum** est in āreā. (11c:9)

With numbers and the words **paucī**, *a few*, **quīdam**, a *certain*, and **nūllus**, *no*, *no one*, the prepositions **ex** or **dē** + ablative are used:

ūnus **ē praedōnibus** (26:24) *one of the pirates*

4. For subordinate clauses that modify nouns, see VIII below.

B. Modifiers of Verbs

1. Adverbs may be used to modify verbs (see Book I-A, page 100):

Laeta est Flāvia quod Cornēlia **iam** in vīllā habitat. (1:5)
Flavia is happy because Cornelia is ***now*** *living in the country house.*

Adverbs may express time (e.g., **adhūc**, *still*), place (e.g., **hīc**, *here*), or manner (e.g., **celeriter**, *quickly*).

2. Dative Case

a. Indirect Object
In Book I-A you met sentences like the following:

Sextus Cornēliam vexat. (4:1) *Sextus annoys Cornelia.*

These sentences consist of a subject (S) in the nominative case, a direct object (DO) in the accusative case, and a transitive verb (TV). In Book I-B this pattern has been expanded with a word or phrase in the dative case (an indirect object, IO; see Book I-B, page 55):

Servī cistās Cornēliōrum **raedāriō** trādidērunt. (22:2)
The slaves handed the chests of the Cornelii over ***to the coachman.***

(The indirect object, **raedāriō**, tells to whom the slaves handed over the chests.)

b. Dative with Intransitive Verbs

Intransitive verbs (IV) and verbs that may be transitive but are used without a direct object may be accompanied by words or phrases in the dative case (see Book I-B, page 55):

(Aulus) **Septimō** clāmāvit. (21:8–9) *(Aulus) shouted* ***to Septimus.***

Aulus in somnō **eī** appāruit. (21:4) *Aulus appeared* ***to him*** *in (his) sleep.*

c. Dative with Intransitive Compound Verbs

Many intransitive compound verbs are accompanied by words or phrases in the dative case (see Book I-B, page 78):

Iam **urbī** appropinquābant. (22:12)
Already they were coming near ***to the city****/approaching* ***the city.***

Ibi fortrasse **patrī tuō** occurrēmus. (24:17)
Perhaps we will meet ***your father*** *there.*

d. Dative with Special Intransitive Verbs (see Book I-B, page 119)

The dative case is also used with special intransitive verbs, such as **nocēre**, *to do harm (to), harm*, **cōnfidere**, *to give trust (to), trust*, and **favēre**, *to (give) favor (to), favor, support*:

"Sī **mihi** nocueritis, pater meus certē vōs pūniet." (26:26–27)
"If you do harm ***to me****, my father will certainly punish you."*
"If you harm ***me****, my father will certainly punish you."*

Frātrī Titō nōn cōnfīdō. (26e:14)
I do not give trust ***to (my) brother Titus.***
I do not trust ***(my) brother Titus.***

Ego **russātīs** favēbō. (27:25)
I will give favor ***to the reds.*** *I will favor/support* ***the reds.***

e. In Book I-A you saw the following use of the dative case with the impersonal verbal phrase **necesse est**:

Cūr **mihi** quoque necesse est ad urbem redīre? (8:13–14)
Why is it necessary ***for me*** *too to return to the city?*

In Book I-B you met a similar use of the dative with impersonal verbs such as **licet** (see Book I-B, page 56):

"Licetne **nōbīs**," inquit Marcus, "hīc cēnāre?" (20:7)
*"Is it allowed **for us**," said Marcus, "to eat here?"*
"May we eat here?"

3. Nouns or phrases in the ablative case without a preposition may be used to modify verbs (see Book I-A, pages 90–91). Such nouns or phrases may indicate any of the following:

   Time when:

   Etiam in pictūrā est vīlla rūstica ubi Cornēlia **aestāte** habitat. (1:2)
   *Also in the picture is the country house and farm where Cornelia lives **in summer**.*

   Time within which:

   Brevī tempore Flāvia quoque est dēfessa. (2:4–5)
   ***In a short time** Flavia is also tired.*

   Instrument or Means:

   Dāvus Getam **baculō** verberat. (12:17–18)
   *Davus beats Geta **with his stick.***

   Dāvus Getam **tunicā** arripit. (12:17)
   *Davus grabs hold of Geta **by the tunic.***

   Cause (see Book I-B, page 79):

   Tuā culpā raeda est in fossā. (14:7)
   ***Because of your fault** the carriage is in the ditch.*
   It's your fault that the carriage is in the ditch.

   Manner: a phrase consisting of a noun and adjective in the ablative case may be used to indicate *how* something happens. This is called the ablative of manner:

   Tum venit Dāvus ipse et, "Tacēte, omnēs!" **magnā vōce** clāmat. (11:6)
   *Then Davus himself comes, and he shouts **in a loud voice**, "Be quiet, everyone!"*

   The preposition **cum** may be found in this construction when the noun is modified by an adjective, e.g., **magnā cum vōce**.

4. Prepositional phrases also modify verbs. Some prepositions are used with the accusative case (see Book I-A, page 64):

ad **vīllam** (2:7)	*to/toward **the country house***
Iānitor ad **iānuam** vīllae dormit. (9:3)	*The doorkeeper sleeps near/at **the door** of the country house.*
in **piscīnam** (3:8)	*into **the fishpond***
per **agrōs** (9:1)	*through **the fields***
prope **rīvum** (5:3)	*near **the stream***

With names of cities and the word **domus**, *home*, the accusative case is used without the preposition **ad** to express the idea "to":

"Eugepae!" clāmat Sextus, quī **Rōmam** īre vult. (7:14)
"Hurray!" shouts Sextus, who wants to go ***to Rome.***

Prīmum Aurēliam et Cornēliam **domum** dūcam. (23:10)
First I will take Aurelia and Cornelia ***home.***

Some prepositions are used with the ablative case (see Book I-A, pages 64 and 90):

ab **urbe** (13:12)	*from* ***the city***
cum **canibus** (12:9)	*with* ***dogs***
ē **silvā** (see Book I-A, page 64)	*out of* ***the woods***
ex **agrīs** (2:7): (see Book I-A, page 64)	*out of* ***the fields***
in **pictūrā** (1:1): (see Book I-A, page 64)	*in* ***the picture***
sub **arbore** (1:3)	*under* ***the tree***

5. For subordinate clauses that modify verbs, see VIII below.

VI. OTHER USES OF CASES

A. The accusative case is used in exclamations:

Ō **mē miseram**! (9:18) ***Poor me!***

B. The vocative case is used when addressing a person or persons directly (see Book I-A, page 56):

Dēscende, **Sexte!** (4:7) *Come down,* ***Sextus!***

VII. COORDINATING CONJUNCTIONS

Conjunctions are words that join together (Latin **con-,** *together* + **iungere,** *to join*) sentences or elements within a sentence. Coordinating conjunctions join elements that are simply added to one another and are of equal grammatical importance (Latin **co-,** *together, same* + **ōrdō,** *order, rank*):

Cornēlia sedet **et** legit. (1:3)
Cornelia sits ***and*** *reads.*

Etiam Sextus dormit **neque** Cornēliam vexat. (6:2)
Even Sextus is sleeping ***and*** *is* ***not*** *annoying Cornelia.*

Marcus **neque** ignāvus **neque** temerārius est. (5:5–6))
Marcus is ***neither*** *cowardly* ***nor*** *rash.*

Hodiē puellae nōn sedent **sed** in agrīs ambulant. (2:2–3)
Today the girls are not sitting ***but*** *are walking in the fields.*

Servī in vīllā sedent, **nam** dēfessī sunt. (8c:8)
The slaves are sitting in the country house, ***for*** *they are tired.*

Sextus est puer molestus quī semper Cornēliam vexat. Cornēlia **igitur** Sextum nōn amat. (4:1–2)
Sextus is an annoying boy who always annoys Cornelia. Cornelia, ***therefore****, does not like Sextus.*

VIII. SUBORDINATE CLAUSES

A clause is a group of words containing a verb. The following sentence contains two clauses, each of which is said to be a main clause because each could stand by itself as a complete sentence:

Rīdent Marcus et Cornēlia, sed nōn rīdet Sextus. (4:10–11)
Marcus and Cornelia laugh, but Sextus does not laugh.

Subordinate (Latin **sub-,** *below* + **ōrdō,** *order, rank*) clauses are clauses that are of less grammatical importance than the main clause in a sentence. They are sometimes called dependent (Latin **dē-,** *down from* + **pendēre,** *to hang*) clauses because they hang down from the main clause and cannot stand by themselves. They are joined to the main clause by pronouns, adverbs, or conjunctions.

Subordinate clauses are modifiers. They may be descriptive, like adjectives, and modify nouns:

Cornēlia est puella Rōmāna **quae** in Italiā habitat. (1:1–2)
Cornelia is a Roman girl ***who*** *lives in Italy.*

Etiam in pictūrā est vīlla rūstica **ubi** Cornēlia aestāte habitat. (1:2)
Also in the picture is a country house and farm ***where*** *Cornelia lives in the summer.*

But most subordinate clauses are adverbial, that is, they modify the verb of the main clause or the action of the main clause as a whole and are introduced by subordinating conjunctions that express ideas such as the following:

sī, condition:

Sī tū puer strēnuus es, ascende arborem!
If *you are an energetic boy, climb a tree!*

quamquam, concession:

Quamquam dominus abest, necesse est nōbīs strēnuē labōrāre. (11:7)
Although *the master is away, it is necessary for us to work hard.*

dum, ubi, and **cum,** time:

Dum Cornēlia legit, Flāvia scrībit. (1:4–5)
While *Cornelia reads, Flavia writes.*

Dum per viam ībant, Aurēlia et Cornēlia spectābant rūsticōs quī in agrīs labōrābant. (13:3–4)

***While/As long as** they were going along the road, Aurelia and Cornelia were looking at the peasants who were working in the fields.*
(**Dum** with the imperfect tense = *while/as long as*)

Dum puerī cibum dēvorant, subitō intrāvit mīles quīdam. (20:13)
***While** the boys were devouring their food, a certain soldier suddenly entered.*
(Here the present tense verb in the **dum** clause is to be translated with the English past tense that describes ongoing action.) (See Book I-B, page 27.)

Puerī, **ubi** clāmōrem audiunt, statim ad puellās currunt. (5:10)
*The boys, **when** they hear the shout, immediately run to the girls.*

Crās, **ubi** surgētis, puerī, clāmōrem et strepitum audiētis.
*Tomorrow **when** you get up/will get up, boys, you will hear shouting and noise.*

Cum intrāverimus, tandem aurīgās ipsōs spectābimus. (26:17–18)
***When** we enter /will have entered, we will finally watch the charioteers themselves.*
(While the verbs of the subordinate clauses are in the future, **surgētis**, and future perfect, **intrāverimus**, we translate them into English as presents; see Book I-B, page 84. The use of the tenses is more exact in Latin.)

quod, cause:

Cornēlia est laeta **quod** iam in vīllā habitat.
*Cornelia is happy **because** she now lives in the country house.*

Words you have met that may introduce subordinate clauses are:

dum, *as long as* (15:1)
dum, *while* (20:13)
nisi, *if not, unless* (18:16)
postquam, *after* (21:10)
quamquam, *although* (11:7)
quī, masc., **quae,** fem., **quod,** neut., *who, which, that* (1:1)
quod, *because* (1:3)
simulac, *as soon as* (24:1)
sī, *if* (5:1)
ubi, *when* (5:10)
ubi, *where* (1:2)
ut, *as* (16:17)

PRONUNCIATION OF LATIN

Consonants

The Latin alphabet does not have the letters *j* or *w*; the letter *i* before a vowel is a consonant and is pronounced as *y*, and *v* is pronounced as *w*. The letters *k*, *y*, and *z* occur in few Latin words, the latter two letters only in words taken over by the Romans from their neighbors the Greeks.

In pronouncing Latin you will find the following rules of use.

Most consonants are pronounced as in English, but the following should be noted:

- **b** before **s** or **t** is pronounced as English *p*: **urbs, observat.**
- **c** is always hard and pronounced as English *k*: **cadit.**
- **g** is hard, as in English "get": **gemit.**
- **gn** in the middle of a word may be pronounced as the *ngn* in English "hangnail": **magnus.**
- **i** before a vowel is a consonant and is pronounced as English *y*: **iam.**
- **r** should be rolled: **rāmus.**
- **s** is pronounced as in English "sing," never as in "roses": **servus.**
- **v** is pronounced as English *w*: **vīlla.**

Vowels

The following approximations are offered for the pronunciation of short and long vowels. In addition, long vowels should be held approximately twice as long as short vowels.

Short	Long
a = English "alike" (**ad**)	**ā** = English "father" (**clāmat**)
e = English "pet" (**ex**)	**ē** = English "date" (**dēscendit**)
i = English "sip" (**Italia**)	**ī** = English "sleep" (**īrātus**)
o = English "for" (**arborem**)	**ō** = English "holy" (**in hortō**)
u = English "foot" (**ubi**)	**ū** = English "boot" (**fūrtim**)

The diphthong **ae** is pronounced as the *y* in English "sky" (**amīcae**). The diphthong **au** is pronounced as the *ow* in English "how" (**audit**). The diphthong **ei** is pronounced as the "ay" in English "say" (**deinde**).

Syllables

In dividing Latin words into syllables, note the following rules:

1. A single consonant between two vowels usually goes with the second vowel:

   nō-mi-ne Rō-mā-na vī-cī-na

2. Two consonants between vowels are usually divided between the syllables:

   puel-la pic-tū-ra rūs-ti-ca

Accents

Latin words are accented according to simple rules:

1. If the next to the last syllable (the *penult*) has a long vowel or a diphthong, it will receive the accent:

   discḗdō

2. If the penult has a short vowel followed by two consonants, it will usually receive the accent:

   exténdō

3. Otherwise, the accent falls on the third syllable from the end (the *antepenult*):

   Británnicus

4. Almost all words of two syllables are accented on the first syllable:

   For example: **légit**   Exception: **adhū́c**

Careful observations of the long marks (macrons) over the vowels will thus help with both pronunciation and accenting of Latin words.

LATIN TO ENGLISH VOCABULARY

Numbers in parentheses at the end of entries refer to the chapters in which the words appear in vocabulary entries or in Building the Meaning or Forms sections. Roman numerals refer to Review chapters.

A

ā or **ab,** prep. + abl., *from* (13)

ábeō, abī́re, ábiī, or **abī́vī, abitū́rus,** irreg., *to go away* (3,9)

Ábī!/Abī́te! *Go away!* (3)

abhínc, adv., *ago, previously* (25)

ábsum, abésse, ā́fuī, āfutū́rus, irreg., *to be away, be absent, be distant* (11, 25)

áccidit, accídere, áccidit, *it happens* (14, 26)

accū́sō, -ā́re, -ā́vī, -ā́tus, *to accuse* (21)

ad, prep. + acc., *to, toward, at, near* (2, 9)

adhū́c, adv., *still* (5, 13)

ádiuvō, adiuvā́re, adiū́vī, adiū́tus, *to help* (6, 21)

admóveō, admovḗre, admṓvī, admṓtus, *to move toward* (22)

ádsum, adésse, ádfuī, adfutū́rus, irreg., *to be present* (26)

advéniō, advenī́re, advḗnī, adventū́rus, *to reach, arrive (at)* (5, 23)

advesperā́scit, advesperā́scere, advesperā́vit, *it gets dark* (17)

aedifícium, -ī, n., *building* (17)

aedíficō, -ā́re, -ā́vī, -ā́tus, *to build* (24)

aéstās, aestā́tis, f., *summer* (1)

aestā́te, *in summer* (1, 12)

aéstus, -ūs, m., *heat* (24, 25)

áger, ágrī, m., *field* (2)

agnṓscō, agnṓscere, agnṓvī, ágnitus, *to recognize* (18)

ágō, ágere, ḗgī, ā́ctus, *to do, drive* (8, 14, 23)

Áge!/Ágite! *Come on!* (8)

Grā́tiās tíbi ágō! *I thank you! Thank you!* (26)

Quid ágis? *How are you?* (18)

albā́tus, -a, -um, *white* (27)

áliquid, *something* (25)

áliter, adv., *otherwise* (26)

álius, ália, áliud, *another, other* (10)

áliī...áliī..., *some...others...* (9)

álter, áltera, álterum, *a/the second, one (of two), the other (of two), another* (1)

álter...álter, *the one...the other* (16)

ámbulō, -ā́re, -ā́vī, -ātū́rus, *to walk* (2)

amī́ca, -ae, f., *friend* (2)

amī́cus, -ī, m., *friend* (3)

ámō, -ā́re, -ā́vī, -ā́tus, *to like, love* (4)

amphitheā́trum, -ī, n., *amphitheater* (25)

ancílla, -ae, f., *slave-woman* (6)

ánimus, -ī, m., *mind* (16)

ánimum recuperā́re, *to regain one's senses, be fully awake* (21)

in ánimō habḗre, *to intend* (16)

ánteā, adv., *previously, before* (20)

antī́quus, -a, -um, *ancient* (26)

apériō, aperī́re, apéruī, apértus, *to open* (16, 26)

appā́reō, -ḗre, -uī, -itū́rus, *to appear* (15, 18)

appéllō, -ā́re, -ā́vī, -ā́tus, *to call, name* (21)

appropínquō, -ā́re, -ā́vī, -ātū́rus + dat. or **ad** + acc., *to approach, come near (to)* (4, 22)

ápud, prep. + acc., *with, in front of, before* (16, 26)

áqua, -ae, f., *water* (6)

aquaedúctus, -ūs, m., *aqueduct* (23, 25)

árbor, árboris, f., *tree* (1)

árcus, -ūs, m., *arch* (24, 25)

ā́rea, -ae, f., *open space, threshing-floor* (11)

arrípiō, arrípere, arrípuī, arréptus, *to grab hold of, snatch, seize* (5, 19, 26)

ars, ártis, gen. pl., **ártium,** f., *skill* (14)

ascéndō, ascéndere, ascéndī, ascḗnsus, *to climb, climb into (a carriage)* (4, 22)

Ásia, -ae, f., *Asia* (Roman province in western Asia Minor) (21)

at, conj., *but* (23)

átque, conj., *and, also* (22)
ā́trium, -ī, n., *atrium, main room* (26)
atténtē, adv., *attentively, closely* (20)
attónitus, -a, -um, *astonished, astounded* (24)
aúdiō, -ī́re, -ī́vī, -ī́tus, *to hear, listen to* (4, 20)
aúreus, -a, -um, *golden* (25)
aurī́ga, -ae, m., *charioteer* (13)
aúrum, -ī, n., *gold* (21)
aut... aut..., conj., *either...or...* (26)
auxílium, -ī, n., *help* (5, 15)
  Fer/Férte auxílium! *Bring help! Help!* (5)

B

báculum, -ī, n., *stick, staff* (10, 15)
Báiae, -ā́rum, *Baiae*
béne, adv., *well* (22)
bónus, -a, -um, *good* (12)
  bóna, -ṓrum, n. pl., *goods, possessions* (26)
bōs, bóvis, m./f., *ox, cow* (15)
brévis, -is, -e, *short* (2)
  brévī témpore, *in a short time, soon* (2, 12)
Británnia, -ae, f., *Britain* (8)
Británnicus, -a, -um, *British* (3)

C

cádō, cádere, cécidī, cāsū́rus, *to fall* (3, 22)
caélum, -ī, n., *sky* (17)
Caésar, Caésaris, m., *Caesar, emperor* (27)
cálidus, -a, -um, *warm* (5)
Calígula, -ae, m., *Caligula (emperor, A.D. 37-41)* (27)
cánis, cánis, m./f., *dog* (12)
cántō, -ā́re, -ā́vī, -ā́tus, *to sing* (21)
cápiō, cápere, cḗpī, cā́ptus, *to take, capture* (21)
captī́vus, -ī, m., *prisoner* (26)
cáput, cápitis, n., *head* (25)
cāríssimus, -a, -um, *dearest* (16)
caúda, -ae, f., *tail* (18)
caúpō, caupṓnis, m., *innkeeper* (17)
caupṓna, -ae, f., *inn* (17, 20)
caúsa, -ae, f., *reason* (25)
cáveō, cavḗre, cā́vī, caútus, *to be careful, watch out for, beware* (4, 13, 23)
  Cávē!/Cavḗte! *Be careful! Watch out for...! Beware!* (4, 13, 23)
celériter, adv., *quickly* (8, 13)
  celérrimē, adv., *very fast, very quickly* (14)
cḗlō, -ā́re, -ā́vī, -ā́tus, *to hide* (11)
cḗna, -ae, f., *dinner* (19)
cḗnō, -ā́re, -ā́vī, -ā́tus, *to dine, eat dinner* (19)
céntum, *a hundred* (15)
cértē, adv., *certainly* (19)
céssō, -ā́re, -ā́vī, -ātū́rus, *to be idle, do nothing, delay* (14)
cíbus, -ī, m., *food* (6)
circḗnsis, -is, -e, *in the circus* (27)
  lū́dī circḗnsēs, *chariot-racing* (27)
circúmeō, circumī́re, circúmiī or **circumī́vī, circúmitus,** irreg., *to go around* (24)
Círcus Máximus, -ī, m., *Circus Maximus (a stadium in Rome)* (23)
císium, -ī, n., *light two-wheeled carriage* (14, 15)
císta, -ae, f., *trunk, chest* (10)
cī́vis, cī́vis, gen. pl., **cī́vium,** m./f., *citizen* (13)
clā́mō, -ā́re, -ā́vī, -ātū́rus, *to shout* (3)
clā́mor, clāmṓris, m., *shout, shouting* (5)
claúdō, claúdere, claúsī, claúsus, *to shut* (26)
  claúsus, -a, -um, *shut, closed* (24)
clíēns, cliéntis, gen. pl., **cliéntium,** m., *client, dependent* (25)
cṓgitō, -ā́re, -ā́vī, -ā́tus, *to think* (21)
collóquium, -ī, n., *conversation* (26)
cólō, cólere, cóluī, cúltus, *to cultivate* (23)
commṓtus, -a, -um, *moved* (14)
compléxus, -ūs, m., *embrace* (9, 25)
  compléxū, *in an embrace* (9)
cóncidō, concídere, cóncidī, *to fall down* (14)
condū́cō, condū́cere, condū́xī, condúctus, *to hire* (23)
cōnfíciō, cōnfícere, cōnfḗcī, cōnféctus, *to finish* (25)
cōnfī́dō, cōnfī́dere + dat., *to give trust (to), trust* (26)
coníciō, conícere, coniḗcī, coniéctus, *to throw* (21)
cóniūnx, cóniugis, m./f., *husband, wife* (26)
cōnsī́dō, cōnsī́dere, cōnsḗdī, *to sit down* (23)
cōnspíciō, cōnspícere, cōnspéxī, cōnspéctus, *to catch sight of* (4, 21)
cōnstítuō, cōnstitúere, cōnstítuī, cōnstitū́tus, *to decide* (23)
cṓnsulō, cōnsúlere, cōnsúluī, cōnsúltus,

to consult (7)
cónvocō, -ā́re, -ā́vī, -ā́tus, *to call together* (12)
cóquō, cóquere, cóxī, cóctus, *to cook* (6)
Cornēliā́nus, -a, um, *belonging to Cornelius* (10)
Cornḗliī, -ṓrum, m. pl., *the members of the family of Cornelius* (22)
córpus, córporis, n., *body* (21)
crās, adv., *tomorrow* (10, 13)
crótalum, -ī, n., *castanet* (21)
cubículum, -ī, n., *room, bedroom* (8, 15)
cúbitum ī́re, *to go to bed* (19)
cui, *to whom, to him, to her* (19)
Cúius...? *Whose...?* (22)
culī́na, -ae, f., *kitchen* (21)
cúlpa, -ae, f., *fault, blame* (14)
cum, prep. + abl., *with* (12)
cum, conj., *when* (22)
cū́nctī, -ae, -a, *all* (14)
Cūr...? adv., *Why...?* (1)
Cū́ria, -ae, f., *Senate House* (23)
cū́rō, -ā́re, -ā́vī, -ā́tus, *to look after, take care of* (6)
currículum, -ī, n., *race track* (27)
cúrrō, cúrrere, cucúrrī, cursū́rus, *to run* (2, 23)
custṓdiō, -ī́re, -ī́vī, -ī́tus, *to guard* (17)
cústōs, custṓdis, m., *guard* (26)

D

dē, prep. + abl., *down from, concerning, about* (16)
débeō, -ḗre, -uī, -itū́rus + infin., *ought* (26)
décem, *ten* (15)
dēféndō, dēféndere, dēféndī, dēfḗnsus, *to defend* (I)
dēféssus, -a, -um, *tired* (2)
deínde, adv., *then, next* (8, 13)
dēmṓnstrō, -ā́re, -ā́vī, -ā́tus, *to show* (24)
dēscéndō, dēscéndere, dēscéndī, dēscēnsū́rus, *to come/go down, climb down* (4, 23)
dēsī́derō, -ā́re, -ā́vī, -ā́tus, *to long for, miss* (26)
dēvértō, dēvértere, dēvértī, dēvérsus, *to turn aside* (14, 27)
dḗvorō, -ā́re, -ā́vī, -ā́tus, *to devour* (20)
dī́cō, dī́cere, dī́xī, díctus, *to say, tell* (20, 21)
díēs, diḗī, m., *day* (5, 13, 25)
éō díē, *on that day* (25)
dīligénter, adv., *carefully* (19)
discḗdō, discḗdere, discéssī, discessū́rus, *to go away, depart* (9, 22)
díū, adv., *for a long time* (15)
dō, dáre, dédī, dátus, *to give* (21)
sē quiḗtī dáre, *to rest* (23)
dóceō, docḗre, dócuī, dóctus, *to teach* (6, 21)
dóleō, -ḗre, -uī, -itū́rus, *to be sad* (18)
dómina, -ae, f., *mistress, lady of the house* (17)
dóminus, -ī, m., *master, owner* (11)
dómus, -ūs, f., *house* (23, 25)
dómī, *at home* (26)
dómō, *from home* (23)
dómum, *homeward, home* (23)
dórmiō, -ī́re, -ī́vī, -ītū́rus, *to sleep* (4)
dū́cō, dū́cere, dū́xī, dúctus, *to lead, take, bring* (7, 19, 20)
dum, conj., *while, as long as* (1)
dúo, dúae, dúo, *two* (15)

E

ē or **ex,** prep. + abl., *from, out of* (2, 5, 9)
éam, *her, it* (9, 16)
eā́rum, *their* (27)
Écce! *Look! Look at...!* (1)
effúgiō, effúgere, effū́gī, *to flee, run away, escape* (11, 21)
égo, *I* (5, 27)
Ḗheu! *Alas!* (7)
Ého! *Hey!* (25)
éī, *to him/her/it* (21)
éī, éae, éa, *they* (22, 27)
éīs, *to them* (22)
éius, *his, her(s), its* (2, 27)
émō, émere, ḗmī, ḗmptus, *to buy* (21)
énim, conj., *for* (20)
éō, ī́re, iī or **ī́vī, itū́rus,** irreg., *to go* (7, 17, 19, 20, 21)
cúbitum ī́re, *to go to bed* (19)
éō, adv., *there, to that place* (23)
éō díē, *on that day* (25)
éō ípsō témpore, *at that very moment* (10)
eṓrum, *their* (25, 27)
éōs, *them* (5)
epístula, -ae, f., *letter* (7)

équus, -ī, m., *horse* (10)
érat, *(he/she/it) was* (13)
érrō, -ā́re, -ā́vī, -ātū́rus, *to wander, be mistaken* (5, 18)
ērúptiō, ēruptiṓnis, f., *eruption* (26)
ésse (see **sum**)
est, *(he/she/it) is* (1)
Éstō! *All right!* (20)
ēsúriō, -ī́re, -ī́vī, -ītū́rus, *to be hungry* (19)
et, conj., *and* (1)
étiam, adv., *also, even* (1, 6, 13)
Eúgepae! *Hurray!* (7)
éum, *him, it* (5)
ex or **ē,** prep. + abl., *from, out of* (2, 5, 9)
excípiō, excípere, excḗpī, excéptus, *to welcome, receive, catch* (5, 16, 22)
éxcitō, -ā́re, -ā́vī, -ā́tus, *to rouse, wake (someone) up* (8)
  excitā́tus, -a, -um, *wakened, aroused* (25)
exclā́mō, -ā́re, -ā́vī, -ā́tus, *to exclaim, shout out* (10)
éxeō, exī́re, éxiī or **exī́vī, exitū́rus,** irreg., *to go out* (5, 23)
éxplicō, -ā́re, -ā́vī, -ā́tus, *to explain* (19)
  rem explicā́re, *to explain the situation* (19)
exspéctō, -ā́re, -ā́vī, -ā́tus, *to look out for, wait for* (15)
éxstāns, exstántis, *standing out, towering* (23)
exténdō, exténdere, exténdī, exténtus, *to hold out* (18)
éxtrā, prep. + acc., *outside* (23)
éxtrahō, extráhere, extrā́xī, extráctus, *to drag out, take out* (14, 21)

F

fā́bula, -ae, f., *story* (20)
fáciō, fácere, fḗcī, fáctus, *to make, do* (1, 23)
  íter fácere, *to travel* (13)
  Quid fácit...? *What does...do? What is... doing?* (1)
  Quid fḗcit...? *What did...do?* (19)
fáctiō, factiṓnis, f., *company (of charioteers)* (27)
fátuus, -a, -um, *stupid* (13)
fáveō, favḗre, fā́vī, fautū́rus + dat., *to give favor (to), favor, support* (27)
fḗlēs, fḗlis, gen. pl., **fḗlium,** f., *cat* (21)
fḗmina, -ae, f., *woman* (3)
fēriā́tus, -a, -um, *celebrating a holiday* (27)
fériō, -ī́re, -ī́vī, -ī́tus, *to hit, strike,* (16)
férō, férre, túlī, lā́tus, irreg., *to bring, carry, bear* (5, 12, 17, 21)
  Fer/Férte auxílium! *Bring help! Help!* (5)
ferṓciter, adv., *fiercely* (13)
festī́nō, -ā́re, -ā́vī, -ātū́rus, *to hurry* (9)
fī́lia, -ae, f., *daughter* (11)
fī́lius, -ī, m., *son* (11)
fī́niō, -ī́re, -ī́vī, -ī́tus, *to finish* (21)
fortásse, adv., *perhaps* (15)
fórtis, -is, -e, *brave, strong* (18)
Fórum, -ī, n., *the Forum (town center of Rome)* (25)
fóssa, -ae, f., *ditch* (12)
frágor, fragṓris, m., *crash, noise, din* (4)
frā́ter, frā́tris, m., *brother* (11)
frígidus, -a, -um, *cool, cold* (5)
frōns, fróntis, gen. pl., **fróntium,** f., *forehead* (12)
frū́strā, adv., *in vain* (14)
fúgiō, fúgere, fū́gī, fugitū́rus, *to flee* (18, 25)
fúī (see **sum**)
fū́rtim, adv., *stealthily* (4, 13)

G

Gā́dēs, Gā́dium, f. pl., *Gades (Cadiz, a town in Spain)* (21)
gaúdeō, gaudḗre, *to be glad, rejoice* (14)
gaúdium, -ī, n., *joy* (23)
gémō, gémere, gémuī, gémitus, *to groan* (3)
gérō, gérere, géssī, géstus, *to wear* (10)
gládius, -ī, m., *sword* (26)
  gládium stríngere, *to draw a sword* (26)
glṓria, -ae, f., *fame, glory* (27)
Graécia, -ae, f., *Greece* (21)
Graécus, -a, -um, *Greek* (17)
  Graécī, -ṓrum, m. pl., *the Greeks* (I)
grā́tia, -ae, f., *gratitude, thanks* (26)
  Grā́tiās tíbi ágō! *I thank you! Thank you!* (26)

H

habḗnae, -ā́rum, f. pl., *reins* (22)
hábeō, -ḗre, -uī, -itus, *to have, hold* (10, 20, 26)
  in ánimō habḗre, *to intend* (16)
  ōrātiṓnem habḗre, *to deliver a speech* (26)

hábitō, -ā́re, -ā́vī, -ā́tus, *to live, dwell* (1)
hāc, *this* (25)
haéreō, haerḗre, haésī, haesū́rus, *to stick* (14)
hanc, *this* (20)
héri, adv., *yesterday* (20)
hī, *these* (18)
hīc, adv., *here* (9, 13)
hic, haec, hoc, *this, the latter* (18, 19, 20, 25, 26)
hódiē, adv., *today* (2, 13)
hómō, hóminis, m., *man* (18)
  hóminēs, hóminum, m. pl., *people* (15)
hṓra, -ae, f., *hour* (9)
hórtus, -ī, m., *garden* (3)
hóspes, hóspitis, m./f., *guest, host, friend, a person related to one of another city by ties of hospitality* (16)
hūc illū́c, adv., *here and there, this way and that* (23)
húius (genitive of **hic**) (25)
húmī, *on the ground* (27)

I

iáceō, -ḗre, -uī, -itū́rus, *to lie, be lying down* (26)
iáciō, iácere, iḗcī, iáctus, *to throw* (10, 20)
iam, adv., *now, already* (1, 8, 13)
  nōn iam, adv., *no longer* (2, 13)
iánitor, iānitṓris, m., *doorkeeper* (9)
iánua, -ae, f., *door* (9)
íbi, adv., *there* (5, 13)
id (see **is**)
  id quod, *that which, what* (11)
ídem, éadem, ídem, *the same* (3)
idéntidem, adv., *again and again, repeatedly* (13)
ígitur, conj., *therefore* (4)
ignā́vus, -a, -um, *cowardly, lazy* (5)
ílle, ílla, íllud, *that, he, she, it, the former, that famous* (11, 15, 16, 20, 22, 25, 26)
illū́c, adv., *there, to that place* (23)
  hūc illū́c, adv., *here and there, this way and that* (23)
ímber, ímbris, gen. pl., **ímbrium** m., *rain* (23)
ímmemor, immémoris + gen., *forgetful* (22)
immṓbilis, -is, -e, *motionless* (12)
immortā́lis, -is, -e, *immortal* (27)
impédiō, -ī́re, -ī́vī, ītus, *to hinder, prevent* (11)
in, prep. + abl., *in, on* (1, 9)
  in ánimō habḗre, *to intend* (16)
  in itínere, *on a journey* (10)
in, prep. + acc., *into, against* (3, 9)
íncitō, -ā́re, -ā́vī, -ā́tus, *to spur on, urge on, drive* (10)
incólumis, -is, -e, *unhurt, safe and sound* (14)
índuō, indúere, índuī, indū́tus, *to put on* (8, 23)
īnfírmus, -a, -um, *weak, shaky* (4)
íngēns, ingéntis, *huge* (22)
innocéntia, -ae, f., *innocence* (21)
ínquit, *(he/she) says, said* (7)
īnspíciō, īnspícere, īnspéxī, īnspéctus, *to examine* (21)
intérdiū, adv., *during the day, by day* (23)
intéreā, adv., *meanwhile* (10, 13)
interpéllō, -ā́re, -ā́vī, -ā́tus, *to interrupt* (14)
íntrā, prep. + acc., *inside* (22)
íntrō, -ā́re, -ā́vī, -ā́tus, *to enter, go into* (8, 19)
inū́rō, inū́rere, inússī, inústus, *to brand* (12)
invéniō, invenī́re, invḗnī, invéntus, *to come upon, find* (12, 21)
invī́tus, -a, -um, *unwilling* (21)
iócus, -ī, m., *joke, prank* (16)
  per iócum, *as a prank* (16)
ípse, ípsa, ípsum, *himself, herself, itself, themselves, very* (6, 10)
ī́ra, -ae, f., *anger* (11)
īrā́tus, -a, -um, *angry* (3)
ī́re (see **éō**) (7, 17)
is, ea, id, *he, she, it; this, that* (27)
íta, adv., *thus, so, in this way* (3, 13, 21)
  Íta vḗrō! adv., *Yes! Indeed!* (3, 13)
Itália, -ae, f., *Italy* (1)
ítaque, adv., *and so, therefore* (16)
íter, itíneris, n., *journey* (10, 13, 15)
  íter fácere, *to travel* (13)
íterum, adv., *again, a second time* (8, 13)
iúbeō, iubḗre, iússī, iússus, *to order, bid* (10, 19, 21)

L

lábor, labṓris, m., *work, toil* (24)
labṓrō, -ā́re, -ā́vī, -ā́tus, *to work* (3)
  labōrántēs, *working* (7)
lácrimō, -ā́re, -ā́vī, -ā́tus, *to weep, cry* (9)
  lácrimāns, *weeping* (9)

laétus, -a, -um, *happy, glad* (1)
lā́na, -ae, f., *wool* (6)
  lā́nam tráhere, *to spin wool* (6)
lápis, lápidis, m., *stone* (25)
lā́trō, -ā́re, -ā́vī, -ātū́rus, *to bark* (12)
  lātrántēs, *barking* (18)
laúdō, -ā́re, -ā́vī, -ā́tus, *to praise* (18)
lávō, lavā́re, lā́vī, laútus, *to wash* (20)
lectī́ca, -ae, f., *litter* (23)
lectīcā́rius, -ī, m., *litter-bearer* (23)
léctus, -ī, m., *bed, couch* (19)
lēgā́tus, -ī, m., *envoy* (18)
légō, légere, lḗgī, lḗctus, *to read* (1, 24)
léntē, adv., *slowly* (2, 13)
líber, líbrī, m., *book* (24)
lī́berī, -ṓrum, m. pl., *children* (10, 11)
lībértās, lībertā́tis, f., *freedom* (21)
lícet, licḗre, lícuit + dat., *it is allowed* (20, 24)
  lícet nṓbīs, *we are allowed, we may* (20)
líttera, -ae, f., *letter (of the alphabet)* (12)
lóngus, -a, -um, *long* (15)
lū́cet, lūcḗre, lū́xit, *it is light, it is day* (6)
lū́dī, -ṓrum, m. pl., *games* (24)
  lū́dī circḗnsēs, *chariot-racing* (27)
lū́dō, lū́dere, lū́sī, lūsū́rus, *to play* (16)
  pílā lū́dere, *to play ball* (16)
lū́dus, -ī, m., *school* (26)
lúpa, -ae, f., *she-wolf* (II)
lúpus, -ī, m., *wolf* (5)
lútum, -ī, n., *mud* (26)
lūx , lū́cis, f., *light* (21)
  prī́mā lū́ce, *at dawn* (21)

M

magníficus, -a, -um, *magnificent* (24)
mágnus, -a, -um, *big, great, large, loud (voice, laugh)* (4)
  mágnā vṓce, *in a loud voice* (4)
  mágnō rī́sū, *with a loud laugh* (13)
málus, -a, -um, *bad* (21)
  níhil málī, *nothing of a bad thing, there is nothing wrong* (21)
mandā́tum, -ī, n., *order, instruction* (22)
mā́ne, adv., *early in the day, in the morning* (21)
máneō, manḗre, mā́nsī, mā́nsus, *to remain, stay, wait, wait for* (9, 20, 23)
mánus, -ūs, f., *hand* (18, 25)
máppa, -ae, f., *napkin* (27)
mā́ter, mā́tris, f., *mother* (6, 11)
máximus, -a, -um, *greatest, very great, very large* (23)
mē, *me* (4)
  mḗcum, *with me* (9)
médius, -a, -um, *mid-, middle of* (20)
  média nox, médiae nóctis, f., *midnight* (20)
Mégara, -ae, f., *Megara (a city in Greece)* (21)
Mehércule! *By Hercules! Goodness me!* (18)
mélior, mélius, gen., **meliṓris,** *better* (19)
mercā́tor, mercātṓris, m., *merchant* (22)
mḗta, -ae, f., *mark, goal, turning post* (27)
métus, -ūs, m., *fear* (26)
méus, -a, -um, *my, mine* (7)
míhi, *for me, to me* (8)
mī́les, mī́litis, m., *soldier* (20)
mī́lle, *a thousand* (15)
Mínimē! *No! Not at all! Not in the least!* (3, 13)
mī́rus, -a, -um, *wonderful, marvelous, strange* (23)
míser, mísera, míserum, *unhappy, miserable, wretched* (9)
míttō, míttere, mī́sī, míssus, *to send* (9, 20)
módo, adv., *only* (18)
mṓlēs, mṓlis, gen. pl., **mṓlium,** f., *mass, huge bulk* (24)
moléstus, -a, -um, *troublesome, annoying* (4)
  moléstus, -ī, m., *pest* (3)
mōns, móntis, gen pl., **móntium,** m., *mountain, hill* (24)
  Mōns Vesúvius, Montis Vesúviī, m., *Mount Vesuvius (a volcano in southern Italy)* (26)
mṓnstrō, -ā́re, -ā́vī, -ā́tus, *to show* (22)
mors, mórtis, gen. pl., **mórtium,** f., *death* (21)
mórtuus, -a, -um, *dead* (16)
móveō, movḗre, mṓvī, mṓtus, *to move* (14, 24)
mox, adv., *soon, presently* (6, 13)
múlier, mulíeris, f., *woman* (27)
múltī, -ae, -a, *many* (3)
multitū́dō, multitū́dinis, f., *crowd* (23)
múrmur, múrmuris, n., *murmur, rumble* (15)

múrus, -ī, m., *wall* (23)
mūs, múris, m., *mouse* (21)
mússō, -áre, -ávī, -ātúrus, *to mutter* (11)

N

nam, conj., *for* (8)
nārrátor, nārrātóris, m., *narrator* (8)
nárrō, -áre, -ávī, -átus, *to tell (a story)* (20)
  nārrátus, -a, -um, *told* (20)
-ne (indicates a question) (3)
Neápolis, Neápolis, f., *Naples* (15)
necésse, adv. or indecl. adj., *necessary* (6, 13)
nécō, -áre, -ávī, -átus, *to kill* (20)
némō, néminis, m./f., *no one* (9)
néque, conj., *and...not* (6)
  néque...néque, conj., *neither...nor* (5)
nésciō, -íre, -ívī, -ítus, *to be ignorant, not to know* (9)
níhil, *nothing* (4)
  níhil málī, *nothing of a bad thing, there is nothing wrong* (21)
nísi, conj., *unless, if...not, except* (18, 26)
nóbīs, *for us, to us* (9)
  nōbíscum, *with us* (16)
nóceō, -ére, -uī, -itúrus + dat., *to do harm (to), harm* (26)
nócte, *at night* (12)
noctúrnus, -a, -um, *happening during the night* (22)
nólō, nólle, nóluī, irreg., *to be unwilling, not to wish, refuse* (5, 17, 21)
  Nólī/Nōlíte + infin., *Don't...!* (9)
nómen, nóminis, n., *name* (1, 15)
  nómine, *by name, called* (1)
nōn, adv., *not* (2, 13)
  nōn iam, adv., *no longer* (2, 13)
nóndum, adv., *not yet* (6, 13)
Nónne...? *Surely...?* (introduces a question that expects the answer "yes") (19)
nōnnúmquam, adv., *sometimes* (26)
nónus, -a, -um, *ninth* (16)
nōs, *we, us* (8, 27)
nóster, nóstra, nóstrum, *our* (14, 27)
nóvem, *nine* (15)
nóvus, -a, -um, *new* (16)
nox, nóctis, gen. pl., **nóctium,** f., *night* (11)
  íllā nócte, *that night* (11)
  média nox, *midnight* (20)
  nócte, *at night* (12)
núbēs, núbis, gen. pl., **núbium,** f., *cloud* (15)
núllus, -a, -um, *no, none* (9)
númerus, -ī, m., *number* (11)
númquam, adv., *never* (20)
nunc, adv., *now* (6, 13)
núntius, -ī, m., *messenger* (7)

O

ō (used with vocative and in exclamations) (9)
  Ō mē míseram! *Poor me! Oh dear me!* (9)
obdórmiō, -íre, -ívī, -ītúrus, *to go to sleep* (21)
obésus, -a, -um, *fat* (18)
obsérvō, -áre, -ávī, -átus, *to watch* (6)
occupátus, -a, -um, *busy* (7)
occúrrō, occúrrere, occúrrī, occursúrus + dat., *to meet* (24)
óctō, *eight* (15)
óculus, -ī, m., *eye* (26)
olfáciō, olfácere, olfécī, olfáctus, *to catch the scent of, smell, sniff* (12, 18)
ólim, adv., *once (upon a time)* (18)
olīvétum, -ī, n., *olive grove* (14, 15)
ómnis, -is, -e, *all, the whole, every, each* (6, 18)
  ómnēs, ómnia, *all, everyone, everything* (6, 9)
  ómnia quae, *everthing that* (6)
ónus, óneris, n., *load, burden* (15)
oppréssus, -a, -um, *crushed* (25)
óptimus, -a, -um, *best, very good* (20)
  vir óptime, *sir* (20)
ōrátiō, ōrātiónis, f., *oration, speech* (26)
  ōrātiónem habére, *to deliver a speech* (26)
ōrátor, ōrātóris, m., *orator, speaker* (22)

P

Palātínus, -a, -um, *Palatine, belonging to the Palatine Hill* (24)
pálla, -ae, f., *palla* (10)
parátus, -a, -um, *ready, prepared* (10)

párēns, paréntis, m./f., *parent* (11)
párō, -áre, -ávī, -átus, *to prepare, get ready* (5, 20)
sē paráre, *to prepare oneself, get ready* (22)
pars, pártis, gen. pl., **pártium,** f., *part, direction, region* (13)
párvulus, -a, -um, *small, little* (26)
páter, pátris, m., *father* (6, 11)
patrṓnus, -ī, m., *patron* (25)
pátruus, -ī, m., *uncle* (22)
paulísper, adv., *for a short time* (20)
pecū́nia, -ae, f., *money* (21)
per, prep. + acc., *through, along* (6, 9)
per iócum, *as a prank* (16)
perīculṓsus, -a, -um, *dangerous* (17)
perī́culum, -ī, n., *danger* (14, 15)
pernóctō, -áre, -ávī, -ātū́rus, *to spend the night* (17, 18)
pertérritus, -a, -um, *frightened, terrified* (5)
pervéniō, perveníre, pervḗnī, perventū́rus, *to arrive (at), reach* (25)
pēs, pédis, m., *foot* (13)
pétō, pétere, petī́vī, petī́tus, *to look for, seek, head for, aim at, attack* (5, 21)
pictū́ra, -ae, f., *picture* (1)
píla, -ae, f., *ball* (16)
pílā lū́dere, *to play ball* (16)
pīráta, -ae, m., *pirate (21)*
piscína, -ae, f., *fishpond* (3)
plácidē, adv., *gently, peacefully* (14)
plaústrum, -ī, n., *wagon, cart* (15)
plḗnus, -a, -um, *full* (11)
plúit, plúere, plúit, *it rains, is raining* (23)
poḗta, -ae, m., *poet* (25)
Pompéiī, -ṓrum, m. pl., *Pompeii*
pṓnō, pṓnere, pósuī, pósitus, irreg., *to put, place* (10, 21)
pōns, póntis, gen. pl., **póntium,** m., *bridge* (23)
pórta, -ae, f., *gate* (11)
pórtō, -áre, -ávī, -átus, *to carry* (6)
póssum, pósse, pótuī, irreg., *to be able; I can* (5, 14, 21)
póterat, *(he/she/it) was able, could* (13)
pótest, *(he/she/it) is able, can* (5)
post, prep. + acc., *after* (20)
póstis, póstis, gen. pl., **póstium,** m., *door-post* (25)
póstquam, conj., *after* (20)
postrī́diē, adv., *on the following day* (26)
praeclárus, -a, -um, *distinguished, famous* (13)
praecípitō, -áre, -ávī, -átus, *to hurl* (18)
sē praecipitáre, *to hurl oneself, rush* (18)
praecúrrō, praecúrrere, praecúrrī, praecursū́rus, *to run ahead* (18)
praédō, praedṓnis, m., *robber* (26)
praéter, prep. + acc., *except* (21)
praetéreā, adv., *besides, too, moreover* (15)
praetéreō, praeterī́re, praetériī or **praeterī́vī, praetéritus,** *to go past* (15)
praetéxta, tóga, -ae, f., *toga with purple border* (10)
prásinus, -a, -um, *green* (27)
prī́mus, -a, -um, *first* (21)
prī́mā lū́ce, *at dawn* (21)
prī́mum, adv., *first, at first* (23)
prī́nceps, prī́ncipis, m., *emperor* (7)
prócul, adv., *in the distance, far off, far* (15)
prōmíttō, prōmíttere, prōmī́sī, prōmíssus, *to promise* (9)
própe, prep. + acc., *near* (5, 9)
própter, prep. + acc., *on account of, because of* (26)
puélla, -ae, f., *girl* (1)
púer, púerī, m., *boy* (3)
púlvis, púlveris, m., *dust* (15)
pū́niō, -íre, -ívī, -ítus, *to punish* (21)
pū́rgō, -áre, -ávī, -átus, *to clean* (6)

Q

quadrátus, -a, -um, *squared* (25)
quae, *who* (1, 11)
Quális...? Quális...? Quále...? *What sort of...?* (4)
Quam...! adv., *How...!* (13)
Quam...? adv., *How...?*
quámquam, conj., *although* (11)
Quándō...? adv., *When...?* (12, 21)
quās, *which* (24)
quáttuor, *four* (15)
Quem...? *Whom...?* (5)
quem, *whom, which, that* (24)
quī, quae, quod, *who, which, that* (1, 3, 14)
Quī...? *Who...?* (pl.) (6)

Quibúscum...? *With whom...?* (12)
Quid...? *What...?* (1, 4)
  Quid ágis? *How are you?* (18)
  Quid fácit...? *What does...do? What is...doing?* (1)
  Quid fécit...? *What did...do?* (19)
quídam, quaédam, quóddam, *a certain* (10)
quíēs, quiḗtis, f., *rest* (23)
  sē quiḗtī dáre, *to rest* (23)
quiḗscō, quiḗscere, quiḗvī, quiētū́rus, *to rest, keep quiet* (13, 23)
quīngéntī, -ae, -a, *five hundred* (15)
quīnquāgíntā, *fifty* (15)
quī́nque, *five* (15)
quī́ntus, -a, -um, *fifth* (26)
Quis...? Quid...? *Who...? What...?* (1, 4)
  Quid ágis? *How are you?* (18)
  Quid fácit...? *What does...do? What is...doing?* (1)
  Quid fécit...? *What did...do?* (19)
Quō...? adv., *Where...to?* (4)
Quṓcum...? *With whom...?* (12, 26)
quod (see **quī, quae, quod**)
quod, conj., *because*; with verbs of feeling, *that* (1, 13)
Quō īnstrūméntō...? *With what instrument...? By what means...? How?* (12)
Quṓmodo...? adv., *In what manner...? In what way...? How...?* (12)
quóque, adv., *also* (2, 13)
Quōs...? *Whom...?* (7)
Quot...? *How many...?* (15)

R

raéda, -ae, f., *carriage* (10)
raedā́rius, -ī, m., *coachman, driver* (10)
rā́mus, -ī, m., *branch* (4)
recúperō, -ā́re, -ā́vī, -ā́tus, *to recover* (21)
  ánimum recuperā́re, *to regain one's senses, be fully awake* (21)
rédeō, redī́re, rédiī or **redī́vī, réditū́rus,** irreg., *to return, go back* (7, 23)
réditus, -ūs, m., *return* (25)
relínquō, relínquere, relī́quī, relíctus, *to leave behind* (16, 21)
remóveō, removḗre, remṓvī, remṓtus, *to remove, move aside* (21)
repéllō, repéllere, réppulī, repúlsus, *to drive off, drive back* (5)
reprehéndō, reprehéndere, reprehéndī, reprehḗnsus, *to blame, scold* (6)
rēs, réī, f., *thing, matter, situation* (19, 25)
  rem explicā́re, *to explain the situation* (19)
respóndeō, respondḗre, respóndī, respōnsū́rus, *to reply* (5, 21)
révocō, -ā́re, -ā́vī, -ā́tus, *to recall, call back* (7)
rī́deō, rīdḗre, rī́sī, rī́sus, *to laugh (at), smile* (3, 21)
rīmṓsus, -a, -um, *full of cracks, leaky* (23)
rī́sus, -ūs, m., *smile, laugh* (13, 25)
  mágnō rī́sū, *with a loud laugh* (13)
rī́vus, -ī, m., *stream* (5)
rógō, -ā́re, -ā́vī, -ā́tus, *to ask* (12)
  sē rogā́re, *to ask oneself, wonder* (21)
Rṓma, -ae, f., *Rome* (7)
  Rṓmam, *to Rome* (7)
Rōmā́nus, -a, -um, *Roman* (1)
  Rōmā́nī, -ṓrum, m. pl., *the Romans* (III)
róta, -ae, f., *wheel* (15)
russā́tus, -a, -um, *red* (27)
rū́stica, vī́lla, -ae, f., *country house and farm* (1)
rū́sticus, -ī, m., *peasant* (13)

S

saépe, adv., *often* (2, 13)
saltā́trīx, saltātrī́cis, f., *dancer* (21)
sáltō, -ā́re, -ā́vī, -ātū́rus, *to dance* (21)
salū́tō, -ā́re, -ā́vī, -ā́tus, *to greet, welcome* (7)
Sálvē!/Salvḗte! *Greetings! Hello!* (7)
sálvus, -a, -um, *safe* (5)
sátis, adv., *enough* (23)
  sátis témporis, *enough time* (23)
sceléstus, -a, -um, *wicked* (10)
scíō, scī́re, scī́vī, scī́tus, *to know* (16)
scrī́bō, scrī́bere, scrī́psī, scrī́ptus, *to write* (1, 24)
sē, *himself, herself, oneself, itself, themselves* (11)
secúndus, -a, -um, *second* (9)
sed, conj., *but* (2)
sédeō, sedḗre, sḗdī, sessū́rus, *to sit* (1, 21)
sēmisómnus, -a, -um, *half-asleep* (9)

sémper, adv., *always* (4, 13)
senā́tor, senātṓris, m., *senator* (7)
sēnā́tus, -ūs, m., *Senate* (25)
sénex, sénis, m., *old man* (I)
séptem, *seven* (15)
séptimus, -a, -um, *seventh* (13)
sepúlcrum, -ī, n., *tomb* (22)
séquēns, sequéntis, *following* (25)
sḗrō, adv., *late* (21)
sérvō, -ā́re, -ā́vī, -ā́tus, *to save* (26)
sérvus, -ī, m., *slave* (3)
sex, *six* (15)
sī, conj., *if* (5)
  sī vīs, *if you wish, please* (26)
sígnum, -ī, n., *signal* (27)
siléntium, -ī, n., *silence* (15)
sílva, -ae, f., *woods, forest* (5)
símul, adv., *together, at the same time* (9, 13)
símulac, conj., *as soon as* (24)
símulō, -ā́re, -ā́vī, -ā́tus, *to pretend* (21)
síne, prep. + abl., *without* (26)
sóleō, solḗre + infin., *to be accustomed (to), be in the habit of* (10)
sollícitus, -a, -um, *anxious, worried* (4)
sṓlus, -a, -um, *alone* (3)
sómnium, -ī, n., *dream* (21)
sómnus, -ī, m., *sleep* (21)
sónitus, -ūs, m., *sound* (21, 25)
sórdidus, -a, -um, *dirty* (19)
sóror, sorṓris, f., *sister* (11)
spectā́tor, spectātṓris, m., *spectator* (27)
spéctō, -ā́re, -ā́vī, -ā́tus, *to watch, look at* (7)
státim, adv., *immediately* (5, 13)
státua, -ae, f., *statue* (3)
stércus, stércoris, n., *dung, manure* (21)
stértō, stértere, stértuī, *to snore* (25)
stílus, -ī, m., *pen* (25)
stō, stā́re, stétī, statū́rus, *to stand* (10, 22)
stóla, -ae, f., *stola (a woman's outer garment)* (10)
strḗnuus, -a, -um, *active, energetic* (2)
  strḗnuē, adv., *strenuously, hard* (6, 13)
strépitus, -ūs, m., *noise, clattering* (23, 25)
stríngō, stríngere, strī́nxī, stríctus, *to draw* (26)
  gládium stríngere, *to draw a sword* (26)
stúltus, -a, -um, *stupid, foolish* (23)
stúpeō, -ḗre, -uī, *to be amazed, gape* (23)
sub, prep. + abl., *under, beneath* (1, 9)
súbitō, adv., *suddenly* (3, 13)
súī, síbi, sē, sē, *himself, herself, oneself, itself, themselves* (27)
sum, ésse, fúī, futū́rus, irreg., *to be* (1, 14, 20, 21)
sū́mō, sū́mere, sū́mpsī, sū́mptus, *to take, take up, pick out* (22)
sunt, *(they) are* (2)
súprā, prep. + acc., *above* (23)
súprā, adv., *above, on top* (21)
súrgō, súrgere, surrḗxī, surrēctū́rus, *to get up, rise* (6, 21)
súus, -a, -um, *his, her, one's, its, their (own)* (9, 27)

T

tabellā́rius, -ī, m., *courier* (13)
tabérna, -ae, f., *shop* (25)
tablī́num, -ī, n., *study* (26)
táceō, -ḗre, -uī, -itus, *to be quiet* (9)
  Tácē!/Tacḗte! *Be quiet!* (9)
tácitē, adv., *silently* (9, 13)
taédet, taedḗre, *it bores* (16)
tā́lis, -is, -e, *such, like this, of this kind* (23)
támen, adv., *however, nevertheless* (6, 13)
tándem, adv., *at last, at length* (2, 13)
tántum, adv., *only* (15)
tántus, -a, -um, *so great, such a big* (24)
tárdus, -a, -um, *slow* (15)
tē (see **tū**), *you* (4)
temerā́rius, -a, -um, *rash, reckless, bold* (5)
témptō, -ā́re, -ā́vī, -ā́tus, *to try* (9)
témpus, témporis, n., *time* (2, 8, 12, 15)
  brévī témpore, *in a short time, soon* (2, 12)
  éō ípsō témpore, *at that very moment* (10)
  sátis témporis, *enough time* (23)
téneō, tenḗre, ténuī, téntus, *to hold* (9, 25)
térra, -ae, f., *earth, ground* (26)
térreō, terrḗre, térruī, térritus, *to frighten, terrify* (4)
térror, terrṓris, m., *terror, fear* (22)
tértius, -a, -um, *third* (25)
tíbi, *to you, for you* (19)

tímeō, -ḗre, -uī, *to fear, be afraid (to/of)* (5)
tímidus, -a, -um, *afraid, fearful, timid* (21)
tóga, -ae, f., *toga* (8)
tóga praetéxta, -ae, f., *toga with purple border* (10)
tóga virī́lis, tógae virī́lis, f., *toga of manhood, plain white toga* (10)
tṓtus, -a, -um, *all, the whole* (21)
trā́dō, trā́dere, trā́didī, trā́ditus, *to hand over* (7, 22)
tráhō, tráhere, trā́xī, tráctus, *to drag, pull* (6, 12, 25)
lā́nam tráhere, *to spin wool* (6)
trémō, trémere, trémuī, *to tremble* (21)
trēs, trēs, tría, *three* (13, 15)
tríbus diḗbus, *in three days* (12, 13)
Trṓia, -ae, f., *Troy* (I)
Troiā́nus, -a, -um, *Trojan* (I)
Troiā́nī, -ṓrum, m. pl., *the Trojans* (I)
tū (acc. **tē**), *you* (sing.) (4, 27)
túlī (see **férō**)
tum, adv., *at that moment, then* (4, 13)
tumúltus, -ūs, m., *uproar, commotion* (25)
túnica, -ae, f., *tunic* (8)
túrba, -ae, f., *crowd, mob* (23)
túus, -a, -um, *your* (sing.) (9, 27)

U

Úbi...? adv., *Where...?* (10, 12)
úbi, adv., conj., *where, when* (1, 5, 13)
Únde...? adv., *From where...?* (12)
ūndécimus, -a, -um, *eleventh* (17)
úndique, adv., *on all sides, from all sides* (23)
ū́nus, -a, -um, *one* (15)
urbs, úrbis, gen. pl., **úrbium,** f., *city* (7)
ut, adv., *as* (16)
úxor, uxṓris, f., *wife* (11)

V

váldē, adv., *very, very much, exceedingly* (19)
Válē!/Valḗte! *Goodbye!* (9)
veheménter, adv., *very much, violently, hard* (19)
vehículum, -ī, n., *vehicle* (13, 15)
vélle (see **vólō**)
vénetus, -a, -um, *blue* (27)
véniō, venī́re, vḗnī, ventū́rus, *to come* (7, 20)
vérberō, -ā́re, -ā́vī, -ā́tus, *to beat, whip* (11)
verbṓsus, -a, -um, *talkative* (26)
vértō, vértere, vértī, vérsus, *to turn* (16)
vésperī, *in the evening* (18)
véster, véstra, véstrum, *your* (pl.) (22, 27)
vēstī́gium, -ī, n., *track, footprint, trace* (12, 15)
vétō, vetā́re, vétuī, vétitus, *to forbid* (26)
véxō, -ā́re, -ā́vī, -ā́tus, *to annoy* (4)
vía, -ae, f., *road, street* (10)
Vía Áppia, -ae, f., *the Appian Way* (11)
viā́tor, viātṓris, m., *traveler* (18)
vīcī́nus, -a, -um, *neighboring, adjacent* (1)
víctor, victṓris, m., *conqueror, victor* (27)
vídeō, vidḗre, vī́dī, vī́sus, *to see* (4, 21)
vidḗtur, *he/she/it seems* (21)
vígilō, -ā́re, -ā́vī, -ātū́rus, *to stay awake* (19)
vī́licus, -ī, m., *overseer, farm manager* (11)
vī́lla, -ae, f., *country house* (1)
vī́lla rū́stica, -ae, f., *country house and farm* (1)
víncō, víncere, vī́cī, víctus, *to conquer, win* (27)
vī́nea, -ae, f., *vineyard* (12)
vī́num, -ī, n., *wine* (25)
vir, vírī, m., *man, husband* (3, 11)
vir óptime, *sir* (20)
vírga, -ae, f., *stick, rod, switch* (13)
virī́lis, -is, -e, *of manhood* (23)
tóga virī́lis, f., *toga of manhood, plain white toga* (10)
vīs (from **vólō**), *you want* (16)
vī́sitō, -ā́re, -ā́vī, -ā́tus, *to visit* (23)
vī́tō, -ā́re, -ā́vī, -ā́tus, *to avoid* (13)
vix, adv., *scarcely, with difficulty* (24)
vṓbīs, *to you, for you* (pl.) (19)
vólō, vélle, vóluī, irreg., *to wish, want, be willing* (5, 17, 20, 21)
sī vīs, *if you wish, please* (26)
vōs, *you* (pl.) (8)
vōx, vṓcis, f., *voice* (4)
mágnā vṓce, *in a loud voice* (4)
vult (from **vólō**), *(he/she) wishes, wants, is willing* (5, 17)

ENGLISH TO LATIN VOCABULARY

Verbs are usually cited in their infinitive form. For further information about the Latin words in this list, please consult the Latin to English Vocabulary list.

A

able, (he/she/it) was, **póterat**
able, to be, **pósse**
about, **dē**
above, **súprā**
absent, to be, **abésse**
accuse, to, **accūsā́re**
accustomed (to), to be, **solḗre**
active, **strḗnuus**
adjacent, **vīcī́nus**
afraid, **tímidus**
afraid (to/of), to be, **timḗre**
after, **post, póstquam**
again, **íterum**
again and again, **idéntidem**
against, **in**
ago, **abhínc**
aim at, to, **pétere**
Alas! **Ḗheu!**
all, **cū́nctī, ómnis, tṓtus**
All right! **Éstō!**
allowed, it is, **lícet**
allowed, we are, **lícet nṓbīs**
alone, **sṓlus**
along, **per**
already, **iam**
also, **átque, étiam, quóque**
although, **quámquam**
always, **sémper**
amazed, to be, **stupḗre**
amphitheater, **amphitheā́trum**
ancient, **antī́quus**
and, **átque, et**
and...not, **néque**
and so, **ítaque**
anger, **ī́ra**
angry, **īrā́tus**
annoy, to, **vexā́re**
annoying, **moléstus**
another, **álius, álter**
anxious, **sollícitus**
appear, to, **appārḗre**
Appian Way, the, **Vía Áppia**
approach, to, **appropinquā́re**
aqueduct, **aquaedúctus**
arch, **árcus**
are, (they), **sunt**
aroused, **excitā́tus**
arrive (at), to, **advenī́re, pervenī́re**
as, **ut**
as a prank, **per iócum**
as long as, **dum**
as soon as, **símulac**
Asia Minor, **Ásia**
ask, to, **rogā́re**
ask oneself, to, **sē rogā́re**
astonished, **attónitus**
astounded, **attónitus**
at, **ad**
at last, **tándem**
at length, **tándem**
at night, **nócte**
atrium, **ā́trium**
attack, to, **pétere**
attentively, **atténtē**
avoid, to, **vītā́re**
awake, to be fully, **ánimum recuperā́re**

B

bad, **málus**
Baiae, **Báiae**
ball, **píla**

ball, to play, **pílā lū́dere**
bark, to, **lātrā́re**
barking, **lā́trāns**
be, to, **ésse**
be away, to, **abésse**
Be quiet! **Tácē!/Tacḗte!**
bear, to, **férre**
beat, to, **verberā́re**
because, **quod**
because of, **própter**
bed, **léctus**
bed, to go to, **cúbitum ī́re**
bedroom, **cubículum**
before, **ánteā, ápud**
beneath, **sub**
besides, **praetéreā**
best, **óptimus**
better, **mélior**
Beware! **Cávē!/Cavḗte!**
beware, to, **cavḗre**
bid, to, **iubḗre**
big, **mágnus**
big, such a, **tántus**
blame, **cúlpa**
blame, to, **reprehéndere**
blue, **vénetus**
body, **córpus**
bold, **temerā́rius**
book, **líber**
bores, it, **taédet**
boy, **púer**
branch, **rā́mus**
brand, to, **inū́rere**
brave, **fórtis**
bridge, **pōns**
bring, to, **dū́cere, férre**
Bring help! **Fer/Férte auxílium!**
Britain, **Británnia**
British, **Británnicus**
brother, **frā́ter**
build, to, **aedificā́re**
building, **aedifícium**
bulk, huge, **mṓlēs**
burden, **ónus**
busy, **occupā́tus**
but, **at, sed**
buy, to, **émere**
By Hercules! **Mehércule!**
By what means...? **Quō īnstrūméntō...?**

C

Caesar, **Caésar**
Caligula, **Calígula**
call, to, **appellā́re**
call back, to, **revocā́re**
call together, to, **convocā́re**
called, **nṓmine**
can, (he/she/it), **pótest**
can, (I), **póssum**
capture, to, **cápere**
careful! Be, **Cávē!/Cavḗte!**
careful, to be, **cavḗre**
carefully, **dīligénter**
carriage, **raéda**
carriage, light two-wheeled, **císium**
carry, to, **férre, portā́re**
cart, **plaústrum**
castanet, **crótalum**
cat, **fḗlēs**
catch, to, **excípere**
catch sight of, to, **cōnspícere**
certain, a, **quī́dam**
certainly, **cértē**
charioteer, **aurī́ga**
chariot-racing, **lū́dī circḗnsēs**
chest, **císta**
children, **lī́berī**
circus, in the, **circḗnsis**
Circus Maximus, **Círcus Máximus**
citizen, **cī́vis**
city, **urbs**
clattering, **strépitus**
clean, to, **pūrgā́re**
client, **clíēns**
climb, to, **ascéndere**
climb down, to, **dēscéndere**
climb into (a carriage), to, **ascéndere**

closed, **claúsus**
closely, **atténtē**
cloud, **nū́bēs**
coachman, **raedā́rius**
cold, **frī́gidus**
come, to, **venī́re**
come down, to, **dēscéndere**
come near (to), to, **appropinquā́re**
Come on! **Áge!/Ágite!**
come upon, to, **invenī́re**
commotion, **tumúltus**
company (of charioteers), **fáctiō**
concerning, **dē**
conquer, to, **víncere**
conqueror, **víctor**
consult, to, **cōnsúlere**
conversation, **collóquium**
cook, to, **cóquere**
cool, **frī́gidus**
Cornelius, belonging to, **Cornēliā́nus**
Cornelius, the members of the family of, **Cornḗliī**
couch, **léctus**
could, (he/she/it), **póterat**
country house, **vī́lla**
country house and farm, **vī́lla rū́stica**
courier, **tabellā́rius**
cow, **bōs**
cowardly, **ignā́vus**
cracks, full of, **rīmṓsus**
crash, **frágor**
crowd, **multitū́dō, túrba**
crushed, **oppréssus**
cry, to, **lacrimā́re**
cultivate, to, **cólere**

D

dance, to, **saltā́re**
dancer, **saltā́trīx**
danger, **perī́culum**
dangerous, **perīculṓsus**
dark, it gets, **advesperā́scit**
daughter, **fī́lia**
dawn, at, **prī́mā lū́ce**
day, **díēs**
day, during the *or* by, **intérdiū**
day, on that, **éō díē**
day, on the following, **postrī́diē**
day, it is, **lū́cet**
dead, **mórtuus**
dearest, **cāríssimus**
death, **mors**
decide, to, **cōnstitúere**
defend, to, **dēféndere**
delay, to, **cessā́re**
deliver a speech, to, **ōrātiṓnem habḗre**
depart, to, **discḗdere**
dependent, **clíēns**
devour, to, **dēvorā́re**
difficulty, with, **vix**
din, **frágor**
dine, to, **cēnā́re**
dinner, **cḗna**
direction, **pars**
dirty, **sórdidus**
distance, in the, **prócul**
distant, to be, **abésse**
distinguished, **praeclā́rus**
ditch, **fóssa**
do, to, **ágere, fácere**
do?, What did..., **Quid fḗcit...?**
do?, What does..., **Quid fácit...?**
do nothing, to, **cessā́re**
dog, **cánis**
doing?, What is..., **Quid fácit...?**
Don't...! **Nṓlī/Nōlī́te** + infinitive
door, **iā́nua**
door-post, **póstis**
doorkeeper, **iā́nitor**
down from, **dē**
drag, to, **tráhere**
drag out, to, **extráhere**
draw, to, **stríngere**
draw a sword, to, **gládium stríngere**
dream, **sómnium**
drive, to, **ágere, incitā́re**

drive off/back, to, **repéllere**
driver, **raedā́rius**
dung, **stércus**
dust, **púlvis**
dwell, to, **habitā́re**

E

each, **ómnis**
early in the day, **mā́ne**
earth, **térra**
eat dinner, to, **cēnā́re**
eight, **óctō**
either...or, **aut...aut**
eleventh, **ūndécimus**
embrace, **compléxus**
embrace, in an, **compléxū**
emperor, **Caésar, prī́nceps**
energetic, **strḗnuus**
enough, **sátis**
enter, to, **intrā́re**
envoy, **lēgā́tus**
eruption, **ērúptiō**
escape, to, **effúgere**
even, **étiam**
evening, in the, **vésperī**
every, **ómnis**
everyone, **ómnēs**
everything, **ómnia**
everything that, **ómnia quae**
examine, to, **īnspícere**
exceedingly, **váldē**
except, **nísi, praéter**
exclaim, to, **exclāmā́re**
explain, to, **explicā́re**
explain the situation, to, **rem explicā́re**
eye, **óculus**

F

fall, to, **cádere**
fall down, to, **concídere**
fame, **glṓria**
famous, **praeclā́rus**
far (off), **prócul**
fast, very, **celérrimē**
fat, **obḗsus**
father, **páter**
fault, **cúlpa**
favor, to, **favḗre**
fear, **métus, térror**
fear, to, **timḗre**
fearful, **tímidus**
field, **áger**
fiercely, **ferṓciter**
fifth, **quī́ntus**
fifty, **quīnquāgíntā**
find, to, **invenī́re**
finish, to, **cōnfícere, fīnī́re**
first, **prī́mus**
first, (at), **prī́mum**
fishpond, **piscī́na**
five, **quī́nque**
flee, to, **effúgere, fúgere**
following, **séquēns**
following day, on the, **postrī́diē**
food, **cíbus**
foolish, **stúltus**
foot, **pēs**
footprint, **vēstī́gium**
for, **énim, nam**
forbid, to, **vetā́re**
forehead, **frōns**
forest, **sílva**
forgetful, **ímmemor**
former, the, **ílle**
Forum, **Fórum**
four, **quáttuor**
freedom, **lībértās**
friend, **amī́ca, amī́cus, hóspes**
frighten, to, **terrḗre**
frightened, **pertérritus**
from, **ā, ab, ē, ex**
from home, **dómō**
From where...? **Únde...?**
full, **plḗnus**

G

Gades, **Gā́dēs**
games, **lū́dī**
gape, to, **stupḗre**
garden, **hórtus**
gate, **pórta**
gently, **plácidē**
get ready, to, **(sē) parā́re**
get up, to, **súrgere**
gets dark, it, **advesperā́scit**
girl, **puélla**
give, to, **dáre**
give favor (to), to, **favḗre**
glad, **laétus**
glad, to be, **gaudḗre**
glory, **glṓria**
go, to, **ī́re**
go around, to, **circumī́re**
Go away! **Ábī!/Abī́te!**
go away, to, **abī́re, discḗdere**
go back, to, **redī́re**
go down, to, **dēscéndere**
go into, to, **intrā́re**
go out, to, **exī́re**
go past, to, **praeterī́re**
goal, **mḗta**
gold, **aúrum**
golden, **aúreus**
good, **bónus**
good, very, **óptimus**
Goodbye! **Válē!/Valḗte!**
Goodness me! **Mehércule**!
goods, **bóna**
grab hold of, to, **arrípere**
gratitude, **grā́tia**
great, **mágnus**
great, very, **máximus**
greatest, **máximus**
Greece, **Graécia**
Greek, **Graécus**
Greeks, the, **Graécī**
green, **prásinus**
greet, to, **salūtā́re**
Greetings! **Sálvē!/Salvḗte!**
groan, to, **gémere**
ground, **térra**
ground, on the, **húmī**
guard, **cústōs**
guard, to, **custōdī́re**
guest, **hóspes**

H

habit of, to be in the, **solḗre**
half-asleep, **sēmisómnus**
hand, **mánus**
hand over, to, **trā́dere**
happens, it, **áccidit**
happy, **laétus**
hard, **strḗnuē, veheménter**
harm, to, **nocḗre**
have, to, **habḗre**
he, **is, ílle**
head, **cáput**
head for, to, **pétere**
hear, to, **audī́re**
heat, **aéstus**
Hello! **Sálvē!/Salvḗte!**
help, **auxílium**
help!, Bring, **Fer/Férte auxílium!**
help, to, **adiuvā́re**
her, **éam**
her, of, **éius**
her (own), **súa**
her(s), **éius**
her, to, **cui, éī**
here, **hīc**
here and there, **hūc illū́c**
herself, **ípsa, sē, súī**
Hey! **Ého!**
hide, to, **cēlā́re**
hill, **mōns**
him, **éum**
him, to, **cui, éī**
himself, **ípse, sē, súī**
hinder, to, **impedī́re**
hire, to, **condū́cere**

his, **éius**
his (own), **súus**
hit, to, **feríre**
hold, to, **habḗre, tenḗre**
hold out, to, **exténdere**
holiday, celebrating a, **fēriā́tus**
home, at, **dómī**
home(ward), **dómum**
horse, **équus**
host, **hóspes**
hour, **hṓra**
house, **dómus**
house, country, **vī́lla**
How...! **Quam...!**
How...? **Quam...? Quō īnstrūméntō...? Quṓmodo...?**
How are you? **Quid ágis?**
How many...? **Quot...?**
however, **támen**
huge, **íngēns**
hundred, a, **céntum**
hundred, five, **quīngéntī**
hungry, to be, **ēsurī́re**
hurl, to, **praecipitā́re**
hurl oneself, to, **sē praecipitā́re**
Hurray! **Eúgepae!**
hurry, to, **festīnā́re**
husband, **cóniūnx, vir**

I

I, **égo**
I thank you! **Grā́tiās tíbi ágō!**
idle, to be, **cessā́re**
if, **sī**
if...not, **nísi**
ignorant, to be, **nescī́re**
immediately, **státim**
immortal, **immortā́lis**
in, **in**
in a loud voice, **mágnā vṓce**
in front of, **ápud**
in three days, **tríbus diḗbus**
in vain, **frū́strā**
In what manner...? **Quṓmodo...?**
In what way...? **Quṓmodo...?**
Indeed! **Íta vḗrō!**
inn, **caupṓna**
innkeeper, **caúpō**
innocence, **innocéntia**
inside, **íntrā**
instruction, **mandā́tum**
instrument...?, With what, **Quō īnstrūméntō...?**
intend, to, **in ánimō habḗre**
interrupt, to, **interpellā́re**
into, **in**
is, (he/she/it), **est**
is able, (he/she/it), **pótest**
it, **is, ílle**
it, of, **éius**
it, to, **éī**
Italy, **Itália**
its, **éius**
its (own), **súus**
itself, **ípse, sē**

J

joke, **iócus**
journey, **íter**
joy, **gaúdium**

K

keep quiet, to, **quiḗscere**
kill, to, **necā́re**
kind, of this, **tā́lis**
kitchen, **culī́na**
know, not to, **nescī́re**
know, to, **scī́re**

L

lady of the house, **dómina**
large, **mágnus**
large, very, **máximus**
late, **sḗrō**
latter, the, **hic**
laugh, **rī́sus**

laugh (at), to, **rīdḗre**
laugh, with a loud, **mágnō rī́sū**
lazy, **ignā́vus**
lead, to, **dū́cere**
leaky, **rīmṓsus**
leave behind, to, **relínquere**
letter, **epístula**
letter (of the alphabet), **líttera**
lie, to, **iacḗre**
light, **lūx**
light, it is, **lū́cet**
light two-wheeled carriage, **císium**
like, to, **amā́re**
like this, **tā́lis**
listen to, to, **audī́re**
litter, **lectī́ca**
litter-bearer, **lectīcā́rius**
little, **párvulus**
live, to, **habitā́re**
load, **ónus**
long, **lóngus**
long for, to, **dēsīderā́re**
long time, for a, **díū**
look after, to, **cūrā́re**
look at, to, **spectā́re**
look for, to, **pétere**
look out for, to, **exspectā́re**
Look (at...)! **Écce!**
loud, **mágnus**
loud laugh, with a, **mágnō rī́sū**
loud voice, in a, **mágnā vṓce**
love, to, **amā́re**
lying down, to be, **iacḗre**

M

magnificent, **magníficus**
main room, **ā́trium**
make, to, **fácere**
man, **hómō, vir**
man, old, **sénex**
manager, farm, **vī́licus**
manhood, of, **virī́lis**
manner...?, In what, **Quṓmodo...?**
manure, **stércus**
many, **múltī**
mark, **mḗta**
marvelous, **mī́rus**
mass, **mṓlēs**
master, **dóminus**
matter, **rēs**
may, we, **lícet nṓbīs**
me, **mē**
me, to/for, **míhi**
me, with, **mḗcum**
means...?, By what, **Quō īnstrūméntō...?**
meanwhile, **intéreā**
meet, to, **occúrrere**
Megara, **Mégara**
merchant, **mercā́tor**
messenger, **nū́ntius**
mid-, **médius**
middle of, **médius**
midnight, **média nox**
mind, **ánimus**
mine, **méus**
miserable, **míser**
miss, to, **dēsīderā́re**
mistaken, to be, **errā́re**
mistress, **dómina**
mob, **túrba**
moment, at that, **tum**
moment, at that very, **éō ípsō témpore**
money, **pecū́nia**
moreover, **praetéreā**
morning, in the, **mā́ne**
mother, **mā́ter**
motionless, **immṓbilis**
mountain, **mōns**
Mount Vesuvius, **Mōns Vesúvius**
mouse, **mūs**
move, to, **movḗre**
move aside, to, **removḗre**
move toward, to, **admovḗre**
moved, **commṓtus**
mud, **lútum**
murmur, **múrmur**
mutter, to, **mussā́re**
my, **méus**

N

name, **nṓmen**
name, by, **nṓmine**
name, to, **appellā́re**
napkin, **máppa**
Naples, **Neā́polis**
narrator, **nārrā́tor**
near, **ad, própe**
necessary, **necésse**
neighboring, **vīcī́nus**
neither…nor, **néque…néque**
never, **númquam**
nevertheless, **támen**
new, **nóvus**
next, **deínde**
night, **nox**
night, at, **nócte**
night, happening during the, **noctúrnus**
night, that, **íllā nócte**
nine, **nóvem**
ninth, **nṓnus**
no, **nū́llus**
no longer, **nōn iam**
no one, **nḗmō**
No! **Mínimē!**
noise, **frágor, strépitus**
none, **nū́llus**
not, **nōn**
Not at all! **Mínimē!**
Not in the least! **Mínimē!**
not yet, **nṓndum**
nothing, **níhil**
nothing, to do, **cessā́re**
nothing wrong, there is, **níhil málī**
nothing of a bad thing, **níhil málī**
now, **iam, nunc**
number, **númerus**

O

often, **saépe**
Oh dear me! **Ō mē míseram!**
old man, **sénex**
olive grove, **olīvḗtum**
on, **in**
on a journey, **in itínere**
on account of, **própter**
on top, **súprā**
once (upon a time), **ṓlim**
one, **ū́nus**
one (of two), **álter**
one…the other, the, **álter…álter**
oneself, **súī**
only, **módo, tántum**
open, to, **aperī́re**
open space, **ā́rea**
oration, **ōrā́tiō**
orator, **ōrā́tor**
order, **mandā́tum**
order, to, **iubḗre**
other, **álius**
other (of two), the, **álter**
otherwise, **áliter**
ought, they, **dḗbent**
our, **nóster**
out of, **ē, ex**
outer garment, woman's, **stóla**
outside, **éxtrā**
overseer, **vī́licus**
owner, **dóminus**
ox, **bōs**

P

Palatine, belonging to the Palatine Hill, **Palātī́nus**
palla, **pálla**
parent, **párēns**
part, **pars**
patron, **patrṓnus**
peacefully, **plácidē**
peasant, **rū́sticus**
pen, **stílus**
people, **hóminēs**
perhaps, **fortásse**
person related to one of another city by ties of hospitality, **hóspes**
pest, **moléstus**
pick out, to, **sū́mere**
picture, **pictū́ra**

pirate, **pīrā́ta**
place, to, **pṓnere**
place, to that, **éō**
plain white toga, **tóga virī́lis**
play, to, **lū́dere**
play ball, to, **pílā lū́dere**
poet, **poḗta**
Pompeii, **Pompéiī**
Poor me! **Ō mē miseram!**
please, **sī vīs**
possessions, **bóna**
praise, to, **laúdō**
prank, **iócus**
prank, as a, **per iócum**
prepare, to, **parā́re**
prepare oneself, to, **sē parā́re**
prepared, **parā́tus**
present, to be, **adésse**
presently, **mox**
pretend, to, **simulā́re**
prevent, to, **impedī́re**
previously, **abhínc, ánteā**
prisoner, **captī́vus**
promise, to, **prōmíttere**
pull, to, **tráhere**
punish, to, **pūnī́re**
purple-bordered toga, **tóga praetéxta**
put, to, **pṓnere**
put on, to, **indúere**

Q

quickly, **celériter**
quickly, very, **celérrimē**
quiet, to be, **tacḗre**
quiet, to keep, **quiḗscere**
quiet! Be, **Tácē!/Tacḗte!**

R

race-course, **currículum**
rain, **ímber**
rains/is raining, it, **plúit**
rash, **temerā́rius**
reach, to, **advenī́re**
read, to, **légere**
ready, **parā́tus**
ready, to get, **(sē) parā́re**
reason, **caúsa**
recall, to, **revocā́re**
receive, to, **excípere**
reach, to, **pervenī́re**
reckless, **temerā́rius**
recognize, to, **agnṓscere**
recover, to, **recuperā́re**
red, **russā́tus**
refuse, to, **nṓlle**
region, **pars**
regain one's senses, to, **ánimum recuperā́re**
reins, **habḗnae**
rejoice, to, **gaudḗre**
remain, to, **manḗre**
remove, to, **removḗre**
repeatedly, **idéntidem**
reply, to, **respondḗre**
rest, **quíēs**
rest, to, **quiḗscere, sē quiḗtī dáre**
return, **réditus**
return, to, **redī́re**
rise, to, **súrgere**
road, **vía**
robber, **praédō**
rod, **vírga**
Roman, **Rōmā́nus**
Romans, the, **Rōmā́nī**
Rome, **Rṓma**
Rome, to, **Rṓmam**
room, **cubículum**
room, main, **ā́trium**
rouse, to, **excitā́re**
rumble, **múrmur**
run, to, **cúrrere**
run ahead, to, **praecúrrere**
run away, to, **effúgere**
rush, to, **sē praecipitā́re**

S

sad, to be, **dolḗre**
safe, **sálvus**

safe and sound, **incólumis**
said, (he/she), **ínquit**
same time, at the, **símul**
same, the, **ídem**
save, to, **serváre**
say, to, **dícere**
says, said, (he/she), **ínquit**
scarcely, **vix**
scent of, to catch the, **olfácere**
school, **lúdus**
scold, to, **reprehéndere**
second, **secúndus**
second, a/the, **álter**
second time, a, **íterum**
see, to, **vidére**
seek, to, **pétere**
seems, (he/she/it), **vidétur**
seize, to, **arrípere**
-self, -selves, **ípse, sē**
Senate, **senátus**
Senate House, **Cúria**
senator, **senátor**
send, to, **míttere**
seven, **séptem**
seventh, **séptimus**
shaky, **īnfírmus**
she, **éa, ílla**
she-wolf, **lúpa**
shop, **tabérna**
short, **brévis**
short time, for a, **paulísper**
short time, in a, **brévī témpore**
shout(ing), **clámor**
shout, to, **clāmáre**
shout out, to, **exclāmáre**
show, to, **dēmōnstráre, mōnstráre**
shut, **claúsus**
shut, to, **claúdere**
sides, from all, **úndique**
sides, on all, **úndique**
signal, **sígnum**
silence, **siléntium**
silently, **tácitē**
sing, to, **cantáre**
sir, **vir óptime**
sister, **sóror**
sit, to, **sedére**
sit down, to, **cōnsídere**
situation, **rēs**
six, **sex**
skill, **ars**
sky, **caélum**
slave, **sérvus**
slave-woman, **ancílla**
sleep, **sómnus**
sleep, to, **dormíre**
sleep, to go to, **obdormíre**
slow, **tárdus**
slowly, **léntē**
small, **párvulus**
smell, to, **olfácere**
smile, **rísus**
smile, to, **rīdére**
snatch, to, **arrípere**
sniff, to, **olfácere**
snore, to, **stértere**
so, **íta**
so great, **tántus**
soldier, **míles**
some...others, **áliī...áliī**
something, **áliquid**
sometimes, **nōnnúmquam**
son, **fílius**
soon, **brévī témpore, mox**
sound, **sónitus**
space, open, **área**
speaker, **ōrátor**
spectator, **spectátor**
speech, **ōrátiō**
speech, to deliver a, **ōrātiónem habére**
spend the night, to, **pernoctáre**
spin wool, to, **lánam tráhere**
spur on, to, **incitáre**
squared, **quadrátus**
staff, **báculum**
stand, to, **stáre**
standing out, **éxstāns**
statue, **státua**

stay, to, **manḗre**
stay awake, to, **vigilā́re**
stealthily, **fū́rtim**
stick, **báculum, vírga**
stick, to, **haerḗre**
still, **adhū́c**
stola, **stóla**
stone, **lápis**
story, **fā́bula**
strange, **mī́rus**
stream, **rī́vus**
street, **vía**
strenuously, **strḗnuē**
strike, to, **ferī́re**
strong, **fórtis**
study, **tablī́num**
stupid, **fátuus, stúltus**
such, **tā́lis**
suddenly, **súbitō**
summer, **aéstās**
summer, in, **aestā́te**
support, to, **favḗre**
switch, **vírga**
sword, **gládius**
sword, to draw a, **gládium stríngere**

T

tail, **caúda**
take, to, **cápere, dū́cere**
take care of, to, **cūrā́re**
take out, to, **extráhere**
take (up), to, **sū́mere**
talkative, **verbṓsus**
teach, to, **docḗre**
tell, to, **dī́cere**
tell (a story), to, **nārrā́re**
ten, **décem**
terrified, **pertérritus**
terrify, to, **terrḗre**
terror, **térror**
Thank you! **Grā́tiās tíbi agō!**
thanks, **grā́tia**
that, **is, ílle**
that (rel. pron.), **quī**
that (with verbs of feeling), **quod**
that famous, **ílle**
that night, **íllā nócte**
that place, to, **illū́c**
that which, **id quod**
their, **eṓrum**
their (own), **súus**
them, **éōs,**
them, of, **eṓrum,**
them, to, **éīs**
themselves, **ípsī, súī**
then, **deínde, tum**
there, **éō, íbi, illū́c**
therefore, **ígitur, ítaque**
these: pl. of **hic**
they: pl. of **is**
thing, **rēs**
think, to, **cōgitā́re**
third, **tértius**
this, **hic, is**
this way and that, **hūc illū́c**
thousand, a, **mī́lle**
three, **trēs**
threshing-floor, **ā́rea**
through, **per**
throw, to, **conícere, iácere**
time, **témpus**
time, enough, **sátis témporis**
time, in a short, **brévī témpore**
timid, **tímidus**
tired, **dēféssus**
to(ward), **ad**
to Rome, **Rṓmam**
to that place, **éō, illū́c**
today, **hódiē**
toga, **tóga**
toga of manhood, **tóga virī́lis**
toga, plain white, **tóga virī́lis**
toga with purple border, **tóga praetéxta**
together, **símul**
toil, **lábor**
told, **nārrā́tus**
tomb, **sepúlcrum**

tomorrow, **crās**
too, **praetéreā**
towering, **éxstāns**
trace, **vēstígium**
track, **vēstígium**
travel, to, **íter fácere**
traveler, **viā́tor**
tree, **árbor**
tremble, to, **trémere**
Trojan, **Troiā́nus**
Trojans, the, **Troiā́nī**
troublesome, **moléstus**
Troy, **Tróia**
trunk, **císta**
trust, to, **cōnfídere**
try, to, **temptā́re**
tunic, **túnica**
turn, to, **vértere**
turn aside, to, **dēvértere**
turning post, **mḗta**
two, **dúo**

U

uncle, **pátruus**
under, **sub**
unhappy, **míser**
unhurt, **incólumis**
unless, **nísi**
unwilling, **invī́tus**
unwilling, to be, **nṓlle**
uproar, **tumúltus**
urge on, to, **incitā́re**
us, to/for, **nṓbīs**
us, with, **nōbíscum**

V

vehicle, **vehículum**
very, **ípse, váldē**
very (much), **váldē, veheménter**
victor, **víctor**
vineyard, **vī́nea**
violently, **veheménter**
visit, to, **vīsitā́re**
voice, **vōx**
voice, in a loud, **mágnā vṓce**

W

wagon, **plaústrum**
wait, to, **manḗre**
wait for, to, **exspectā́re**
wake (someone) up, to, **excitā́re**
wakened, **excitā́tus**
walk, to, **ambulā́re**
wall, **mū́rus**
wander, to, **errā́re**
want, to, **vélle**
want, (you), **vīs**
wants, (he/she), **vult**
warm, **cálidus**
was, (he/she/it), **érat**
was able, (he/she/it), **póterat**
wash, to, **lavā́re**
watch, to, **observā́re, spectā́re**
watch out for, to, **cavḗre**
Watch out! **Cávē!/Cavḗte!**
watchful, to be, **vigilā́re**
water, **áqua**
way, in this, **íta**
way...?, In what, **Quṓmodo...?**
we, **nōs**
weak, **īnfírmus**
wear, to, **gérere**
weep, to, **lacrimā́re**
weeping, **lácrimāns**
welcome, to, **excípere, salūtā́re**
well, **béne**
what, **id quod**
What...? **Quid...?**
What does...do? **Quid fácit...?**
What sort of...? **Quā́lis...?**
wheel, **róta**
when, **cum, úbi**
When...? **Quándō...?**
where, **úbi**
Where...? **Úbi...?**

where…?, From, **Unde…?**
Where…to? **Quō…?**
which, **quī**
while, **dum**
whip, to, **verberā́re**
white, **albā́tus**
who, **quī**
Who…? **Quis…?**
whole, the, **ómnis, tṓtus**
whom, **quem**
Whom…? **Quem…?**
whom, to, (sing.) **cui**
whom…?, With, **Quṓcum…?**
Whose…? **Cúius…?**
Why…? **Cūr…?**
wicked, **sceléstus**
wife, **cóniūnx, úxor**
willing, (he/she) is, **vult**
willing, to be, **vélle**
win, to, **víncere**
wine, **vī́num**
wish, to, **vélle**
wish, if you, **sī vīs**
wish, not to, **nṓlle**
wishes, (he/she), **vult**
with, **ápud, cum**
with a loud laugh, **mágnō rī́sū**
With whom…? **Quṓcum…?**
without, **síne**
wolf, **lúpus**
woman, **fḗmina, múlier**
wonder, to, **sē rogā́re**
wonderful, **mī́rus**
woods, **sílva**
wool, **lā́na**
wool, to spin, **lā́nam tráhere**
work, **lábor**
work, to, **labōrā́re**
working, **labōrántēs**
worried, **sollícitus**
wretched, **míser**
write, to, **scrī́bere**

Y

Yes! **Íta vḗrō!**
yesterday, **héri**
you, (sing.) **tū,** (pl.) **vōs**
you, to/for, (sing.) **tíbi,** (pl.) **vṓbīs**
your, (sing.) **túus**, (pl.) **véster**

INDEX OF GRAMMAR

INDEX OF CULTURAL INFORMATION

CREDITS

Special credit is extended to Derrick Quarles, contemporary American artist, for his permission to reproduce his privately held painting "Roman Street Scene" in *ECCE ROMANI,* and to Jenny Page of The Bridgeman Art Library, London, for her invaluable assistance in locating illustrative materials sought for *ECCE ROMANI.*

The publisher gratefully acknowledges the contributions of the agencies, institutions, and photographers listed below:

Chapter 18
(p.7) "Horatius Cocles Defending the Bridge," Charles Le Brun (1619–90), Dulwich Art Library, London/Bridgeman Art Library, London.

(p.9) "Great Women of Antiquity," Frederick Dudley Walenn (exh. 1894–1930), Christopher Wood Gallery, London/Bridgeman Art Library, London

Chapter 19
(p.21) Landscape Crossed by the Nile, Palestrina, 2nd–3rd Century B.C., mosaic, Museo Archeologico Prenestino, Palestrina/Bridgeman Art Library, London

Chapter 20
(p.30) Open-air triclinium of House of Neptune and Amphitrite at Herculaneum, 1st Century A.D., Museo e Gallerie Nazionali di Capodimonte, Naples/Bridgeman Art Library, London

(p.36) "A Roman Triumph," Peter Paul Rubens (1577–1640), National Gallery, London/Bridgeman Art Library, London

Chapter 21
(p.45) Silver mask, Roman, 1st half of 3rd Century A.D., Louvre, Paris/Bridgeman Art Library, London

(p.46) Noblewoman Playing a Cithara, Roman Wall Painting, ca. 50 B.C., Metropolitan Museum of Art, New York/Bridgeman Art Library, London

Chapter 22
(p.58) Photograph courtesy Elizabeth Lyding Will

(p.59) "Vercingetorix before Caesar, 52 B.C.," Henri-Paul Motte (1846–1922), Musée Crozatier, Le Puy en Velay, France/Giraudon/Bridgeman Art Library London

Chapter 23
(p.68) Detail of reconstructed general view of the Forum Romanum and the Imperial Fora. From *The Ancient City* by Peter Connolly.

(p.73) Photograph courtesy Gilbert Lawall

Chapter 24
(p.81) "Funerary Portrait of a Man," ca. 1st Century A.D., Faiyum, encaustic painting on linen, The Cleveland Museum of Art, John L. Severence Fund, 71.135

"Portrait from Faiyum," Egyptian, wood and wax, Roman period, 30 B.C.– 337 A.D., Louvre, Paris/Bridgeman Art Library, London

(p.82) "Hannibal Swearing Eternal Enmity to Rome," Jacopo Amigoni (c. 1675/82–1752), Agnew & Sons, London/Bridgeman Art Library, London

(p.87) "Paris Pursued by Menelaus and Saved by Venus," tapestry, Pierre and François Van der Borght, from the Atelier Bruxellais, ca. 1740, Musée Jacquemart-André, Paris/Bridgeman Art Library, London

(p.88) "View of Rome," John Vanderlyn, New York State Office of Parks, Recreation, and Historic Preservation, Senate House State Historic Site, Albany

Chapter 25
(p.96) "Roman Street Scene," Derrick Quarles, Private Collection.

(p.97) Roman funerary stele, 3rd century CE. Museo Ostiense, Ostia, Italy. Erich Lessing/Art Resource, NY

(p. 98) Photograph courtesy Elizabeth Lyding Will

(p. 99) "Roman Art Lover," Sir Lawrence Alma-Tadema (1836–1912), Milwaukee Art Center, Wisconsin/Bridgeman Art Library, London

(p.101) Photograph courtesy Elizabeth Lyding Will

Chapter 26
(p.111) Roman Sarcophagus showing frieze with the Nine Muses, Louvre, Paris/Bridgeman Art Library, London

(p.112) "The Continence of Scipio," Nicolas Poussin (1594–1665), Pushkin Museum, Moscow/Bridgeman Art Library, London

Chapter 27
(p.116) The Campana Relief: A Chariot Race in the Circus, Roman Relief Sculpture, British Museum, London/Bridgeman Art Library, London

(p.117) Photograph courtesy Elizabeth Lyding Will

(p.118) Photograph Birney Lettick © National Geographic Society, NGM 1962/12, 816–7, Washington D.C.